IMAGES
of America

AMES

A RIDE THROUGH TOWN ON THE "DINKEY"

IMAGES
of America

AMES
A RIDE THROUGH TOWN ON THE "DINKEY"

Farwell T. Brown

ARCADIA
PUBLISHING

ISBN 978-0-7385-1933-3

Published by Arcadia Publishing
Charleston, South Carolina

Printed in the United States of America

Library of Congress Catalog Card Number: 2001093949

For all general information contact Arcadia Publishing at:
Telephone 843-853-2070
Fax 843-853-0044
E-mail sales@arcadiapublishing.com
For customer service and orders:
Toll-Free 1-888-313-2665

Visit us on the Internet at www.arcadiapublishing.com

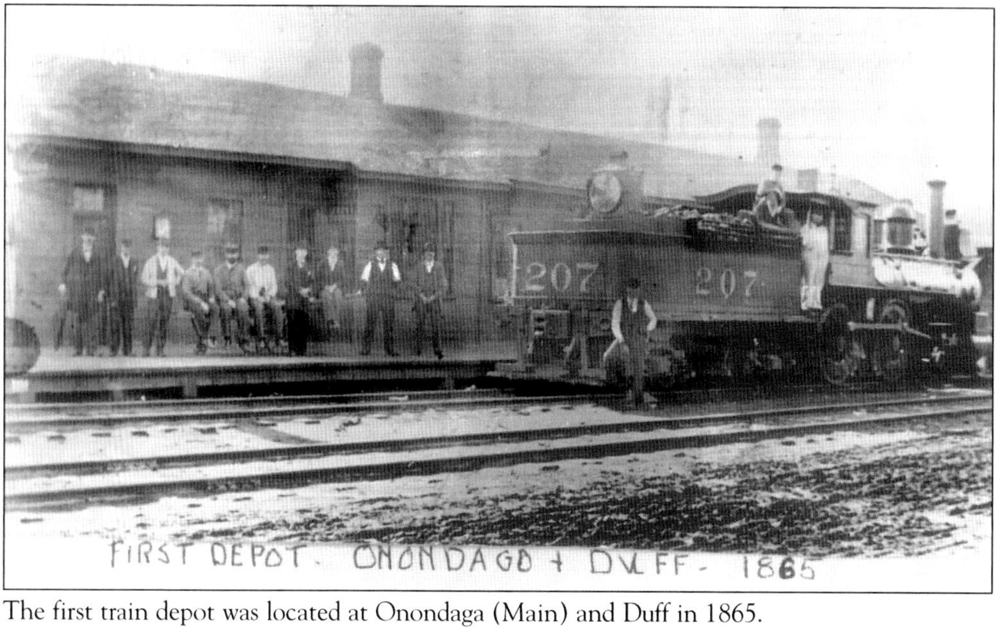

The first train depot was located at Onondaga (Main) and Duff in 1865.

CONTENTS

ACKNOWLEDGMENTS

Complete accuracy of all information contained in this book was striven for. Any errors or omissions are purely unintentional. The following individuals are gratefully acknowledged for their assistance in compiling this book.

Sharon Wirth

Wendy Wirth

Janet Klaas

Kathy Svec

Leslie Suarez

A special thanks also goes to all the people throughout the years who have generously donated photos to the Farwell T. Brown collection.

Also, a thanks goes to the *Daily Tribune* for originally publishing this book.

INTRODUCTION

Pictures from Earlier Days

Pictures provide us with access to the past. History can be interesting, but more than that, it is important. "A society that has lost touch with its past is a society that is in trouble," stated a televised editorial at the time of the nation's bicentennial in 1976. At about that same time, the widow of a Nobel peace prize winner, who was giving her support to the funding of a black history museum in New York, was quoted as saying, "A race that has no past is a race that has no future."

Ames has a significant past. This collection of photographs underlines the presence of the men and women who participated in that past and were contributors to the Ames of today. These pictures must be looked upon as representative of our history; they are symbolic of the larger whole. Historical detail is neither intended nor possible. Browsing through these pages may awaken memories for some older citizens, and others may learn that Ames did not always have paved streets. They will find that the town of Ames and the college, for which it is best known, were once small and that life in the Ames of today developed from the efforts of special early day citizens.

Ames has been referred to as a railroad town; more correctly the railroad came this way at the same moment that the Iowa Agricultural College was taking form in the interests of all Iowa. Ames had its pioneer railroading roots; but it was the college that drew people like Welch, Beardshear, "Tama Jim" Wilson, Charles F. Curtiss, Anson Marston, and their successors. There were many townspeople who were vital in making the community function as a whole. You will meet a few of these people here.

From the early leaders who cast their long shadows over the history of our town have come many accomplishments. You will find examples such as the man who became the nation's first Secretary of Agriculture, and another that left Ames in 1919 to become the first chief of the nation's Bureau of Roads.

Ames had growing pains, but it grew steadily. Ours has been a unique society—the sort of society from which a responsibility for the future of a larger society falls in more apparent ways today then ever before. All in all, many Ames folks, both past and present, would agree that Ames has been, and is, a great place to live.

WATCH OUR SMOKE

Nothing is too poor for our Customers

Our Pullman observation is run on special occasions.

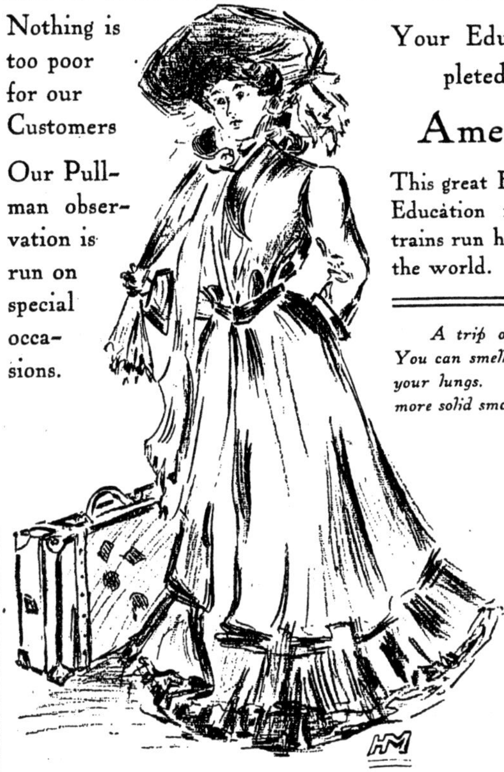

Your Education is Only Half Completed unless you patronize the

Ames & College Ry.

This great East and West Thoroughfare is an Education in Itself. Magnificent, palatial trains run hourly over the finest road-bed in the world.

A trip on the A. & C. is a picturesque reality. You can smell real smoke and breathe live cinders into your lungs. Our system of coach lighting produces more solid smoke than any other system ever invented. There is no extra charge if you have to to stand up or hang on to the rear end. It is a distinct pleasure to ride over this great trunk line, where business-blocks, city-parks, railroad-yards, forests, rivers, fields and pastures blend into a harmonious whole on account of our smoke.

See that your ticket reads

via *The* A. & C.

One

In the Beginning

It seems certain that it was the railroad builder, John I. Blair, who determined where he would locate the town and what name it should be given. That was in 1864. A year before that he had brought Massachusetts congressman Oakes Ames out this way on an inspection trip. The college campus that lay beyond the Squaw Creek floodplain to the west was not in the original town of Ames.

The town, however, was where most of the people lived. Students and faculty were housed on campus in the earliest days. In 1891, a group of citizens organized the little steam railroad, affectionately known as the "Dinkey," to operate between the town and campus. Soon, in 1893, an area including the campus was incorporated into the town of Ames.

After we see the first Chicago & North Western Depot in downtown Ames we can look at pictures of early Ames and then, when the Dinkey comes by, take a ride to the campus. From then on, as pages are turned, pictures depict the scene that once met the eye of daily patrons of the train that traveled what was once referred to as the most scenic passenger route in Iowa. It traveled from downtown Ames out across the Squaw Creek, through the wooded lowland area, and on to the hill where the central campus was then, and still is.

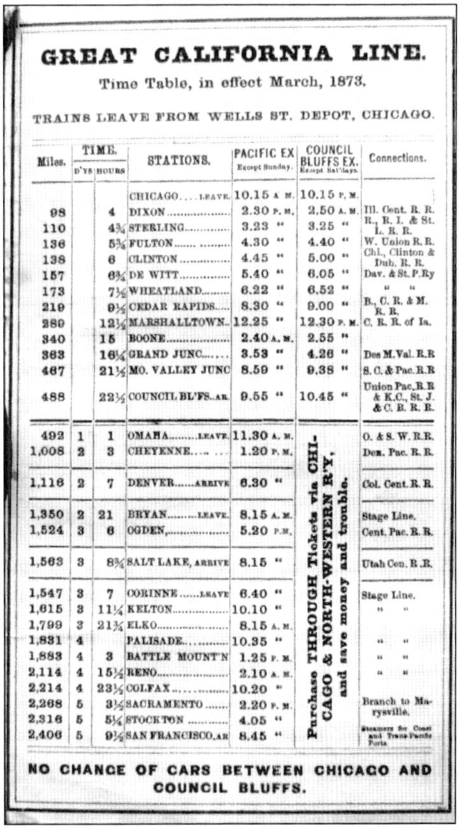

GREAT CALIFORNIA LINE.

Time Table, in effect March, 1873.

TRAINS LEAVE FROM WELLS ST. DEPOT, CHICAGO.

Miles.	TIME. D'YS	TIME. HOURS	STATIONS.	PACIFIC EX Except Sunday.	COUNCIL BLUFFS EX. Except Sat'days.	Connections.
			CHICAGO.... LEAVE.	10.15 A. M.	10.15 P. M.	
98		4	DIXON	2.30 P. M.	2.50 A. M.	Ill. Cent. R. R.
110		4¾	STERLING	3.23 "	3.25 "	R., R. I. & St. L. R. R.
136		5¾	FULTON	4.30 "	4.40 "	W. Union R. R.
138		6	CLINTON	4.45 "	5.00 "	Chi., Clinton & Dub. R. R.
157		6¾	DE WITT	5.40 "	6.05 "	Dav. & St. P. Ry
173		7½	WHEATLAND	6.22 "	6.52 "	" "
219		9½	CEDAR RAPIDS	8.30 "	9.00 "	B., C. R. & M. R. R.
280		12½	MARSHALLTOWN	12.25 "	12.30 P. M.	C. R. R. of Ia.
340		15	BOONE	2.40 A. M.	2.55 "	
363		16¼	GRAND JUNC	3.53 "	4.26 "	Des M. Val. R. R
467		21½	MO. VALLEY JUNC	8.59 "	9.38 "	S. C. & Pac. R. R
488		22½	COUNCIL BL'FS. AR.	9.55 "	10.45 "	Union Pac. R. R & K.C., St. J. & C. B. R. R.
492	1	1	OMAHA.......LEAVE.	11.30 A. M.		O. & S. W. R. R.
1,008	2	3	CHEYENNE	1.20 P. M.		Den. Pac. R. R.
1,116	2	7	DENVER......ARRIVE	6.30 "		Col. Cent. R. R.
1,350	2	21	BRYAN.......LEAVE.	8.15 A. M.		Stage Line.
1,524	3	6	OGDEN	5.20 P. M.		Cent. Pac. R. R.
1,563	3	8¾	SALT LAKE, ARRIVE	8.15 "		Utah Cen. R. R.
1,547	3	7	CORINNE......LEAVE	6.40 "		Stage Line.
1,615	3	11¼	KELTON	10.10 "		" "
1,799	3	21¾	ELKO	8.15 A. M.		
1,831	4		PALISADE	10.35 "		" "
1,883	4	3	BATTLE MOUNT'N	1.25 P. M.		" "
2,114	4	15½	RENO	2.10 A. M.		" "
2,214	4	23½	COLFAX	10.20 "		
2,268	5	3½	SACRAMENTO	2.20 P. M.		Branch to Marysville.
2,316	5	5¼	STOCKTON	4.05 "		
2,406	5	9½	SAN FRANCISCO, AR	8.45 "		Steamers for Coast and Trans-Pacific Ports

Purchase THROUGH Tickets via CHICAGO & NORTH-WESTERN R'Y, and save money and trouble.

NO CHANGE OF CARS BETWEEN CHICAGO AND COUNCIL BLUFFS.

This is an 1873 C & N W Railroad time card.

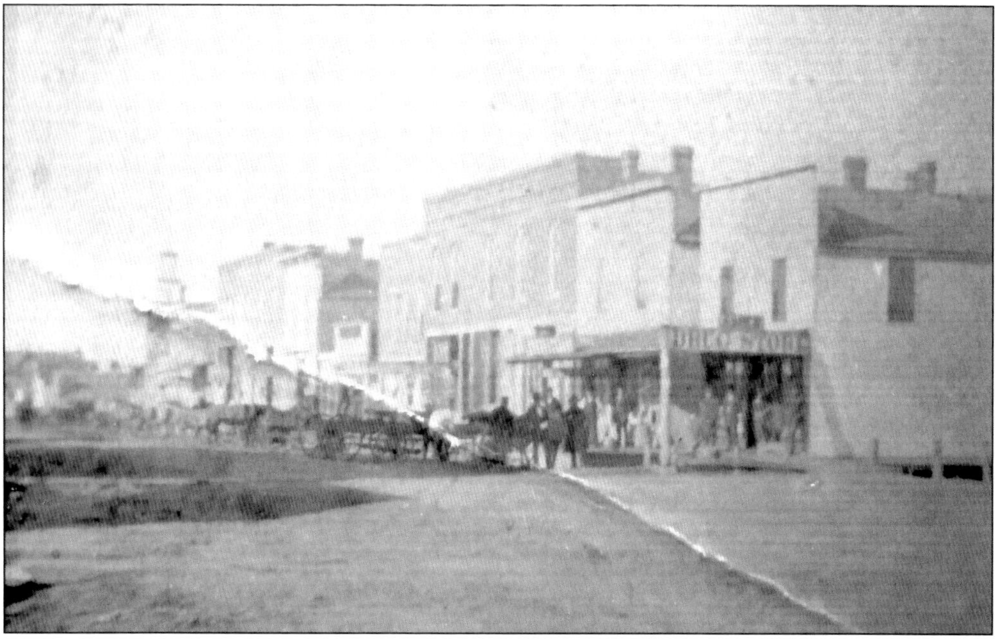

S.O. Osborn operated the Ames Drug Store on the corner of Onondaga (Main) and Douglas, around 1875. D.A. Bigelow, H.C. Huntington, and George G. Tilden owned the mercantile business next door from 1869 to 1883. Tilden became sole owner in 1883.

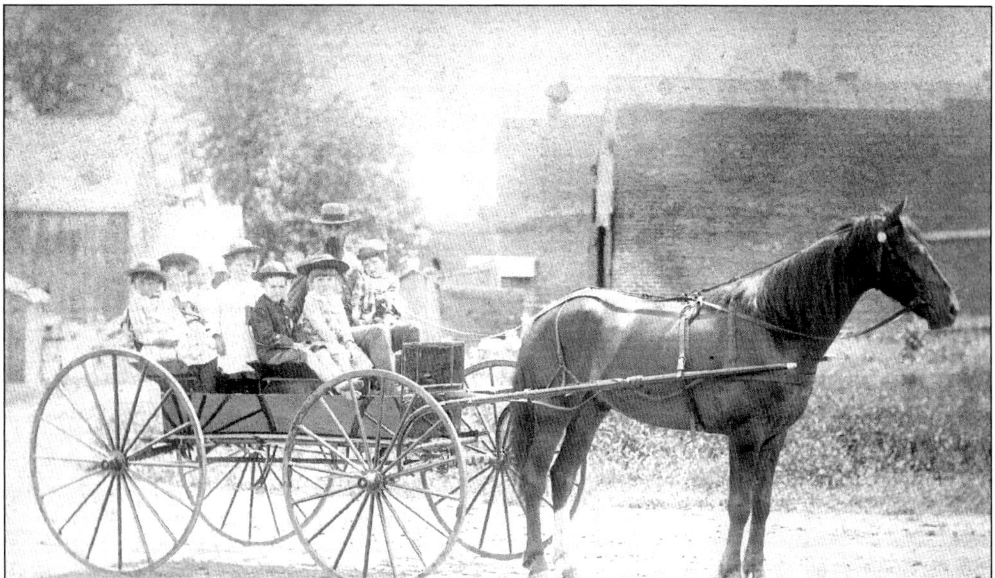

Riding with Dr. Albert Richmond in 1885 is Tommy Watts, son of the editor of the *Intelligencer*, and Mary and Winifred Tilden are seated in front. Dr. Richmond, a graduate of the University of Vermont Medical School, came to Ames in 1870. The Richmond Addition is now the site of the Mary Greeley Medical Center and McFarland Clinic.

George Nichols, better known as Fatty Nichols, was one of the Nichols Livery brothers. Weighing close to 500 pounds, he had his own sideshow in midwest county and state fairs. A 1915 news report stated that he had a seven-foot waistline.

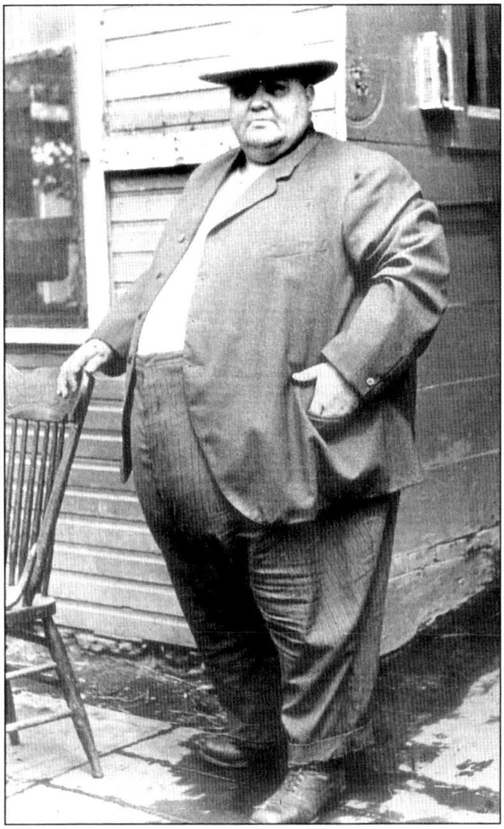

Nichols Livery, shown here on July 2, 1889, later became Morris Livery. The brougham in front was used for prominent local citizens, often conveying them in funeral processions.

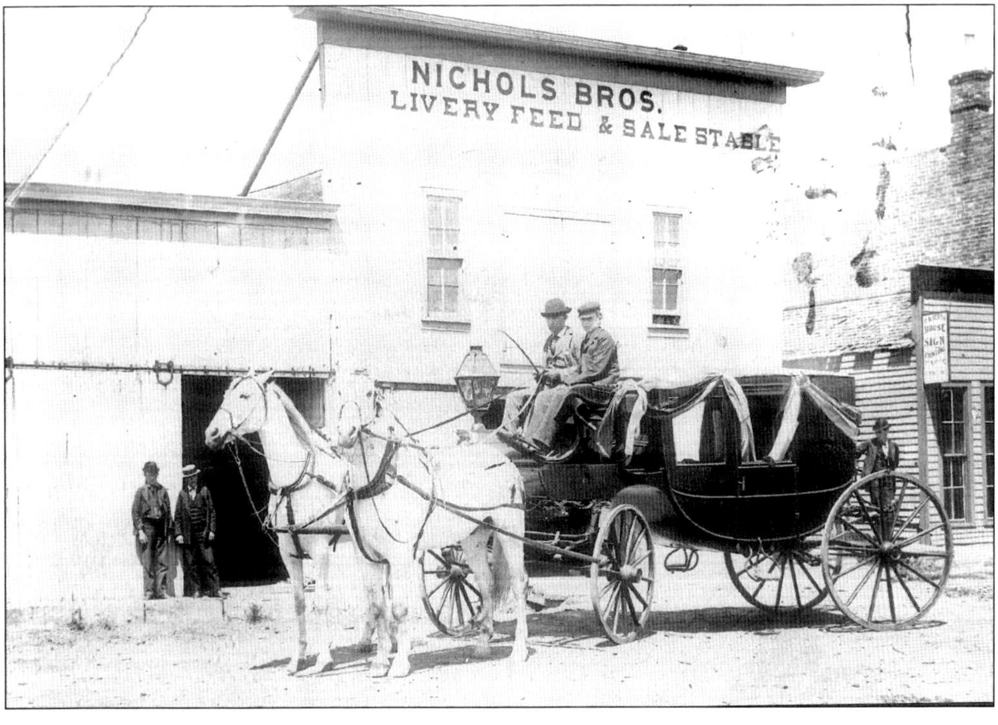

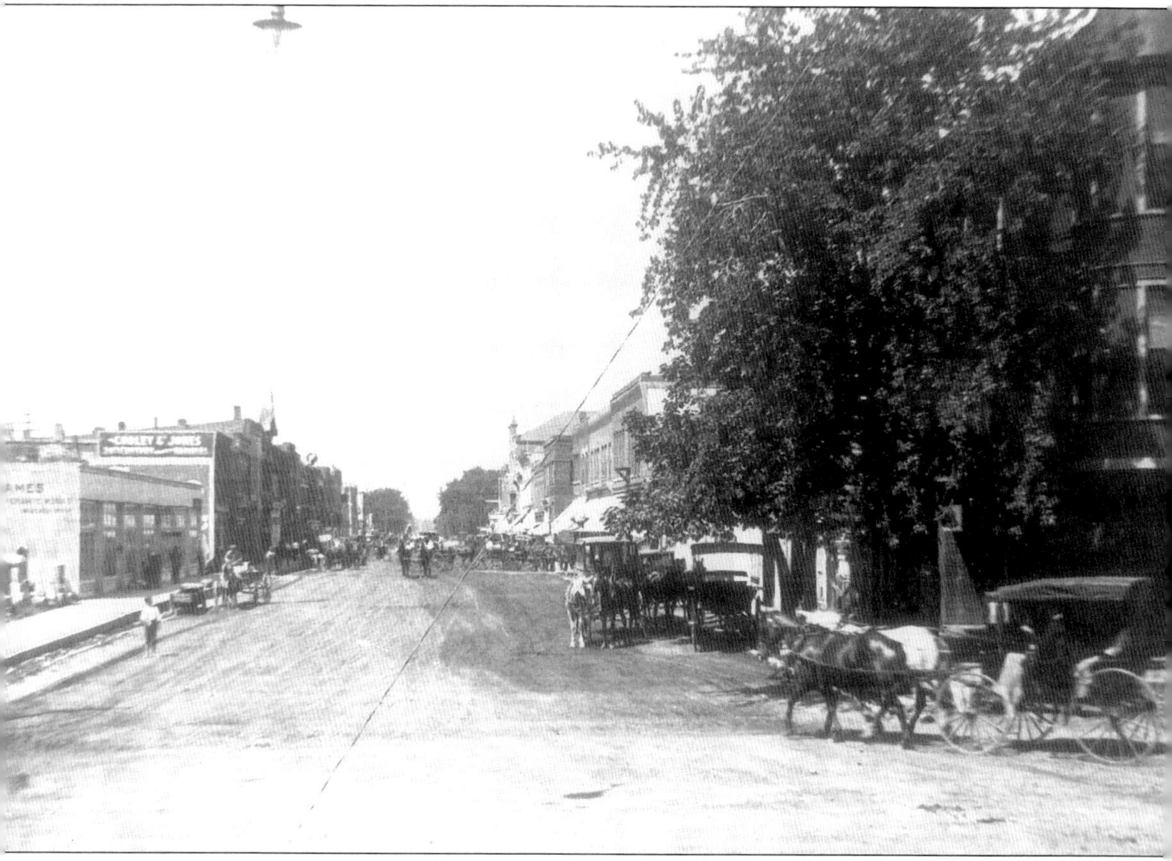

Looking west down Onondaga (Main) Street from Duff Avenue around 1912, one could see the old Ames Hotel on the right. The Odd Fellows Building is further down on the right, and the five identical storefronts on the left gave the illusion of a tall building on its side and was known as the Skyscraper Building.

Two

Steam Dinkey

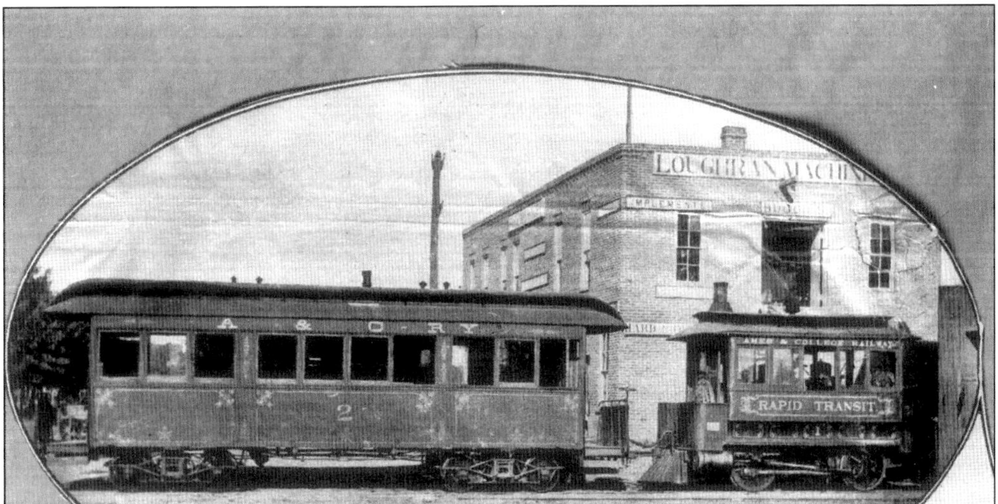

The Ames and College Railway was known as the Dinkey. For a nickel a passenger, this donkey engine pulled cars between the town of Ames and Iowa State College. This image is from c. 1900.

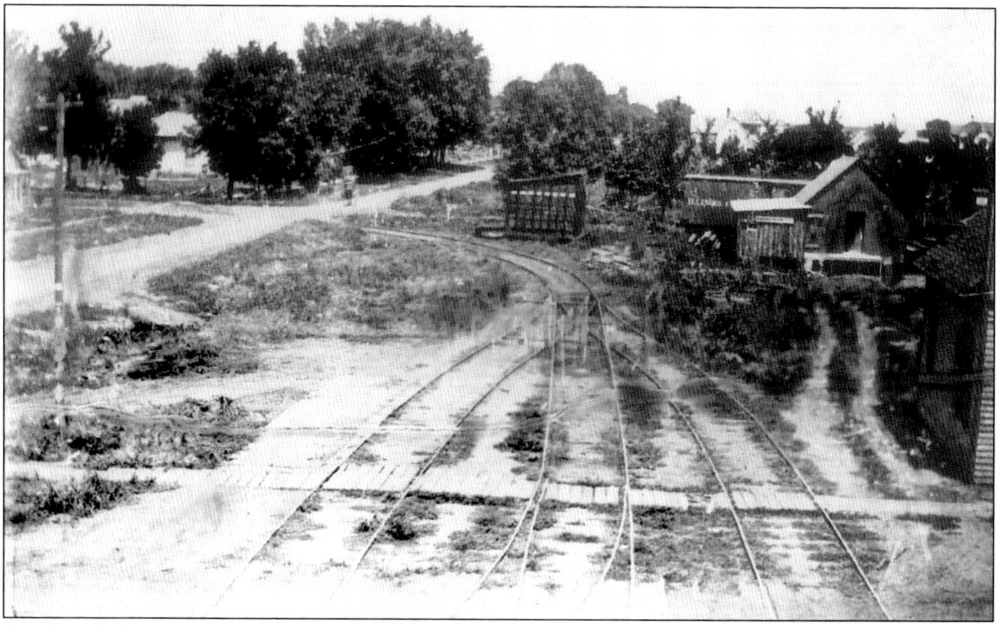

Tracks of the Ames & College (the Dinkey) Railroad's switching yard running north/south along Duff Avenue at Onondaga (Main) Street were photographed around 1900. The building on the right was later part of the Munn Lumber Company.

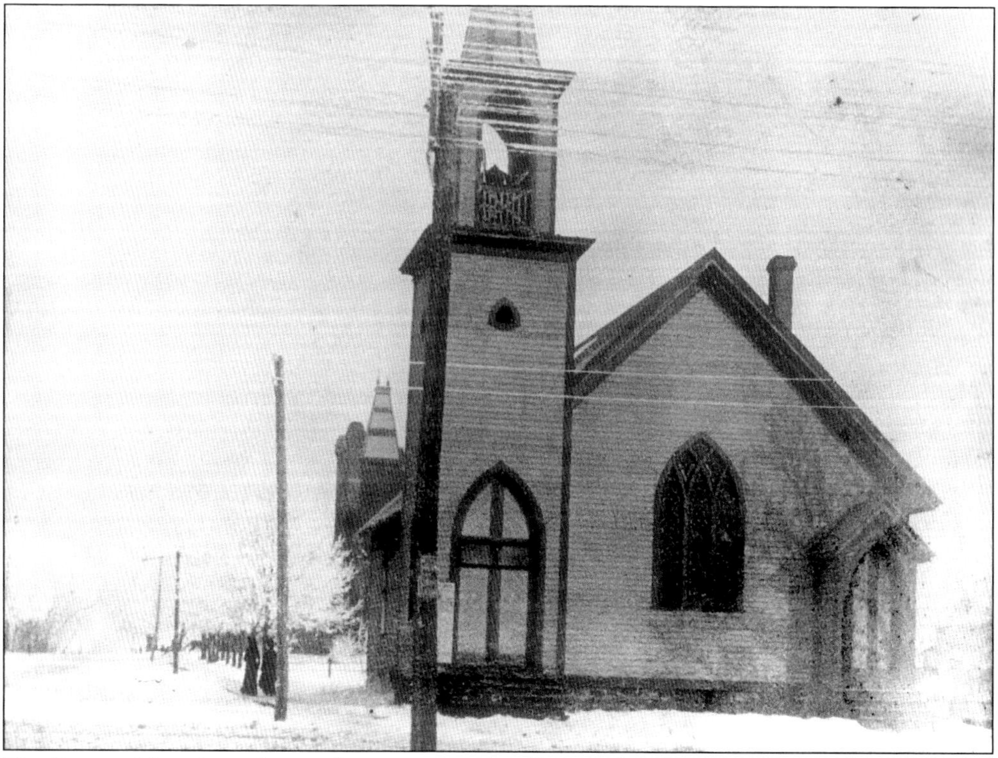

The Baptist Church on the northeast corner of Kellogg and Fifth Street was built in 1872. The Dinkey tracks were on Fifth Street from 1891 until 1907.

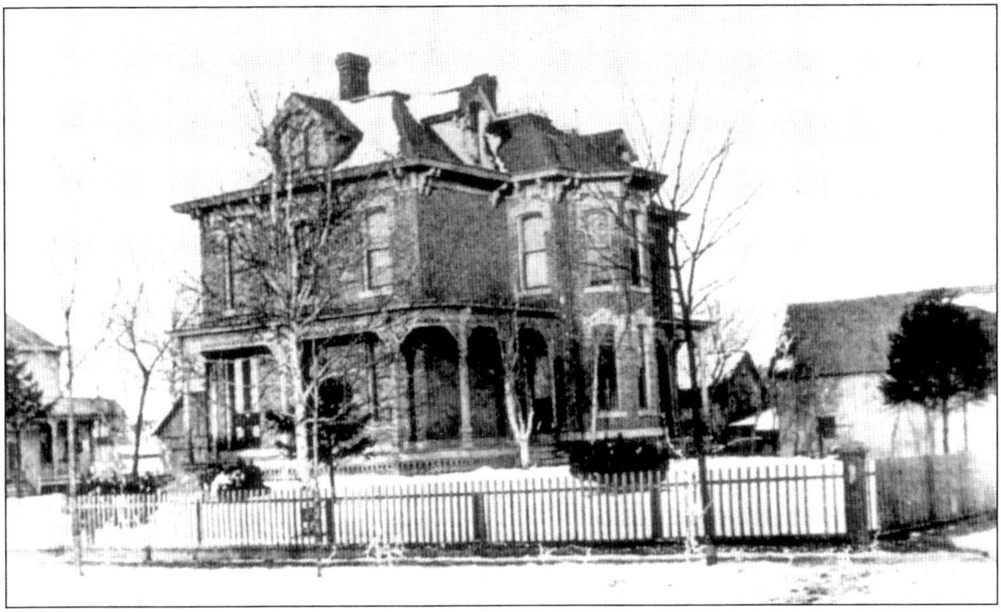

Wallace Greeley built this home in 1882 (the image is from *c.* 1897) and it now houses the Adams Funeral Home on the corner of Douglas and Fifth Street.

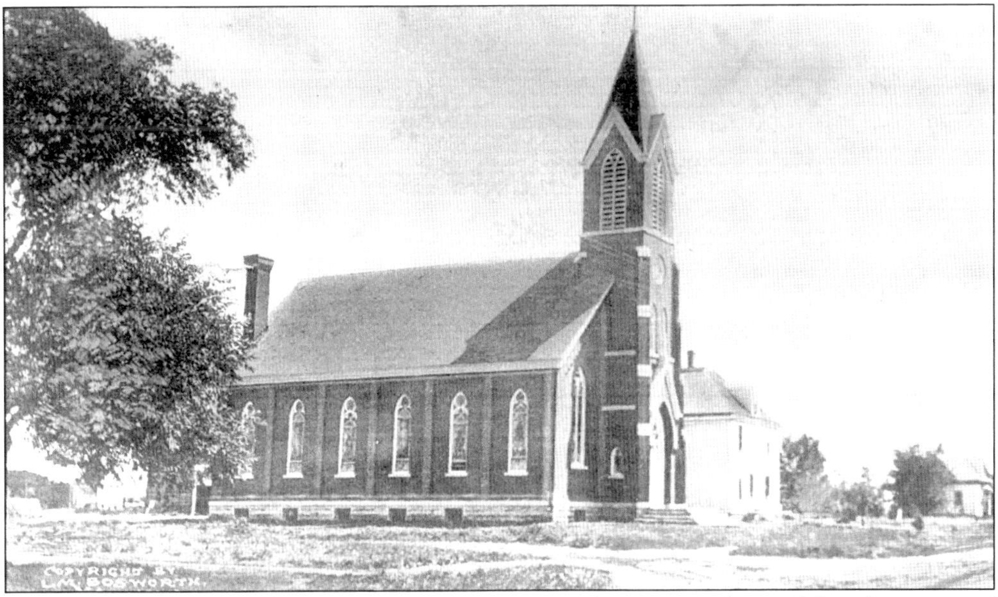

This is St. Cecilia Catholic Church and its rectory as they appeared in 1906 at the corner of Lincoln Way and Oak.

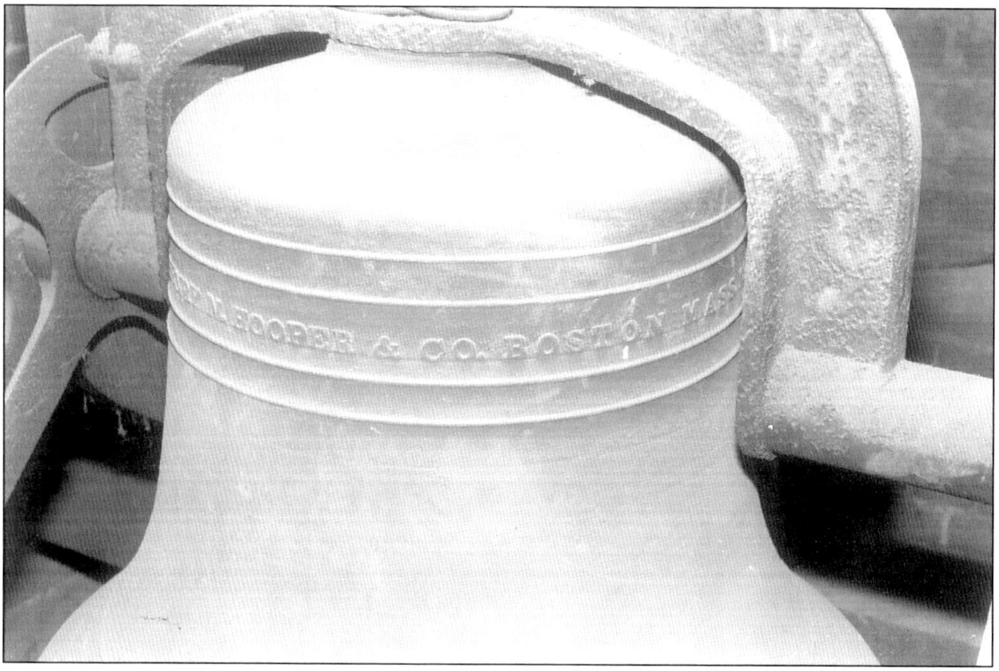

Congressman Oakes Ames gave this bell to the Congregational Church, the first church built in the town named after him. The bell still rings in the United Church of Christ Congregational at its original location at Sixth and Kellogg.

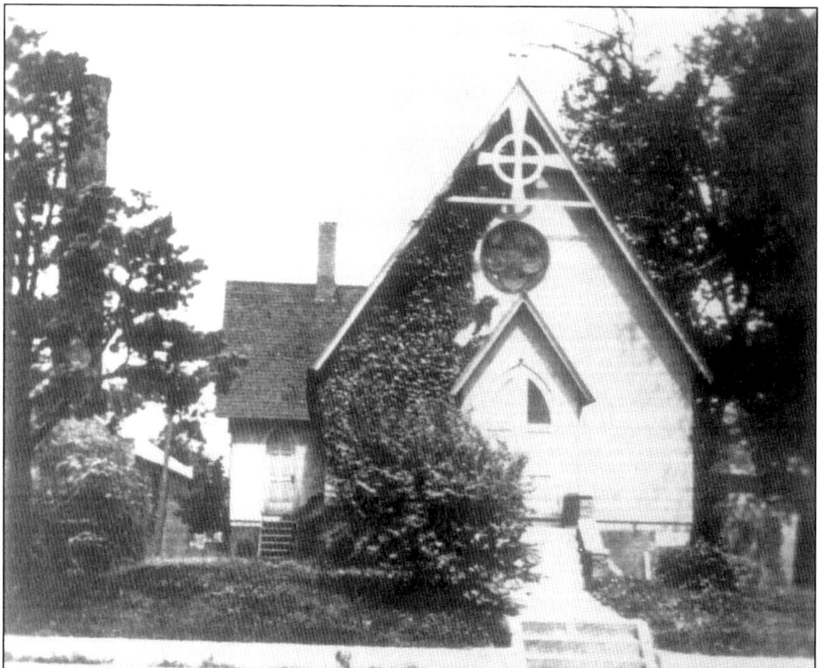

The Episcopal Church on the north side of Fifth Street between Burnett and Clark is shown as it appeared *c.* 1922. Today, the building has been divided into two small residences at 320 and 324 East Sixth Street.

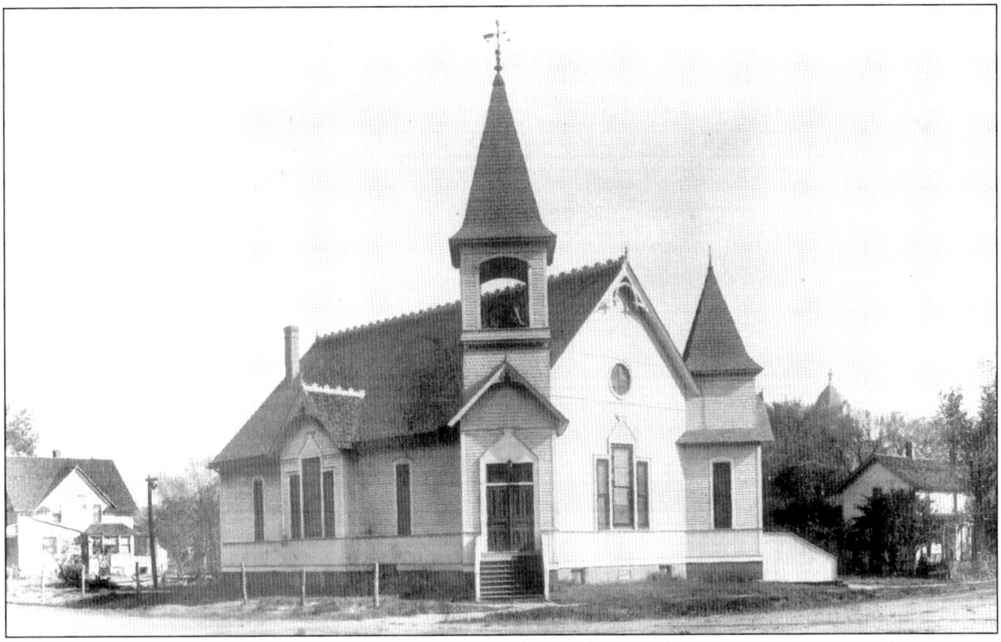

The Christian Church dedicated this new church on the northeast corner of Fifth Street and Burnett Avenue on September 9, 1894. A farewell service was held here June 17, 1928, the same day the church held a dedication ceremony for its present location at Clark and Sixth. The image is from c. 1907.

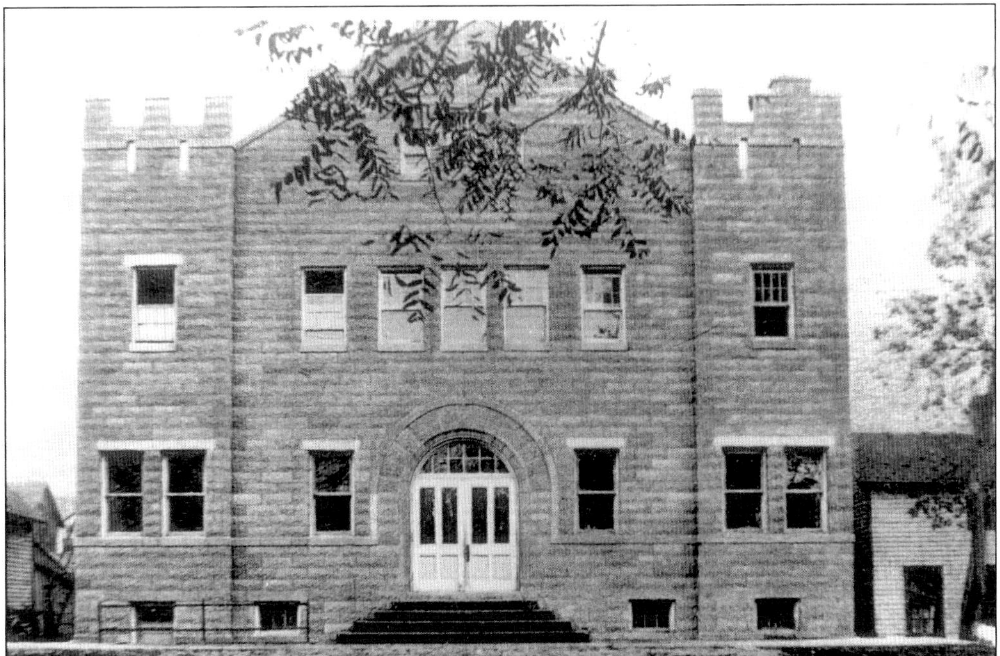

The National Guard in 1905 was located on Fifth Street across from the present-day Tribune Building. Iowa State men and women played their first interscholastic basketball game here in 1907. It later became the O'Neil Dairy until the building was razed in 1985.

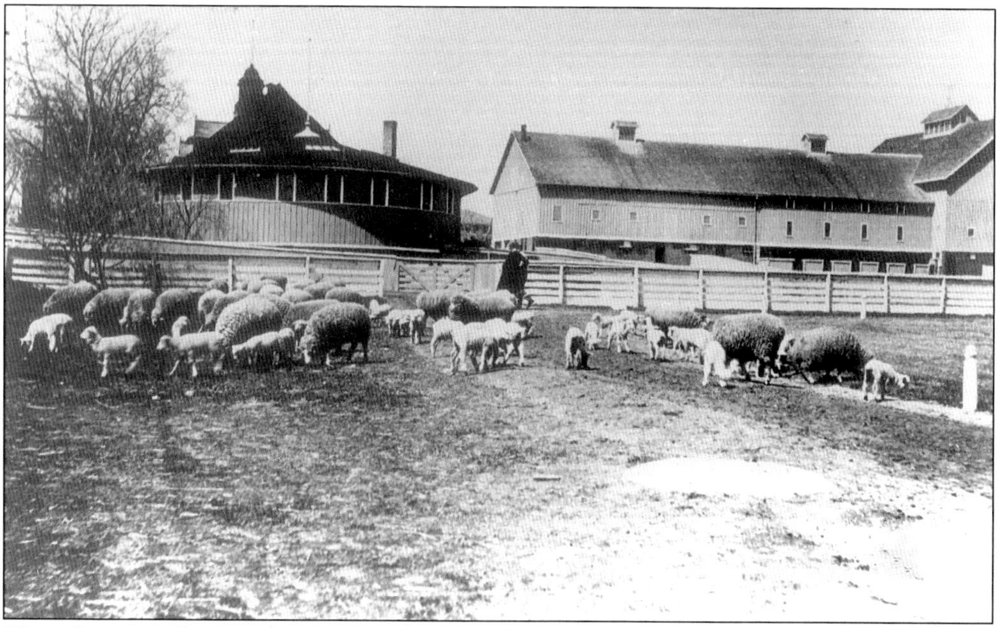

The judging pavilion on the Iowa State campus is now the site of Hamilton Hall. The structure was photographed c. 1920.

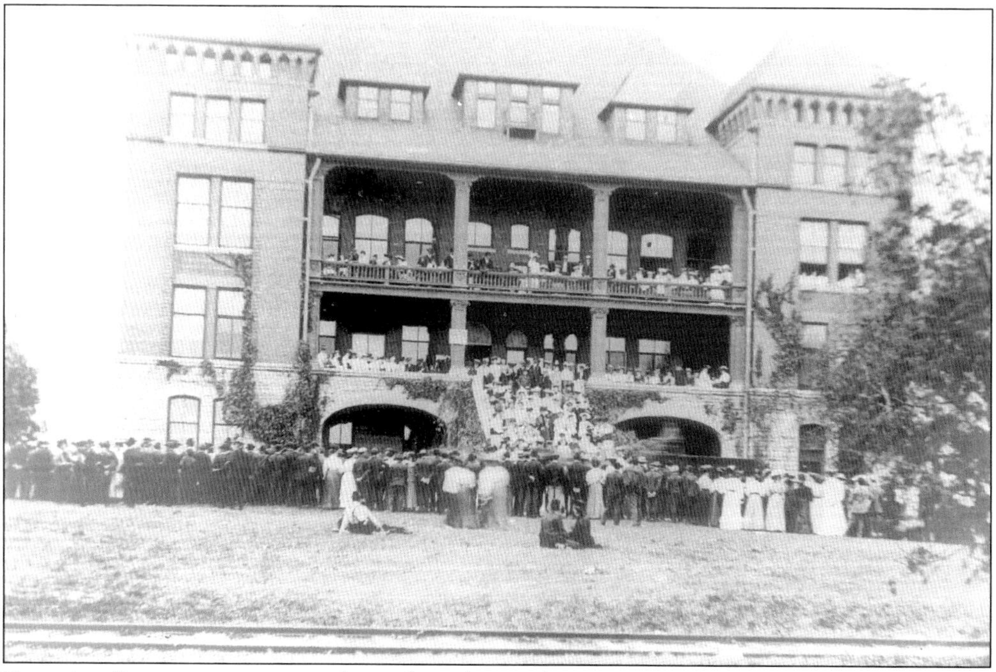

Excursion Days participants are shown here during the 1904–05 school year at the Agricultural Hall, which was constructed in 1892.

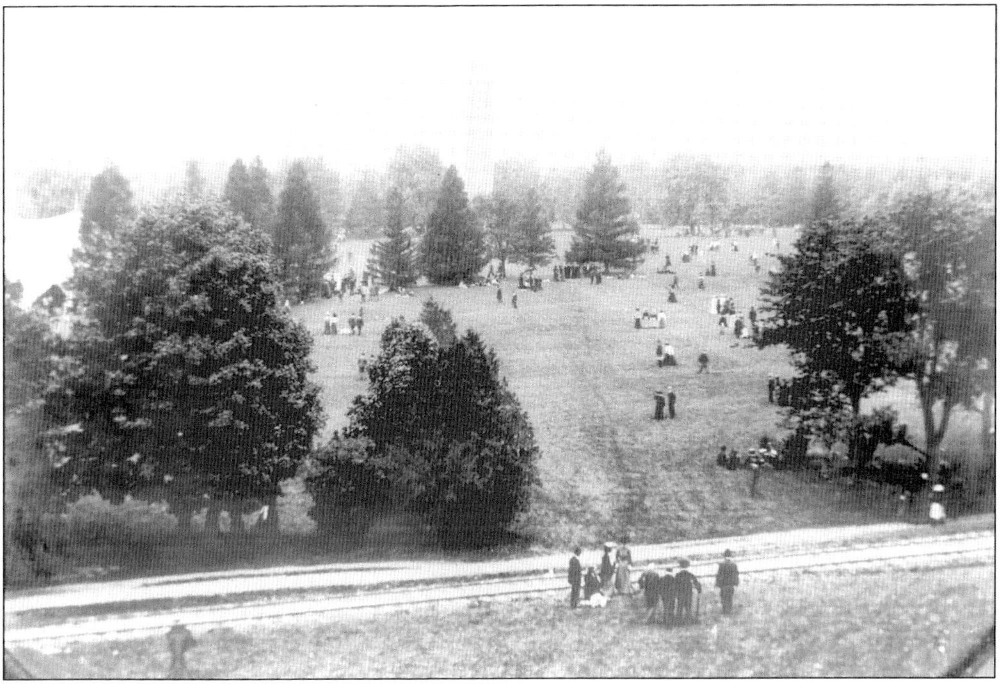

Excursion Days on the ISC campus in 1904 preceded the VEISHA student festival, which began in 1922.

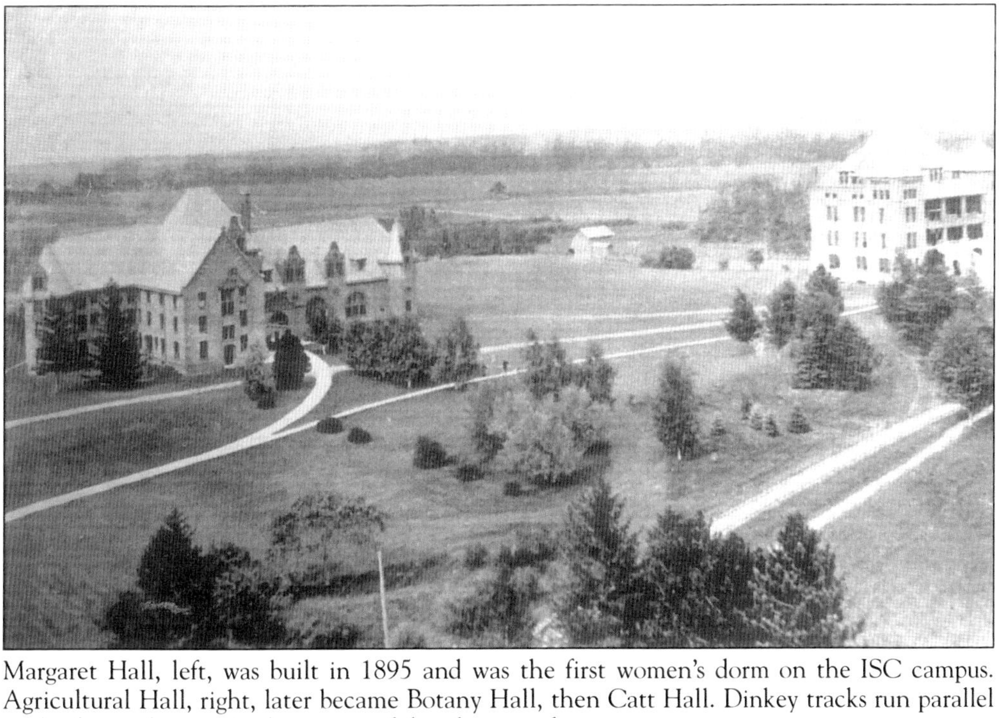

Margaret Hall, left, was built in 1895 and was the first women's dorm on the ISC campus. Agricultural Hall, right, later became Botany Hall, then Catt Hall. Dinkey tracks run parallel to the footpath, seen in the center of the photograph.

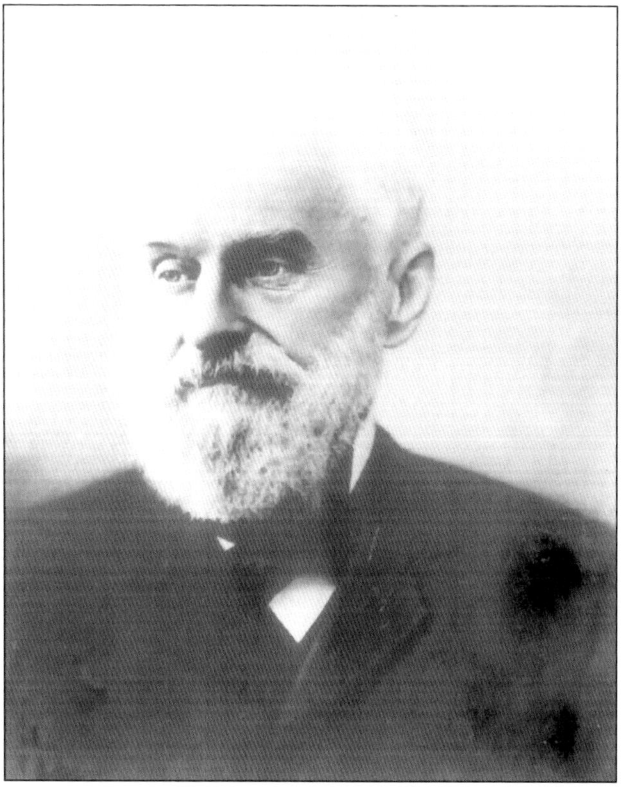

Adonijah S. Welch was the first president of Iowa State Agricultural College from 1869 to 1883. Classes began with 173 students selected from 55 Iowa counties, with women admitted on an equal basis with men. Iowa State was the first coeducational land grant college.

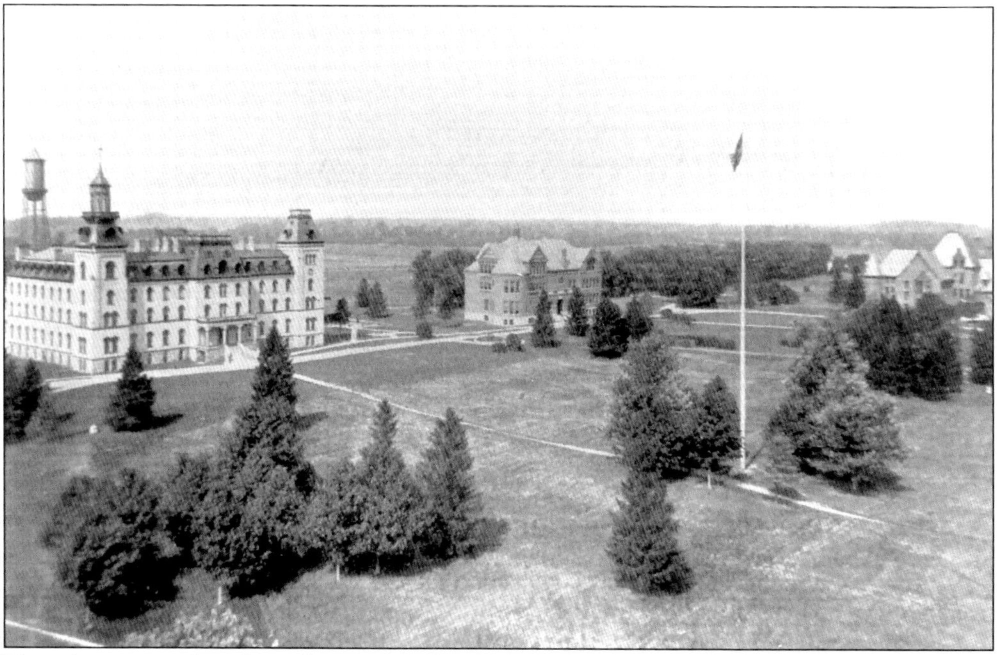

This photo was taken from the Campanile, showing Old Main, left, and Morrill Hall, center, on the ISC campus.

William Miller Beardshear was president of Iowa State Agricultural College from 1891 to 1902.

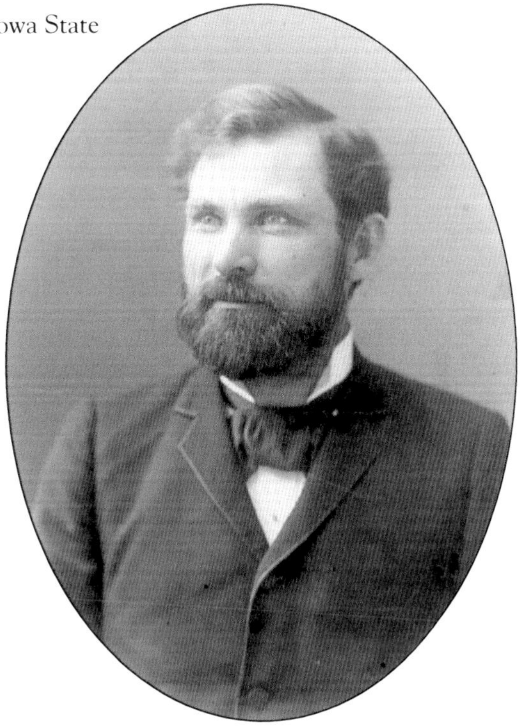

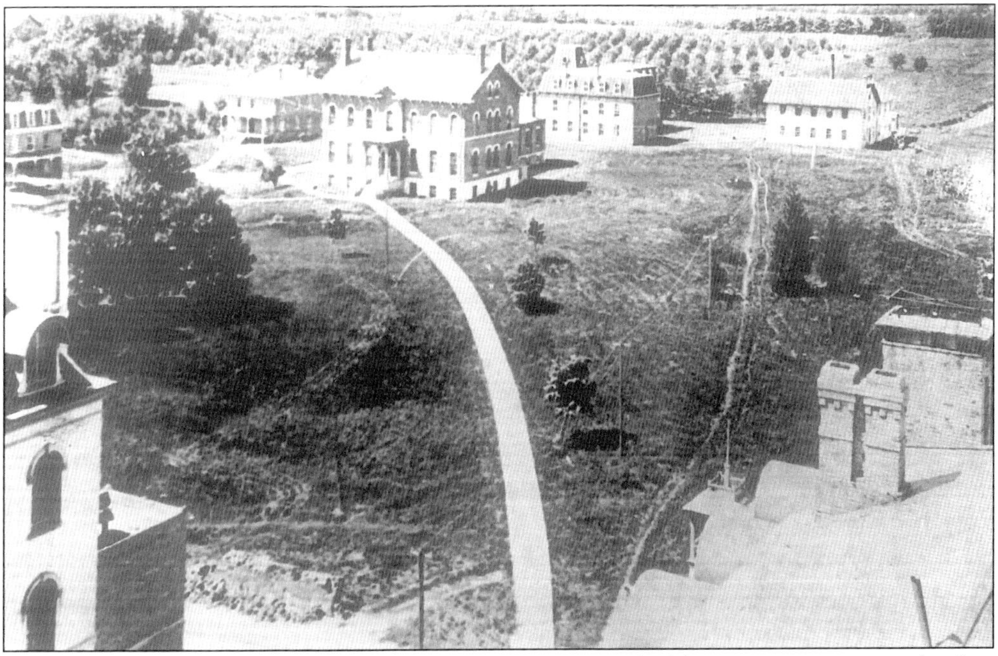

The chemistry building is shown in 1882, from the top of Old Main. It is next to the first engineering building, which today is on the National Register jof Hisotric Buildings.

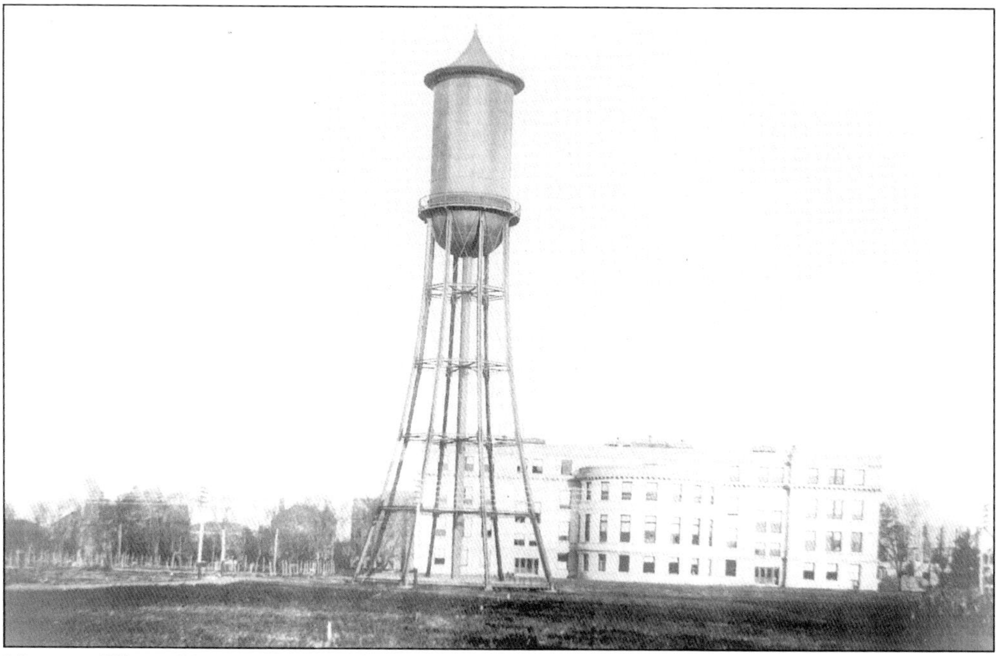

Marston Water Tower was completed in 1897. Behind it is Engineering Hall, which was constructed in 1900 through 1903, and was renamed Marston Hall in 1947.

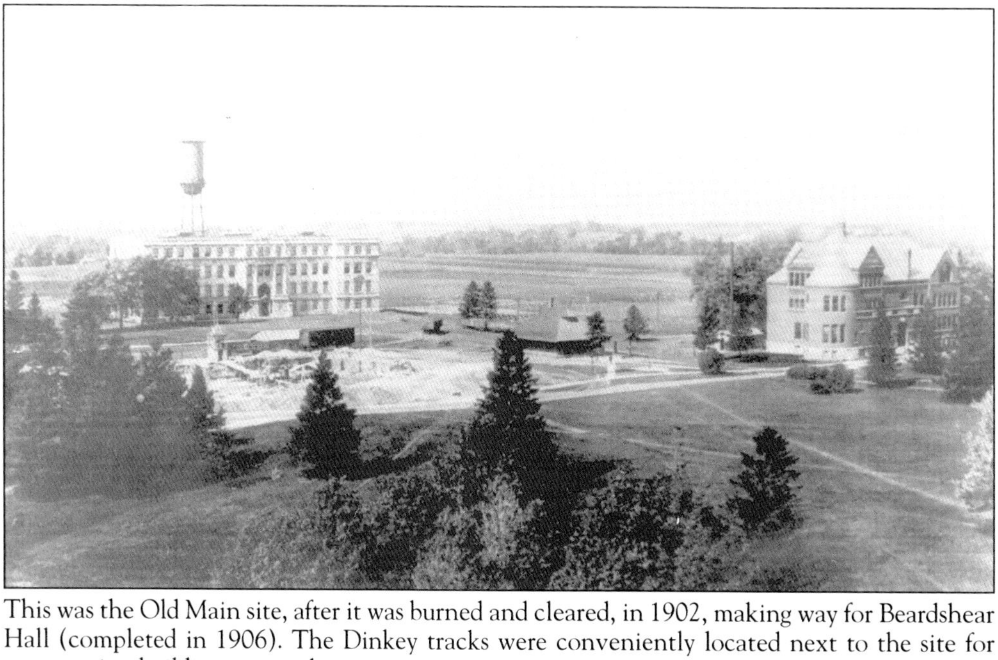

This was the Old Main site, after it was burned and cleared, in 1902, making way for Beardshear Hall (completed in 1906). The Dinkey tracks were conveniently located next to the site for transporting building materials.

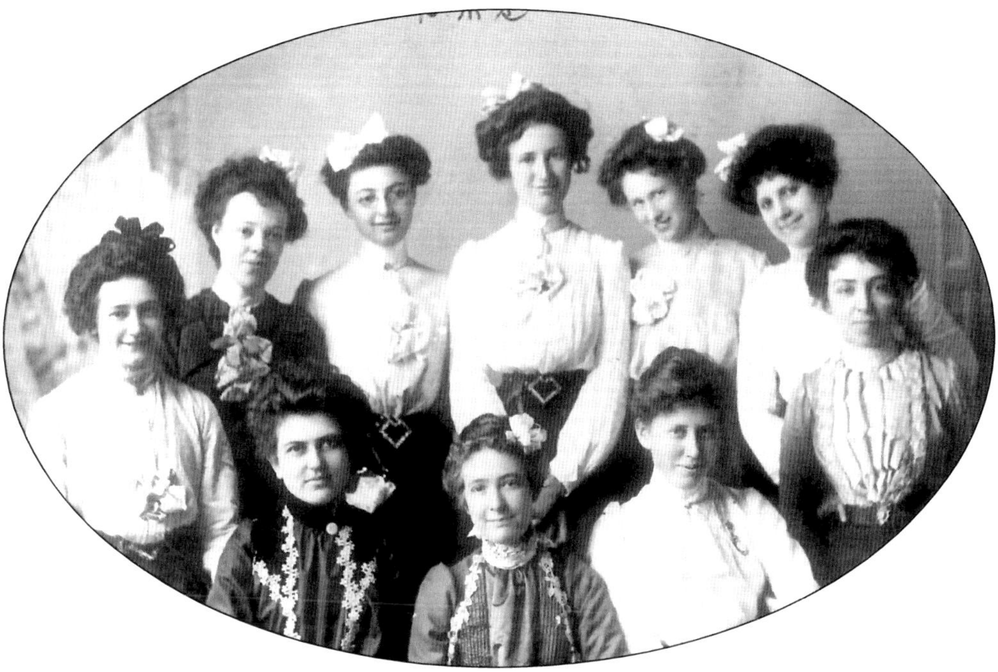

The Bachelor Maids Club is seen here in 1902. The popular Ames girls are seen, from left to right, as follows: (front row) Nettie Bauge Ritchie, Jess Martin, and Mildred Graham Wortman; (back row) Ethel Underwood Meeker, Inis Hunter Grove, Kate McMichael Cole, Catherine Cole, Jess Cole Augustine, Minnie Perkins, and Emma Selby Keltner.

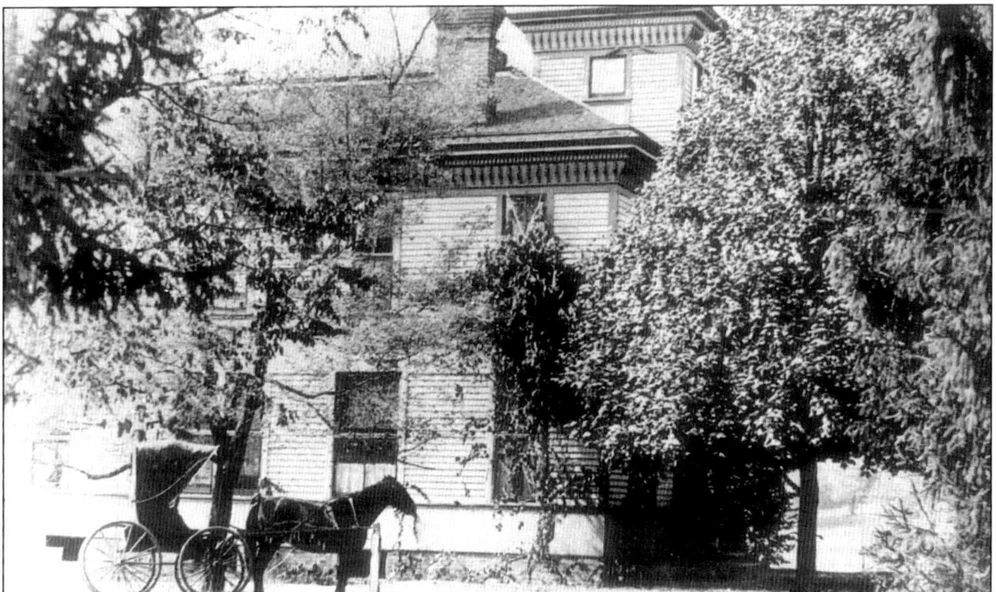

Originally the sanitary building, the music department moved into this building in 1912 after this South Hall burned. The building was razed in 1927 to make room for the new Memorial Union. The horse and buggy in front belonged to Dr. W.E. Harriman, physician at the college from 1895 to 1907.

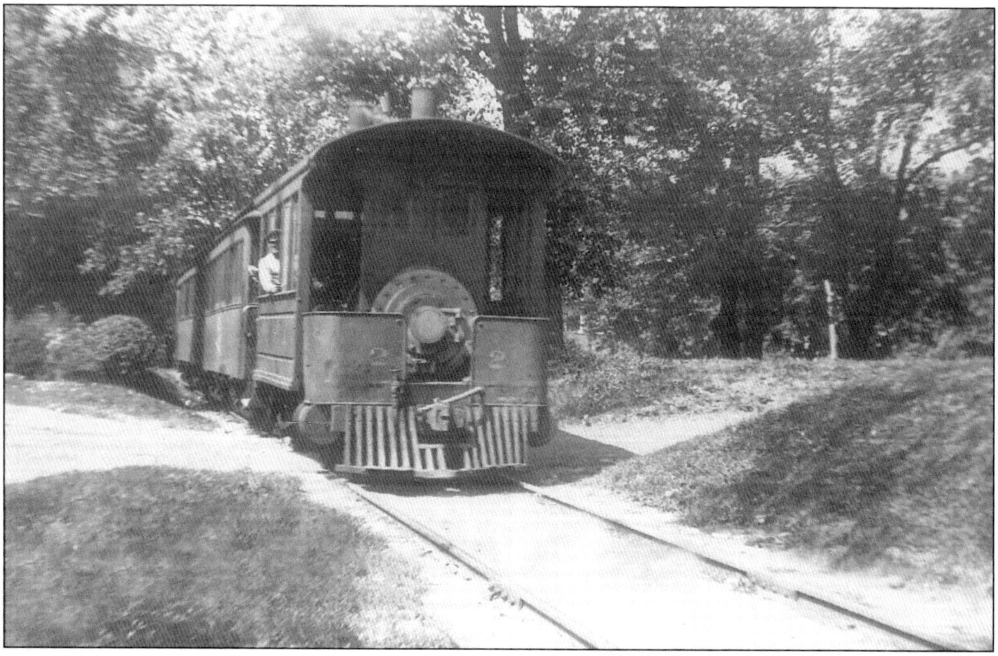

In 1905 the fare was 5¢ to ride the Dinkey, which traveled back and forth from Ames to the ISC campus. The steam engine was replaced by electric cars in 1907.

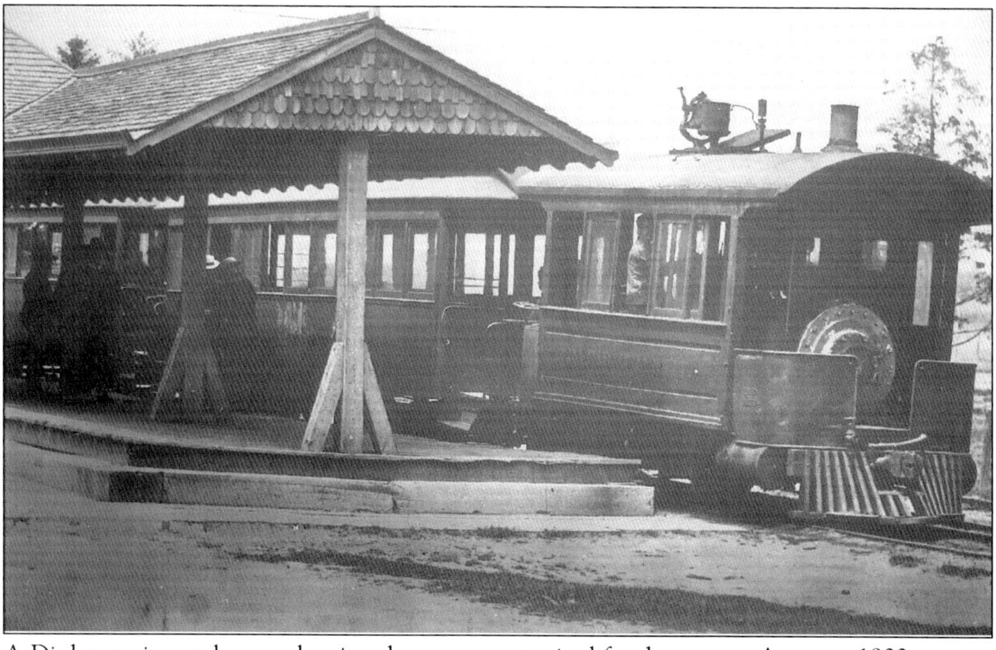

A Dinkey train can be seen leaving the campus terminal for downtown Ames, c. 1900.

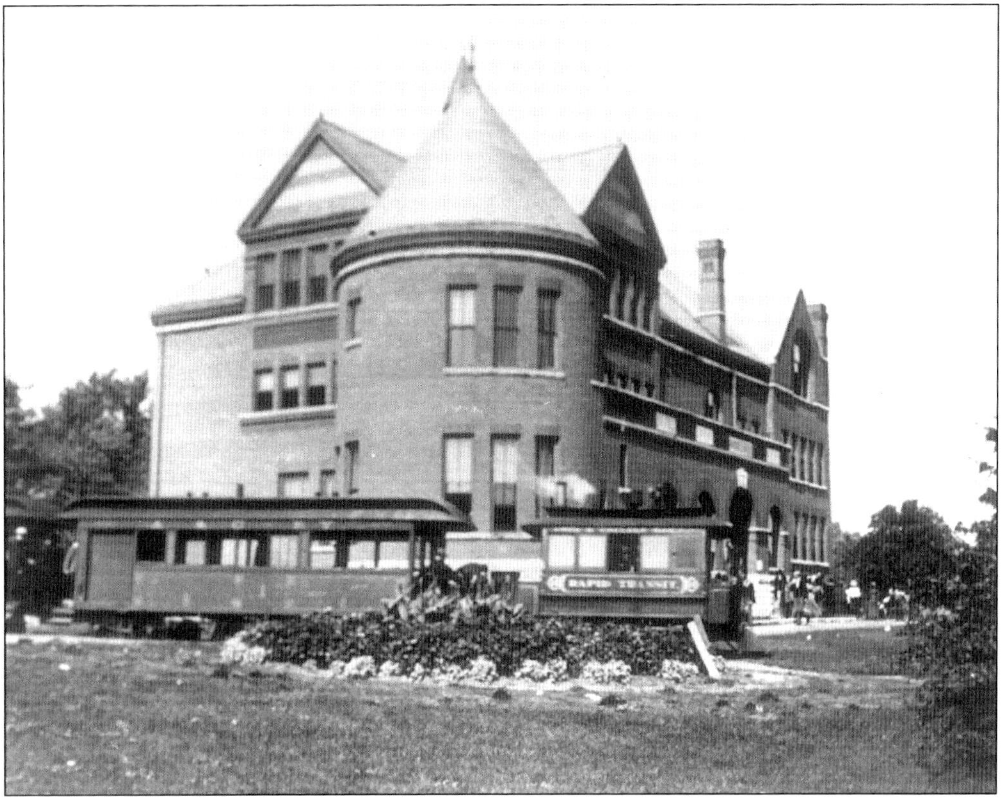

Morrill Hall is a nice backdrop for the Dinkey, running from campus to downtown Ames, *c.* 1900.

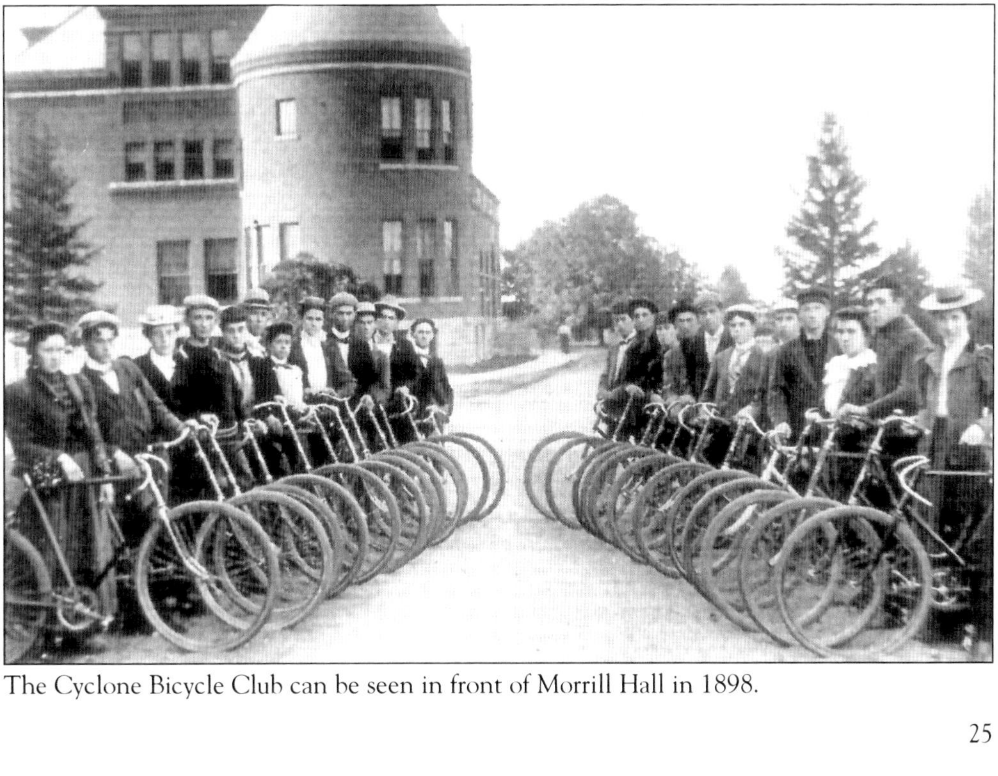

The Cyclone Bicycle Club can be seen in front of Morrill Hall in 1898.

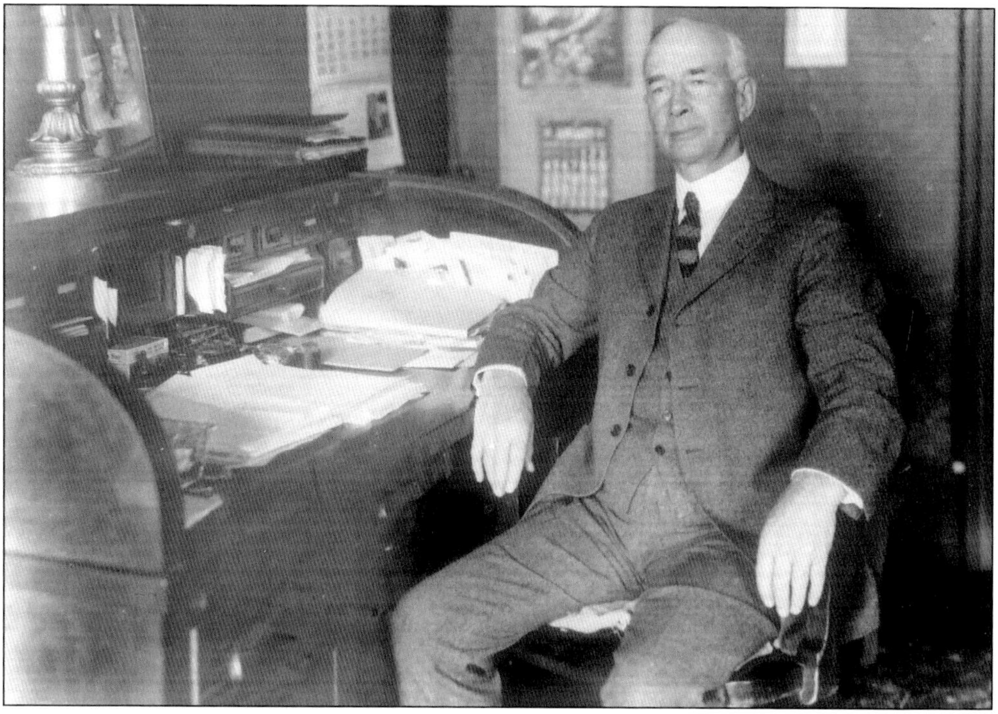

Dean of Agriculture, C.F. Curtiss, and his family resided in the Farm House on the campus during his long tenure at ISC, from 1897 until 1932.

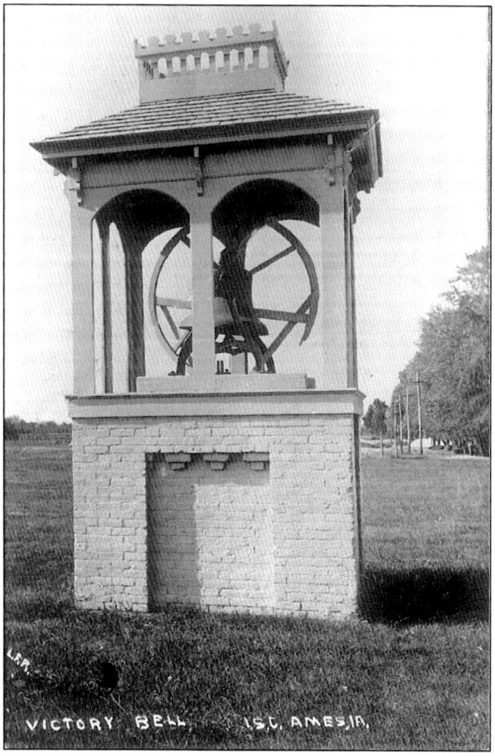

The Victory Bell, west of Beardshear Hall in 1920, was moved when Cyclone Stadium was built in the 1970s.

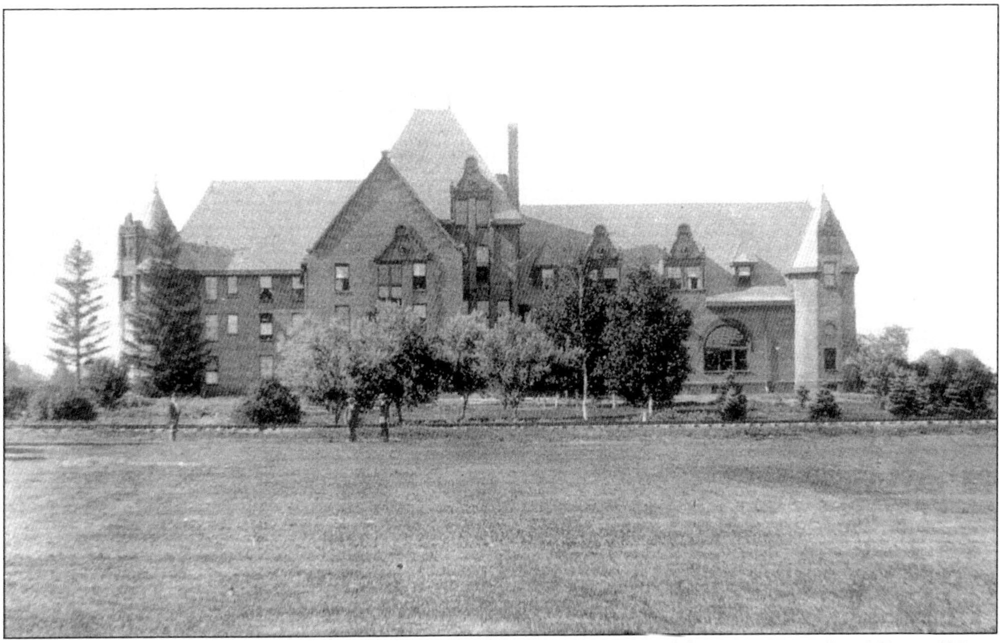

Margaret Hall, built in 1895, was named for Margaret McDonald Stanton, wife of Dean Edgar M. Stanton. Margaret was Preceptress of Iowa State College in 1877, and at her death on July 25, 1895, was the last original faculty member of the college.

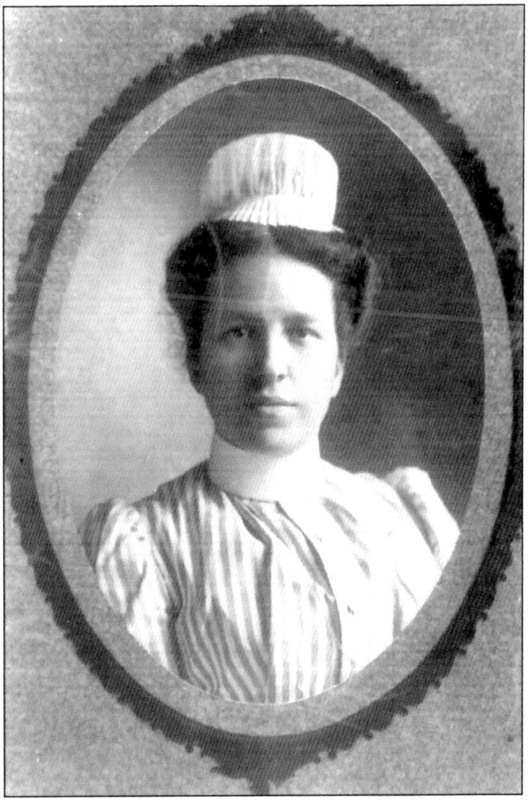

Mrs. Devers (first name unknown) was the first nursing superintendent at Iowa State College Hospital, from 1884 to 1907.

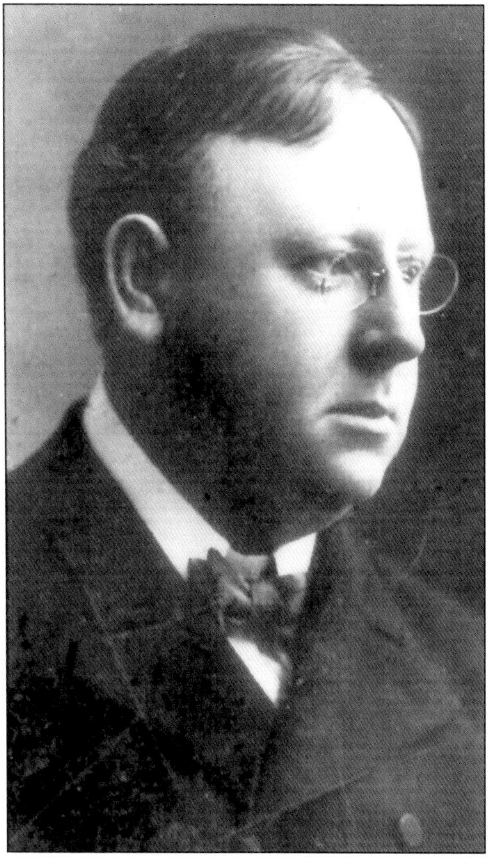

Dr. W.E. Harriman served as physician at Iowa State College from 1895 to 1907. An 1893 graduate of Iowa State, he received his medical training at Jefferson Medical College in Philadelphia.

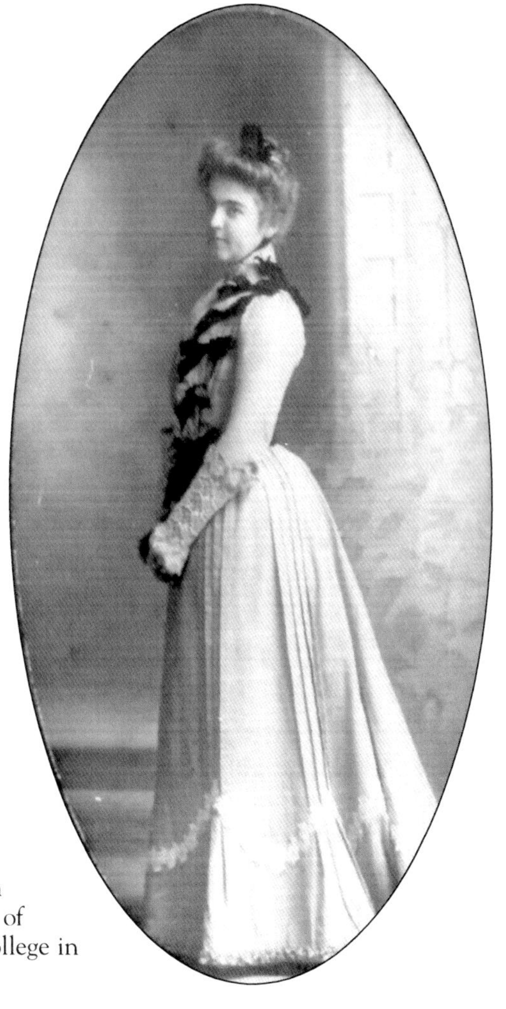

Winifred Tilden is seen here at graduation from Mount Holyoke College. She became the head of physical education for women at Iowa State College in 1904 and headed the department until 1944.

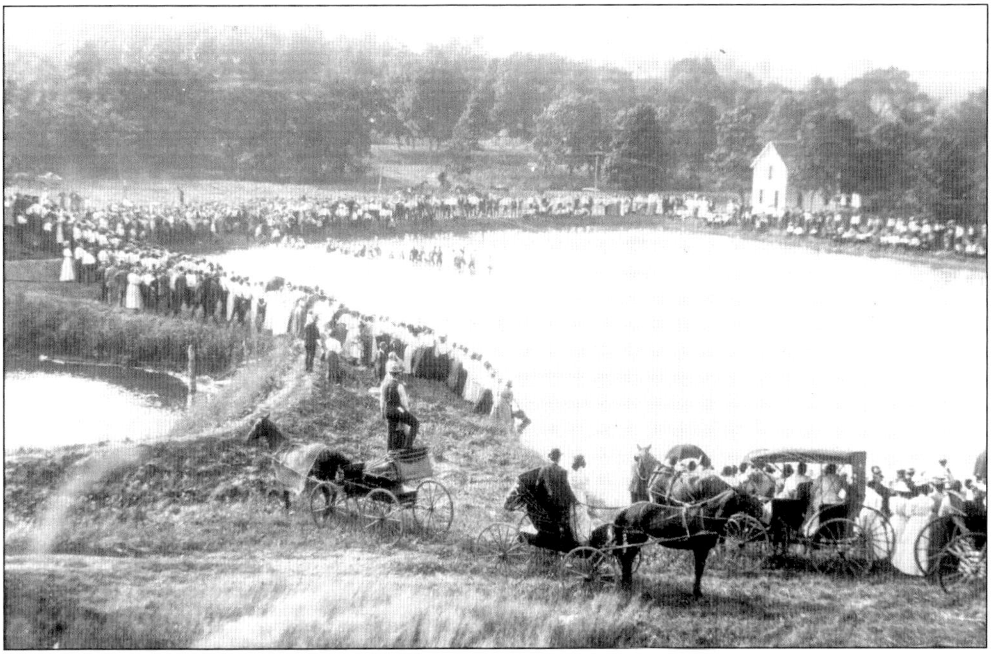

Briley's Pond, which no longer exists, was the site for many years for a tug-of-war between the freshmen and the sophomores at ISC. The pond was formed after clay was removed to make bricks for campus buildings, including the Farm House.

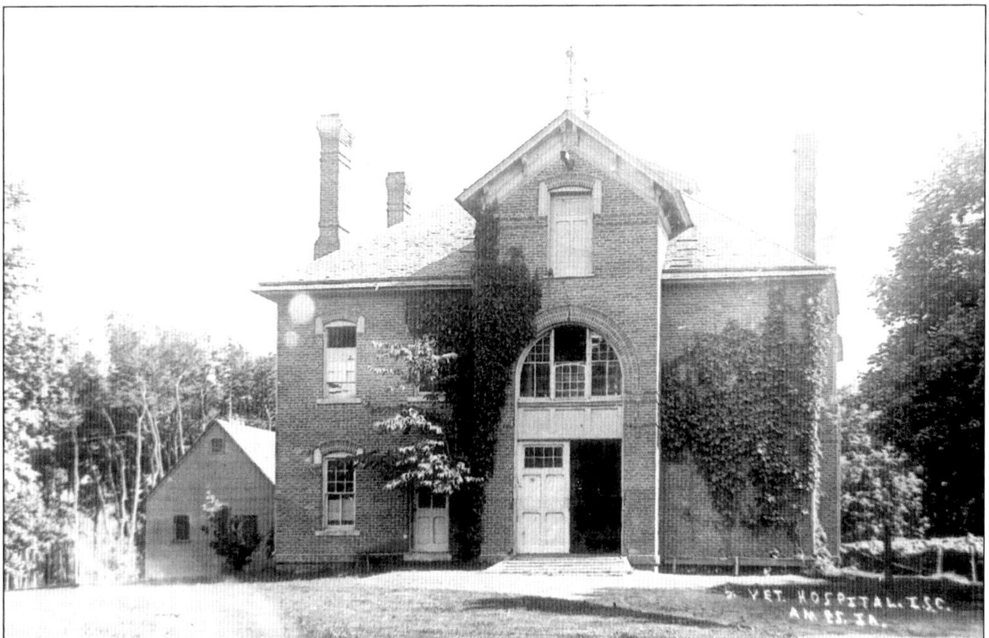

Construction of the Veterinary Hospital was begun in 1879 and completed in 1884. This first building of ISC's Veterinary College was in use until 1912 when it became the college's carpentry shop. It was finally razed in 1926 to make room for the construction of the Memorial Union.

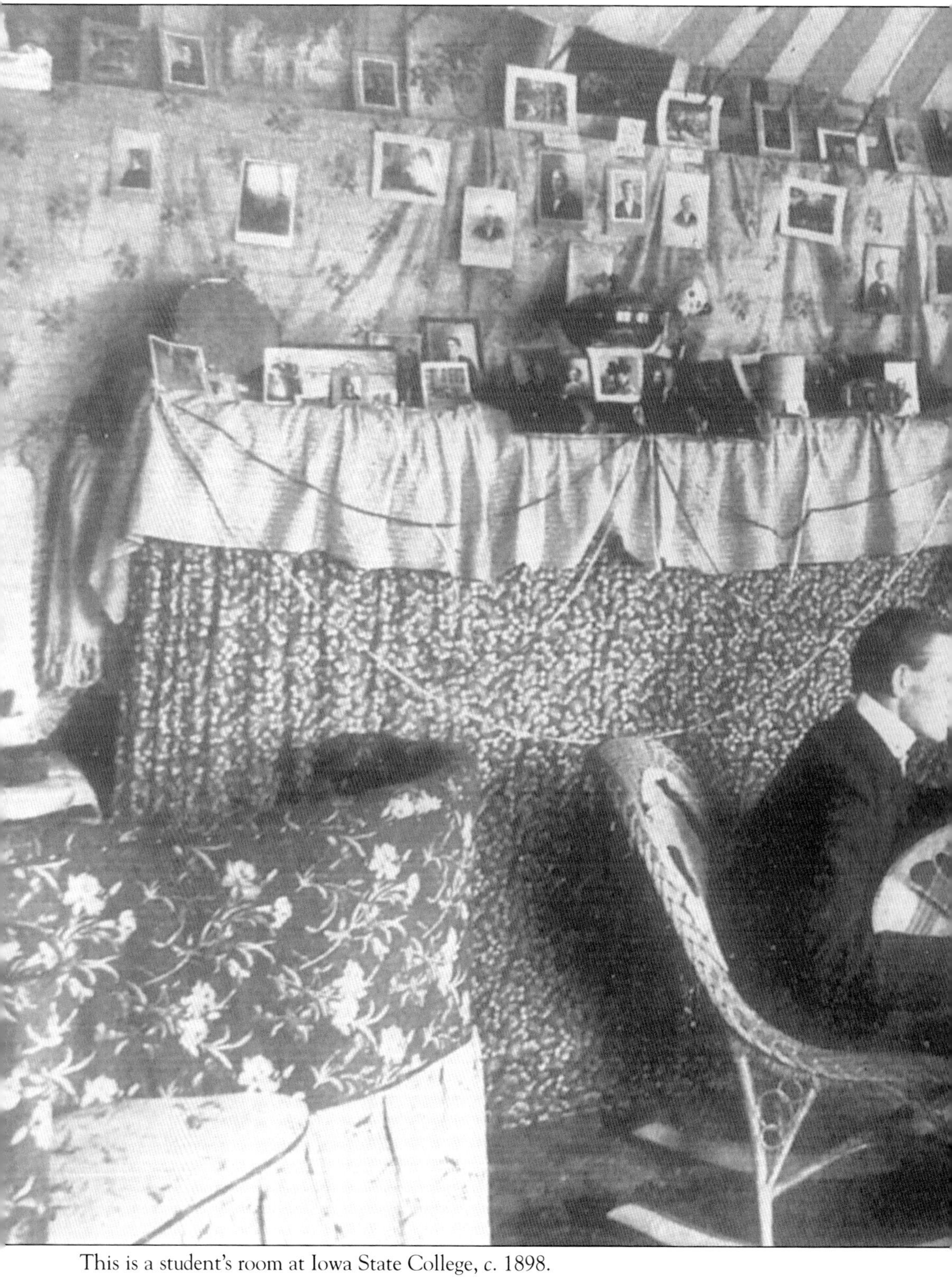

This is a student's room at Iowa State College, *c.* 1898.

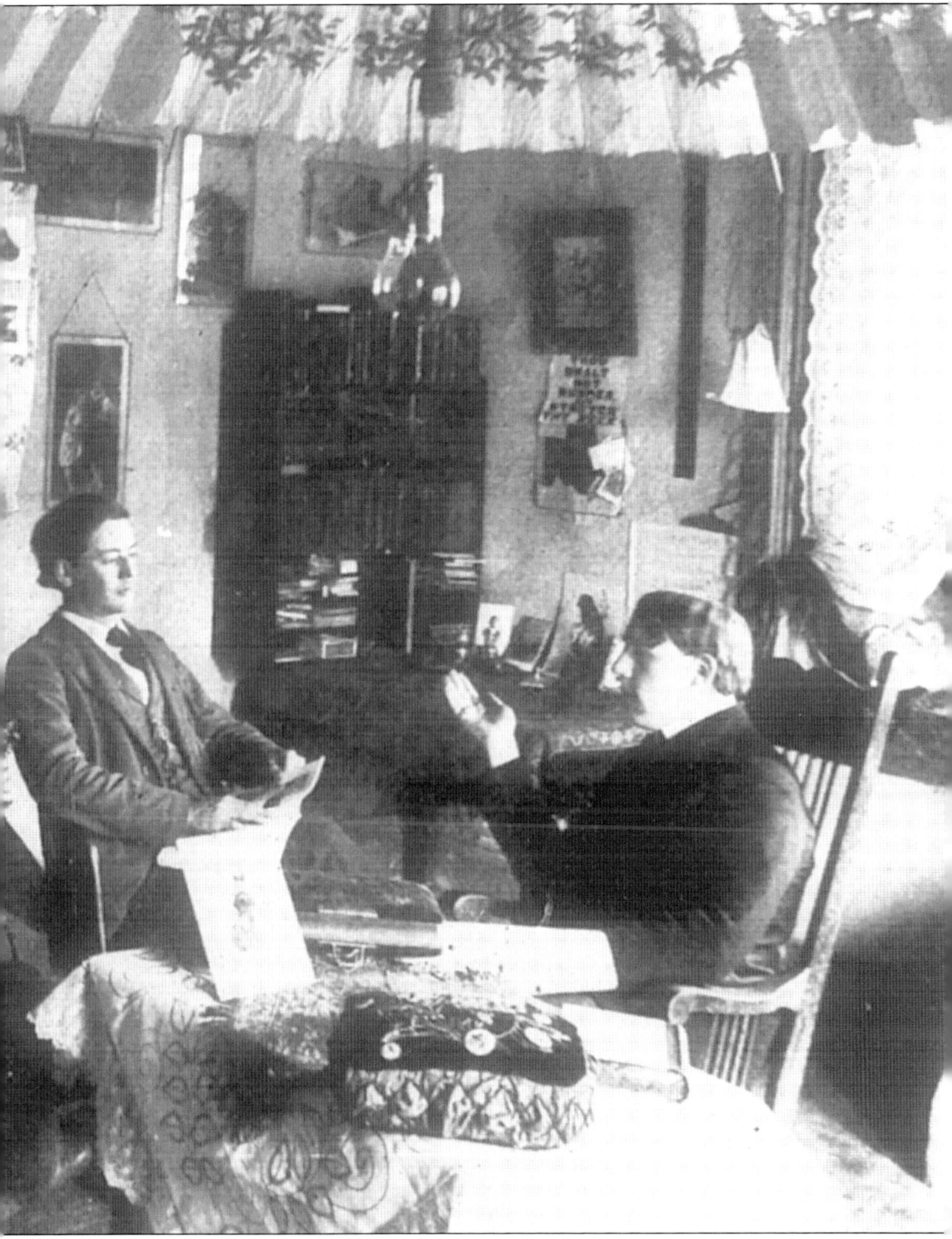

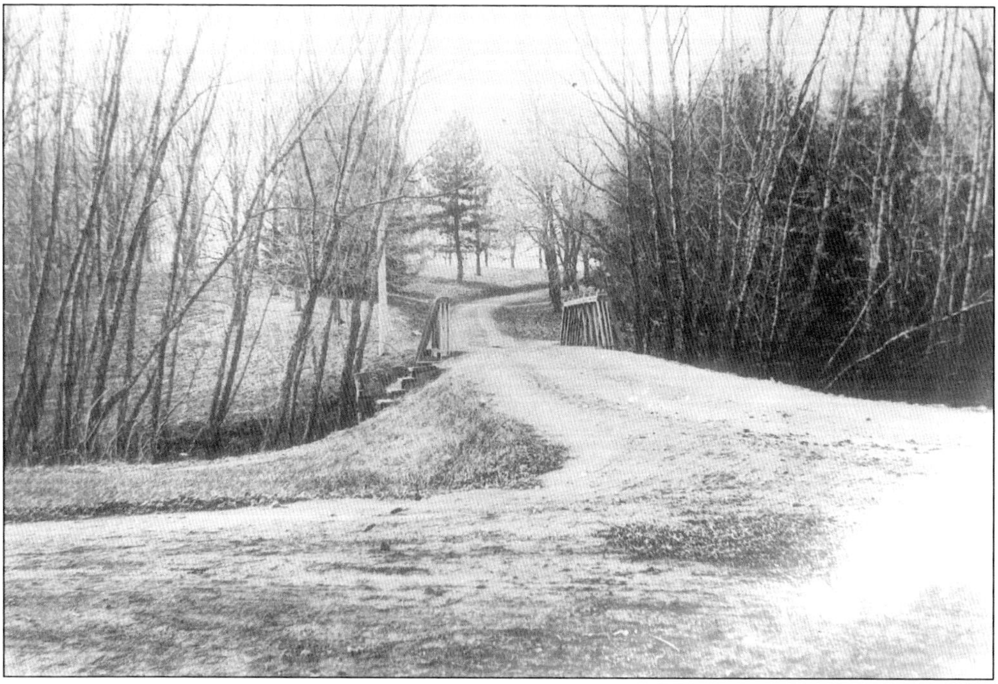

This 1904 view looking south from College Creek looks quite different today with dorms to the left and the Iowa State University president's home to the right.

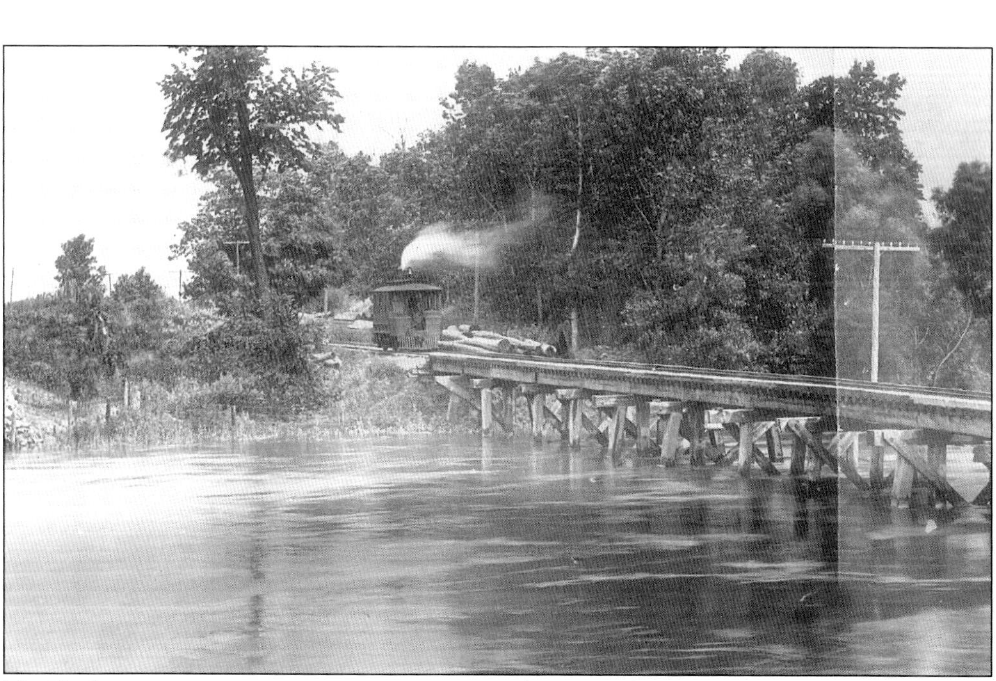

The Dinkey, minus passenger cars, is seen cautiously approaching Squaw Creek Bridge at a time when the creek was at flood stage, *c.* 1907. The line was electrified by July of that year.

Carrie Chapman Catt, an 1880 ISC graduate, was an American leader in the women's suffrage movement. In 1920, she founded the League of Women Voters.

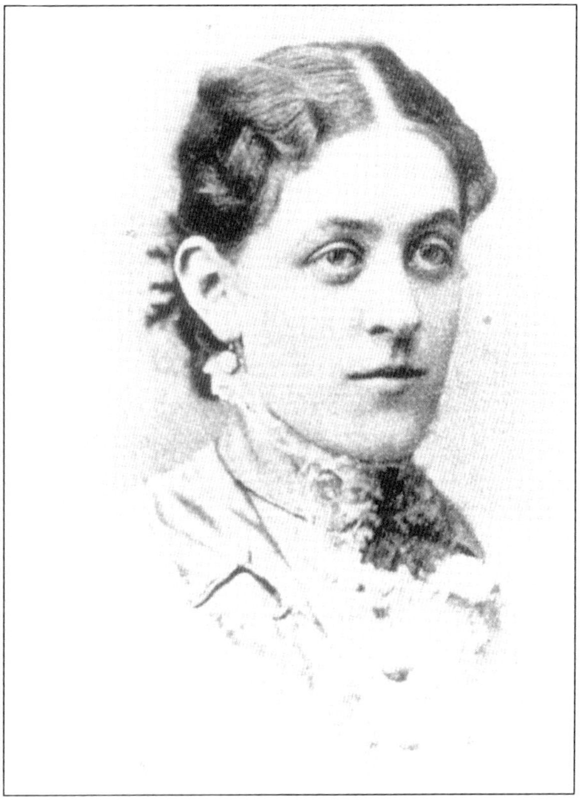

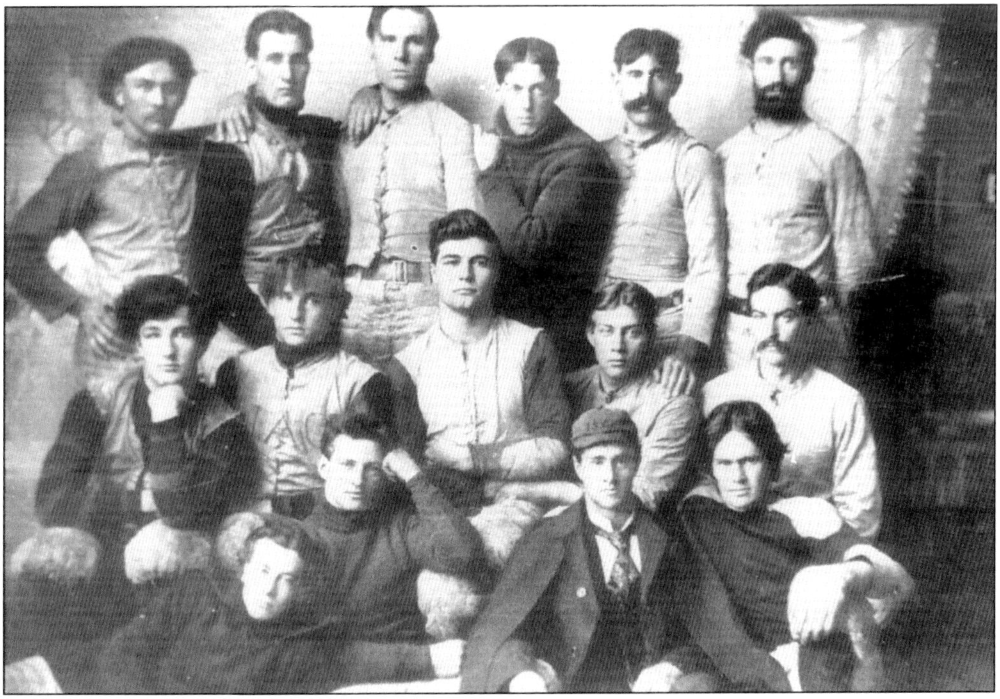

The first ISC football team to be called the Cyclones is seen here in 1895.

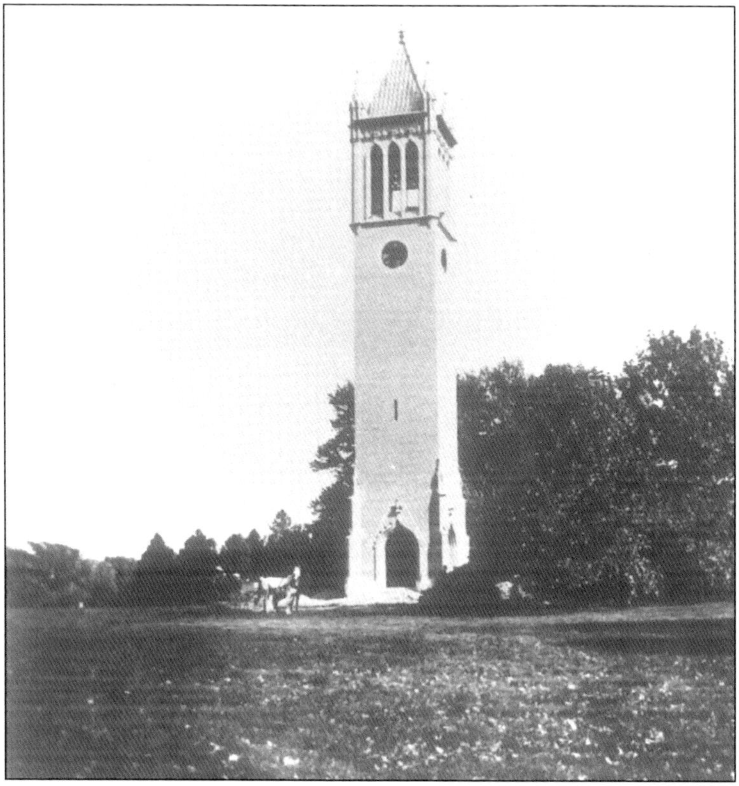

The ISC Campanile was built in 1897. The tower clocks, not yet installed, were purchased in 1899.

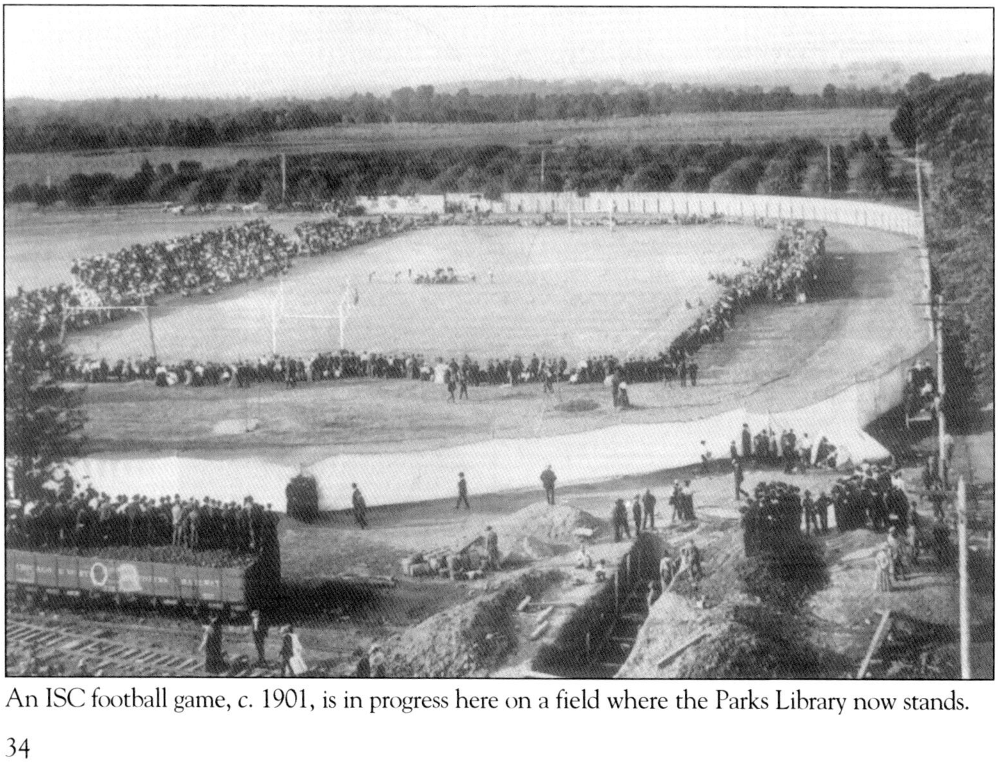

An ISC football game, c. 1901, is in progress here on a field where the Parks Library now stands.

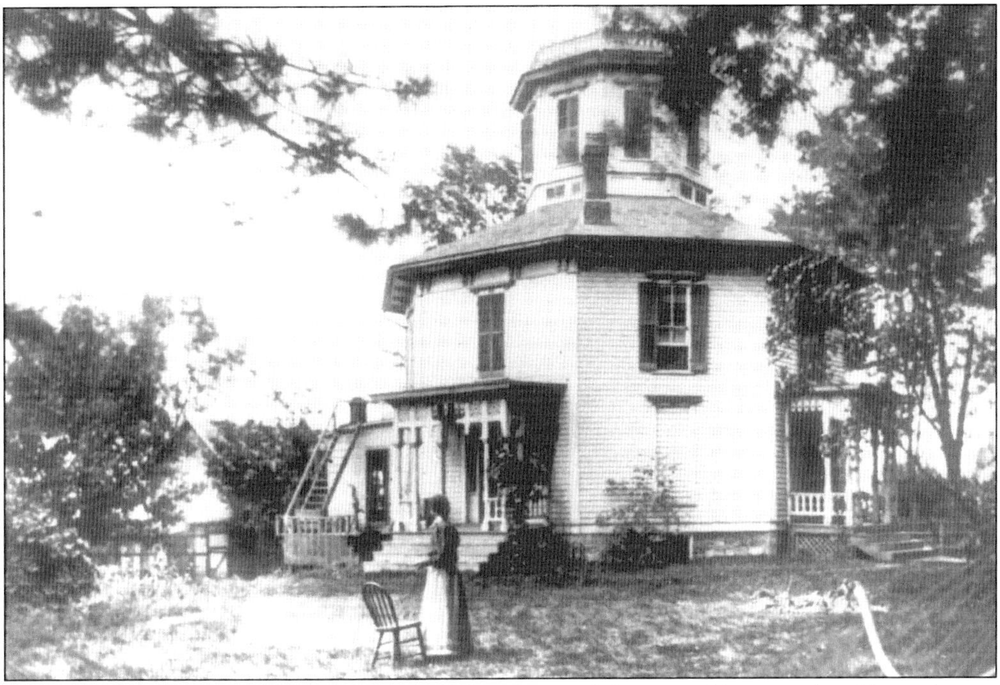

Dr. S.J. Starr built this house in the 1870s. The octagonal shape used less wood and heated more efficiently then contemporary rectangular houses. The Octagon Center for the Arts began and was located here from 1966 to 1968.

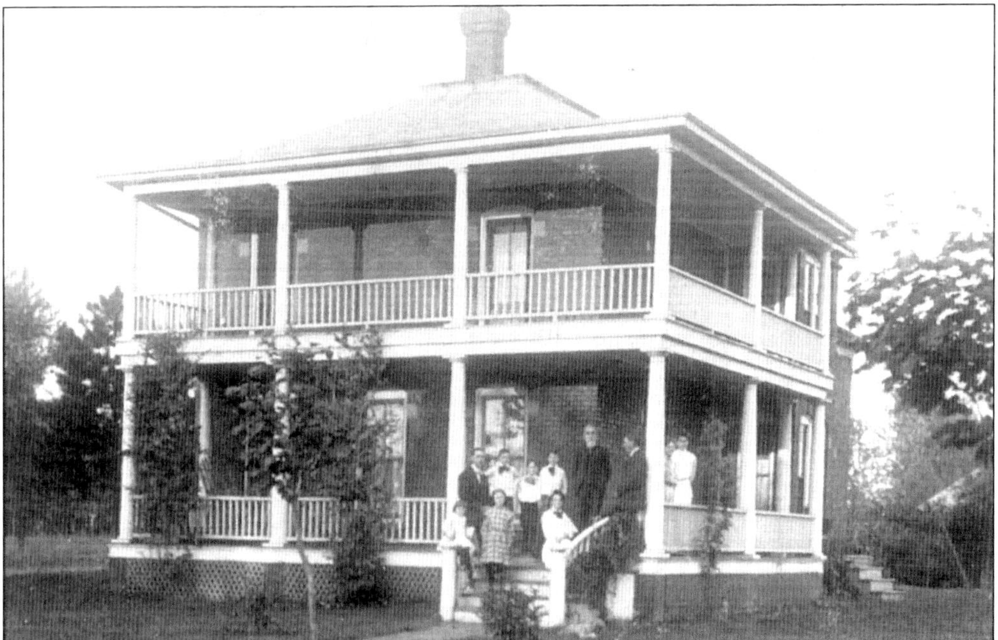

Edmund Loughran Sr. (with beard) stands on the porch of his home, located on the southeast corner of Sixth and Carroll across from the Bandshell Park. The house was built in about 1885 by Dr. Beverly, an early Ames physician.

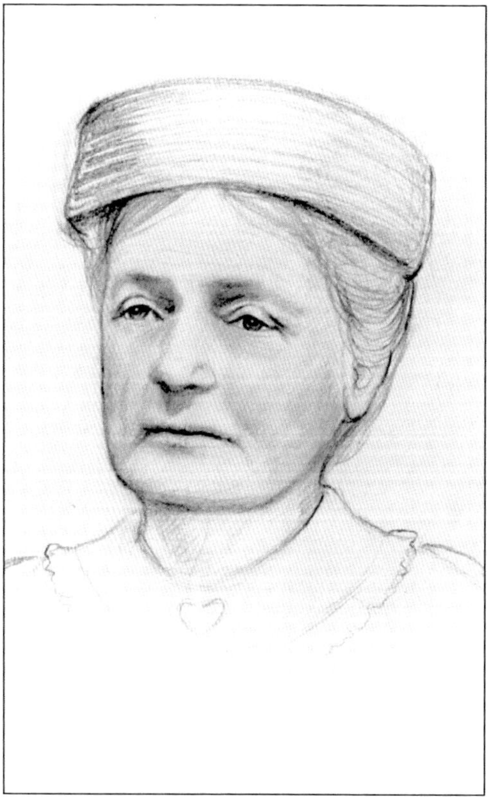

Cynthia Olive Duff (1820–1907) came to what later became Ames with her husband, Alexander, in 1863. She is sometimes referred to as one of the founders of Ames.

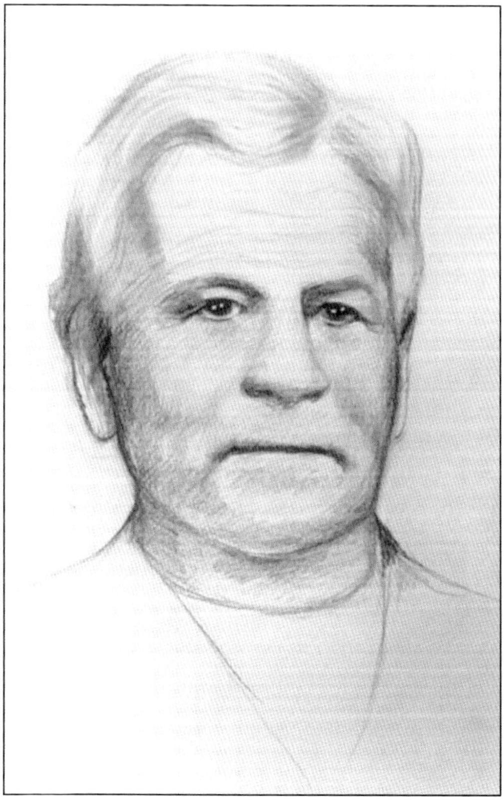

Alexander Duff (1814–1896), along with his wife, Cynthia, farmed land at the north edge of Ames.

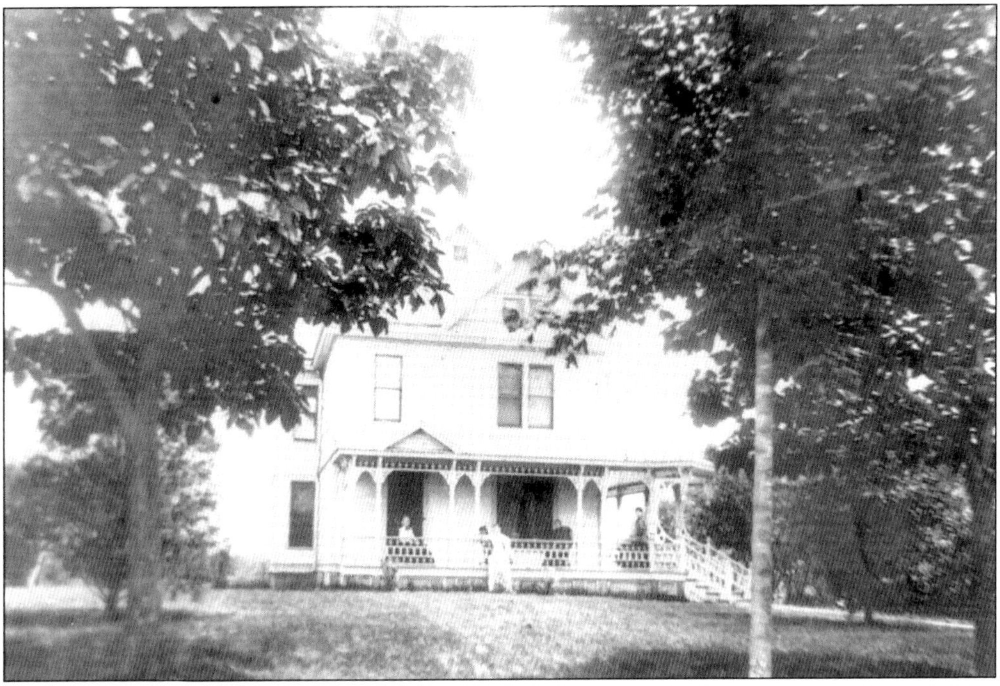

The H.L. Munn house on Duff just north of Eighth Street was built by its namesake, *c.* 1897.

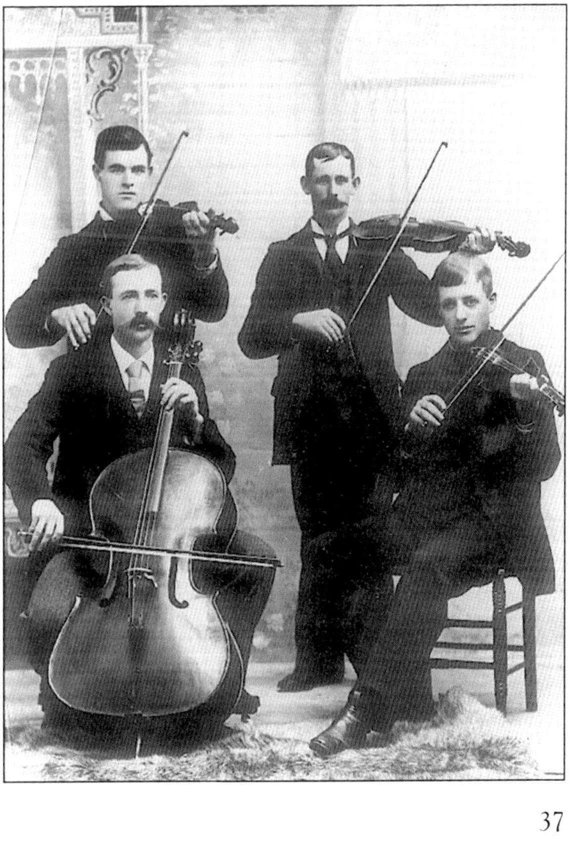

A popular string quartet of the 1890s is seen here, from left to right, as follows: (front row) Roy Taylor and Fay Taylor; (back row) George Miller and Jack Boyd. Miller managed a grocery business in Ames; Roy Taylor was a longtime barber on Main Street and his brother Fay was a farmer northeast of Ames.

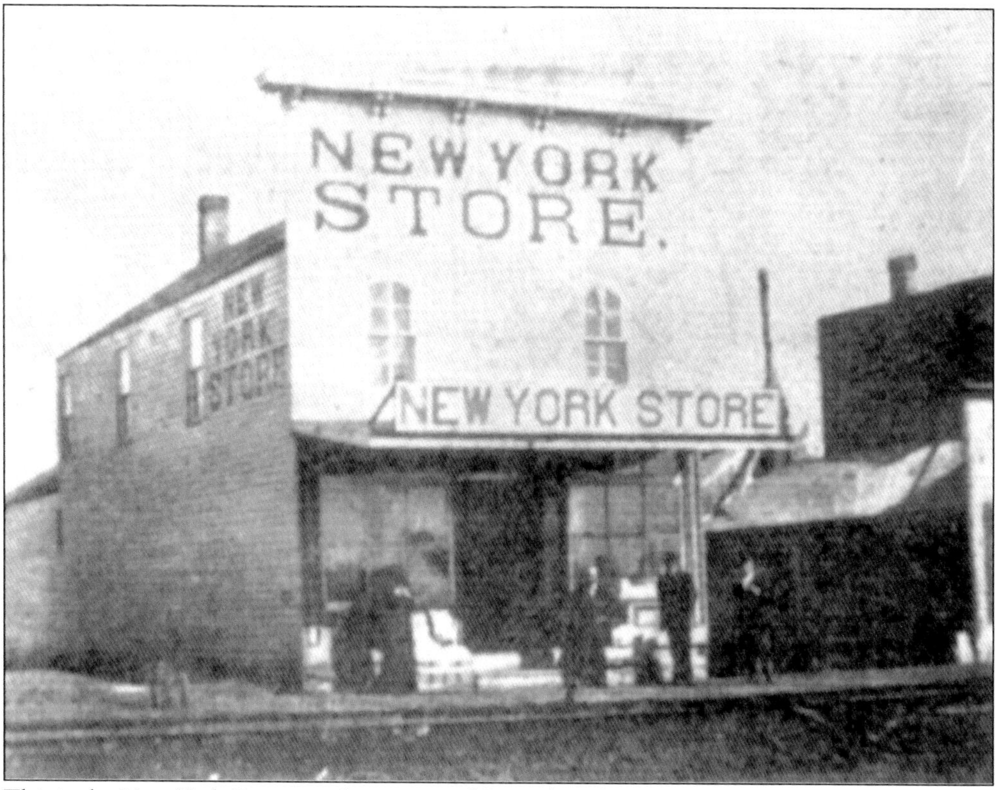

This is the New York Store, on the corner of Onondaga (Main) and Kellogg, c. 1870.

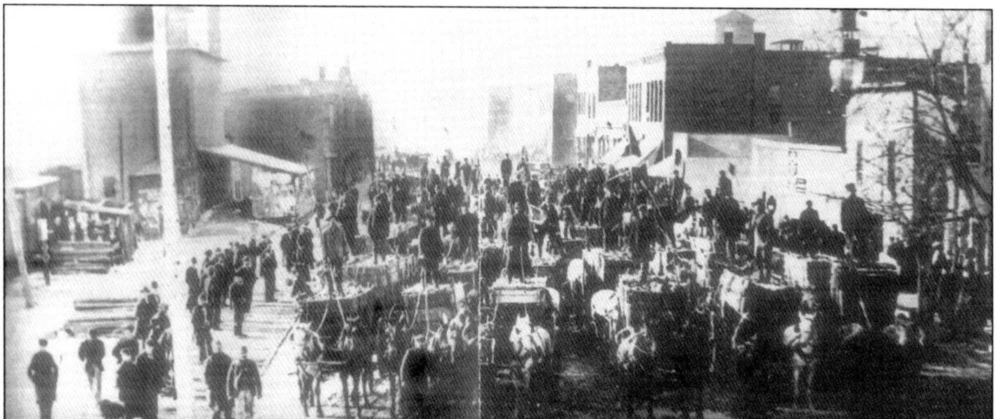
In January 1897, 47 loads of corn were sold to the Lockwood Grain Co. at 11¢ a bushel, by George Bell of Ames. Friends and neighbors had picked 2,204 bushels when Mr. Bell was ill. This photo looks from Duff down Onondaga (Main).

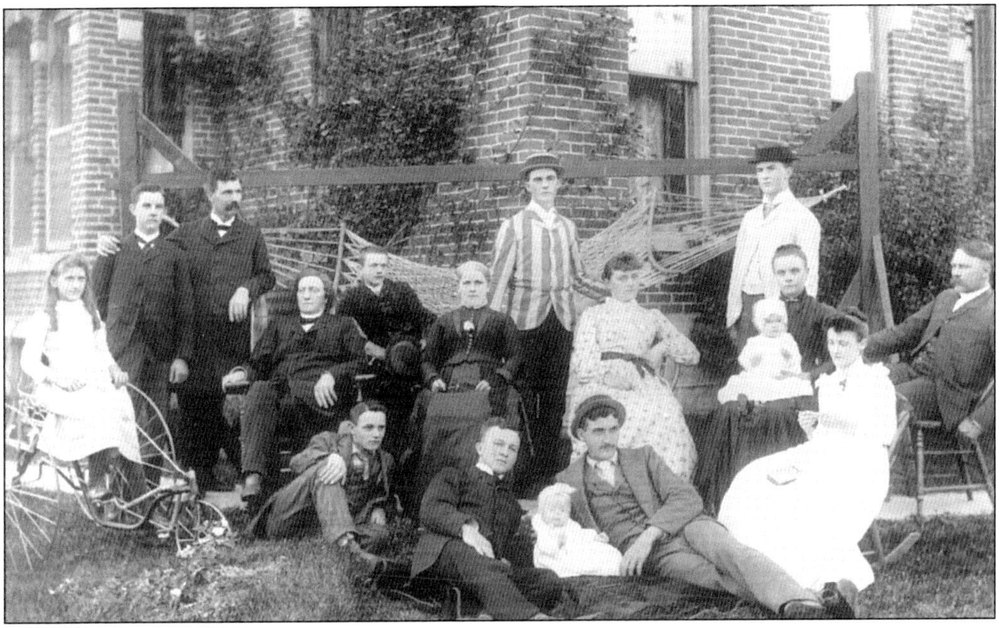

The K.W. Brown home in 1891 was host to this family gathering, with the partygoers, from left to right, as follows: (front row) Gates M. Brown, Clinton G. Brown, Faith Loughram (baby), Stephen L. Loughram, and Lillian Brown Loughram; (back row) Daisy D. Brown (on tricycle), Rolla R. Brown, Dwight P. Brown, Rev. Loren G. Brown, Harry F. Brown, Martha J. Brown (wife of L.G.), Charles S. Brown (seen standing), Josie Brown (wife of Charles), Velora O. Brown (also standing), Margaret M. Brown (wife of K.W.), Lydia B. Brown (in Margaret's lap), and Kendrick W. Brown.

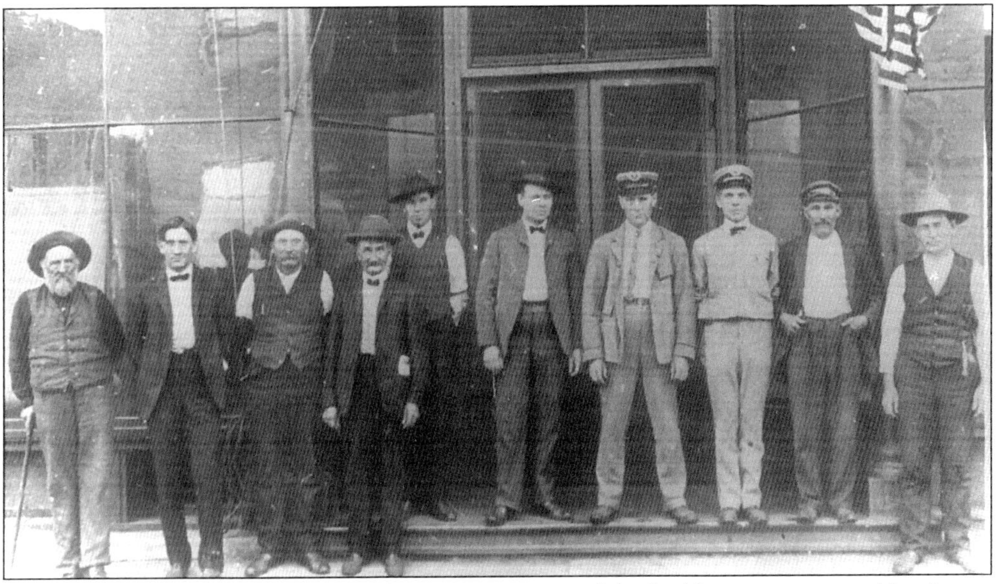

The post office was located on Douglas Avenue in part of the building now occupied by the gas office until 1912. The postal officials, seen here in this early photograph, from left to right are as follows: Henry May (Ames' first schoolteacher, who was later a rural mail carrier), Mr. Coon, Uford Rich, Ben Keltner, and Racine Goble. The remaining people are unidentified.

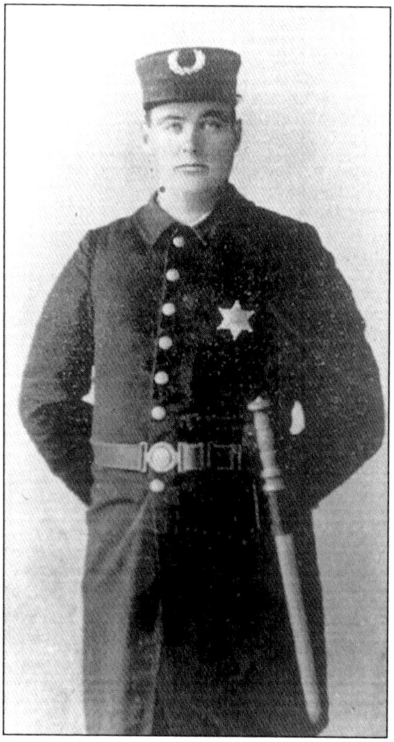

Town Marshall William A. Ricketts, affectionately known as "Big Bill," was a one-person police force from 1896 until 1903, when Ames' population was 2,400. Ricketts spent his time corralling brawlers, chastising bootleggers, and nabbing thieves.

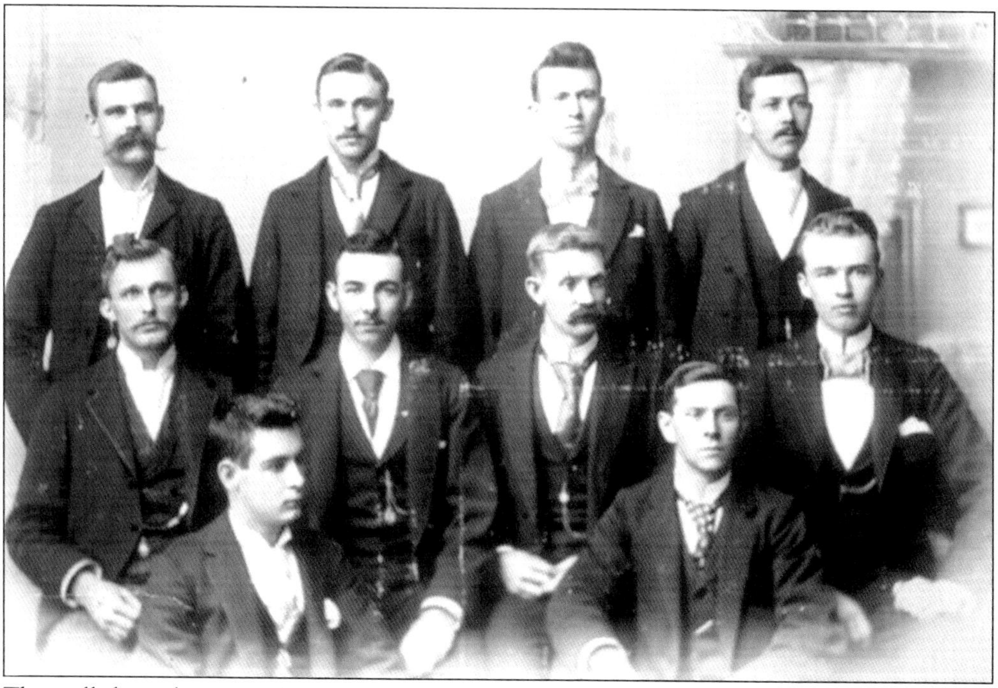

The well-dressed men in this photograph pose for the camera, c. 1905. They are, from left to right, as follows: (front row) B.J. Sheldon and M.J. Adams; (middle row) Robert McCarthy, L.C. Tilden, Harley Stuckslager, and A.H. Munn; (back row) S.G. Hamilton, Elmer Sowers, Mr. Henderson, and George E. Baker.

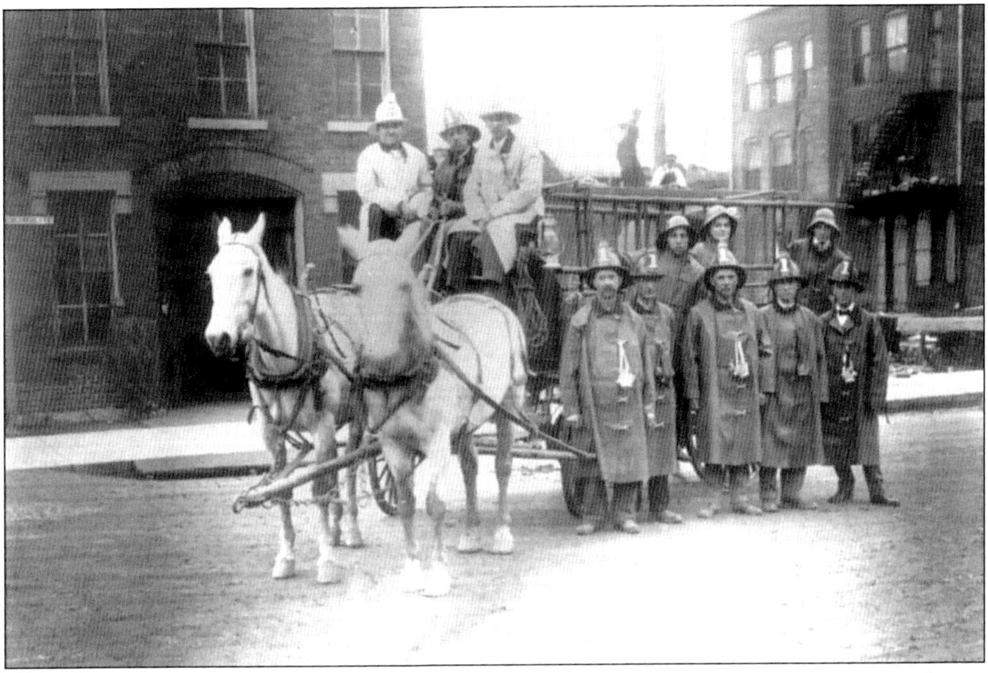

Seen here in front of the first city hall is the volunteer fire department, *c.* 1915. Lynn Morris, the first fire chief, is seated at left.

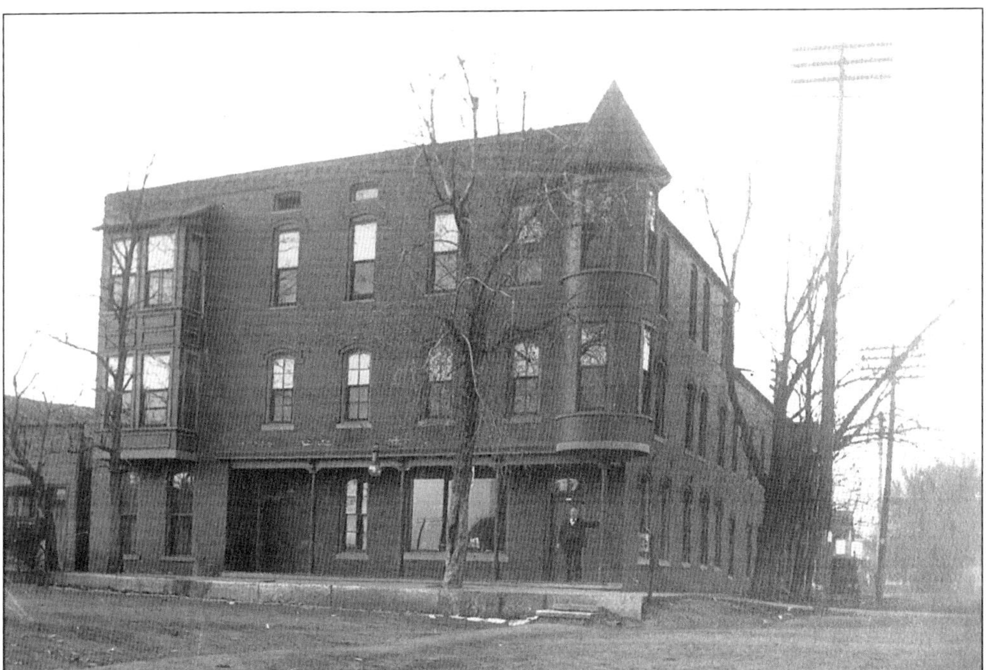

The Ames Hotel, previously known as the Davis Hotel, is seen here *c.* 1902.

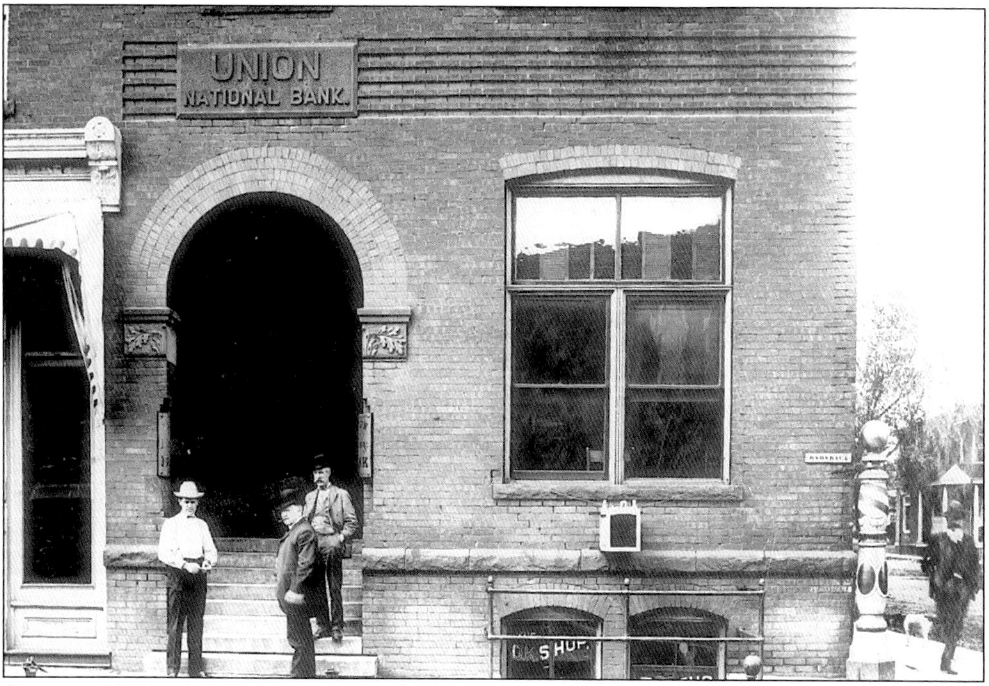

Captain Wallace M. Greeley, captured for the camera in a derby hat in this photo from 1905, was founder and president of the Union National Bank on the corner of Douglas and Onondaga (Main). Lon Hardin (on the left), publisher and editor of the *Ames Evening Times*, and Van Chanderlain, lumber dealer, chat with Mr. Greeley.

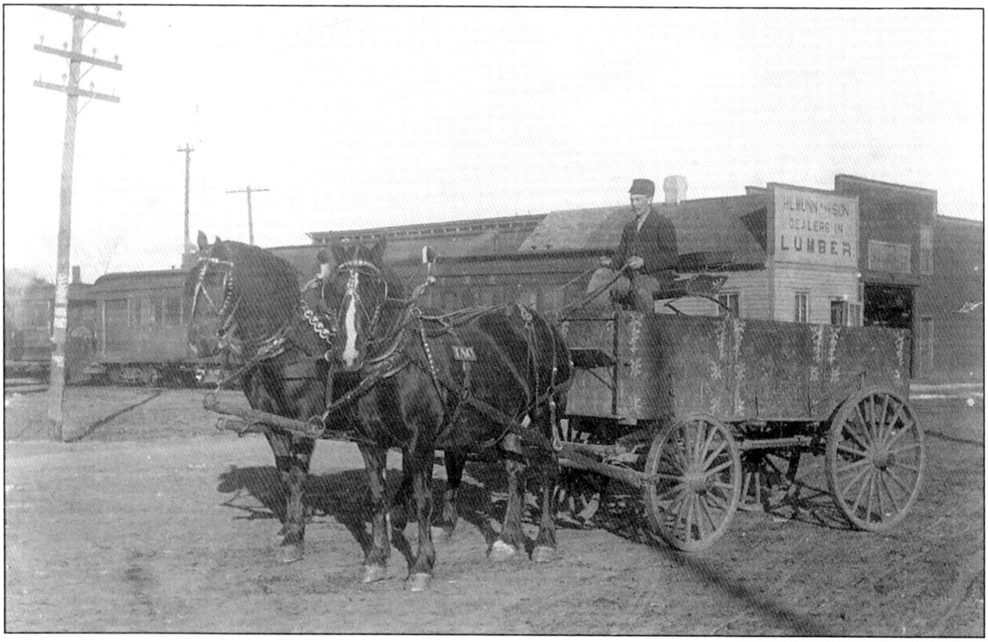

This Iowa State College horse and wagon team is seen leaving H.L. Munn and Son lumberyard in 1906. Iowa Agricultural College became Iowa State College in 1898, but notice the brass IAC insignia on the harness.

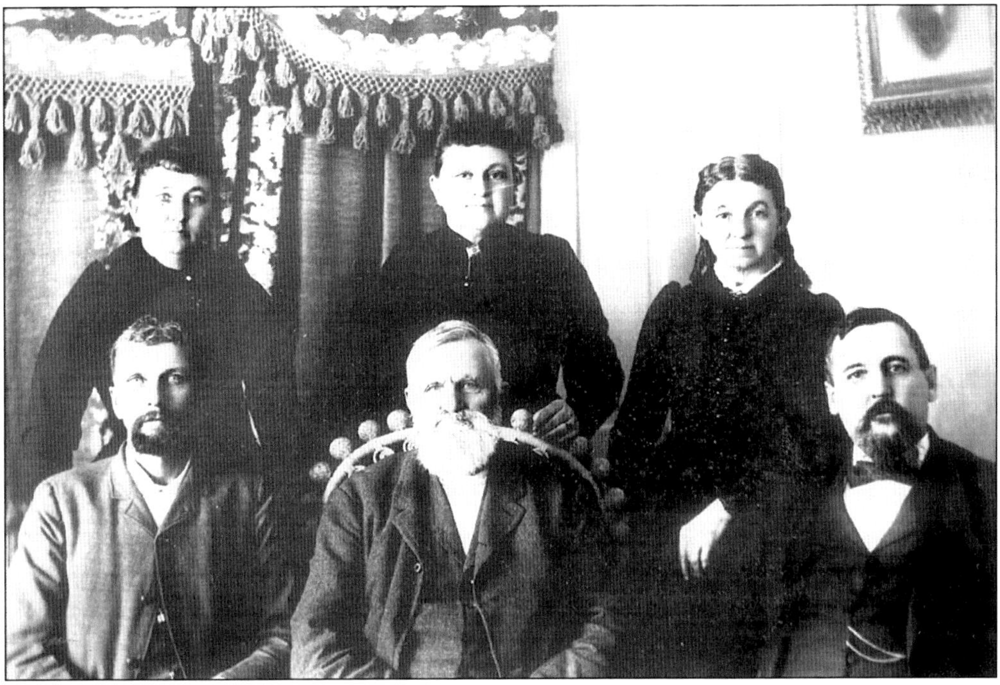

Julius Tilden poses with his sons and daughters on Christmas Day, 1891. From left to right, they are as follows: (front row) Fred Tilden, Julius C. Tilden, and George G. Tilden; (back row) Abbie Tilden Drake, Julia Tilden McClain, and Susan Tilden Goodnow. George Tilden founded the Tilden Department Store that operated from 1869 to 1971.

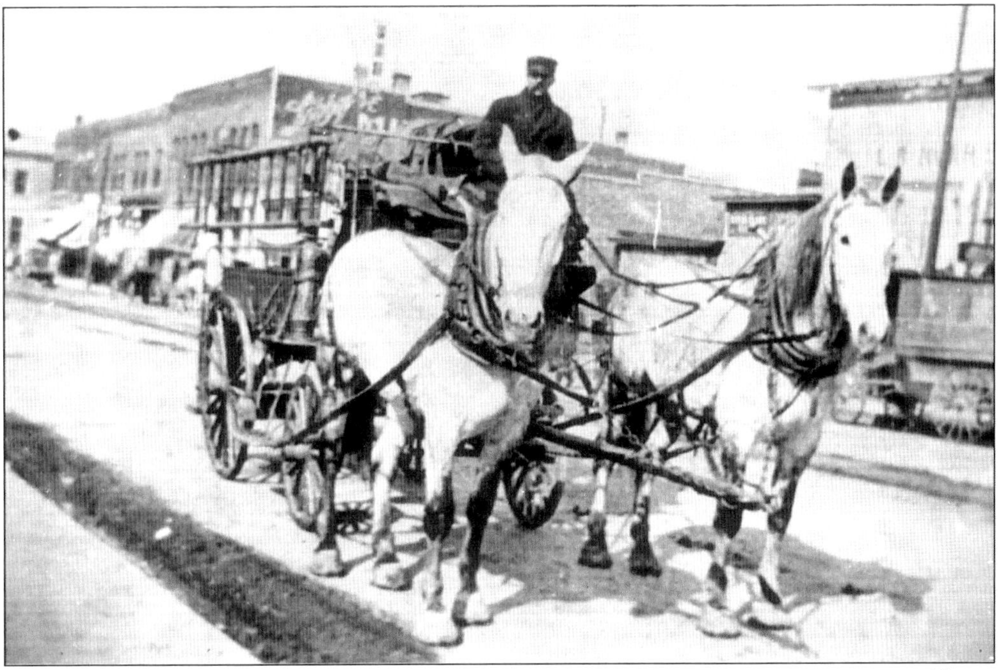

Art McCoy drives the Ames fire wagon in 1912 in front of the Lynn Morris Livery Stable on east Onondaga (Main) Street.

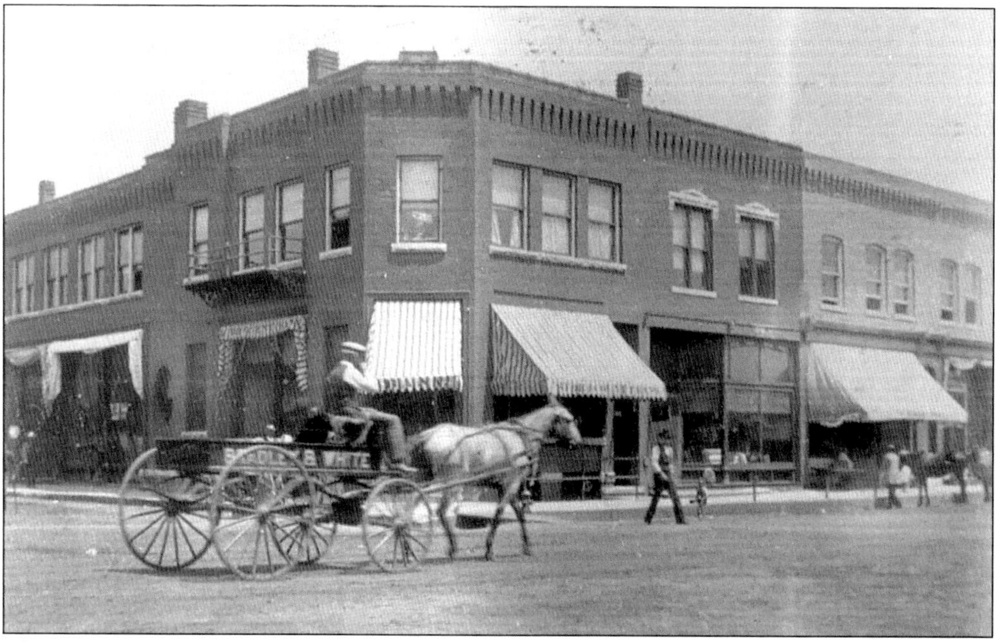

This is Parley Sheldon's Story Country Bank, on the corner of Douglas Avenue and Onondaga (Main) Street, *c.* 1905. It is the present-day Alliant Energy office. The delivery wagon is headed for the Bradley and White Grocery down the street (with the awning). On the second floor were the offices of law firm McCarthy and Lee.

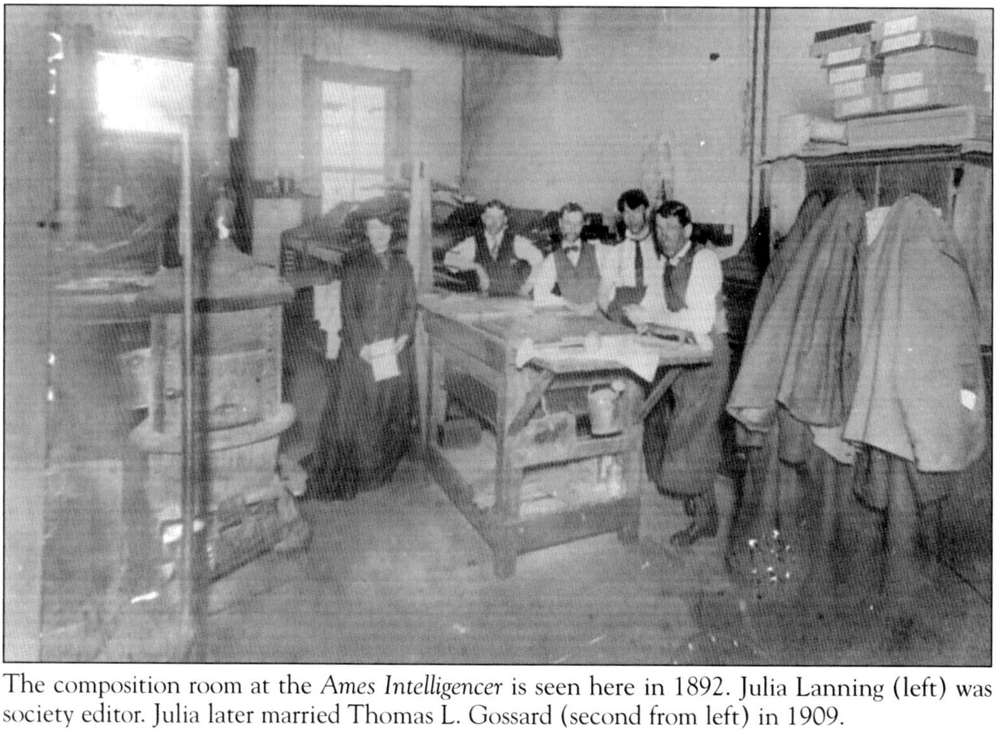

The composition room at the *Ames Intelligencer* is seen here in 1892. Julia Lanning (left) was society editor. Julia later married Thomas L. Gossard (second from left) in 1909.

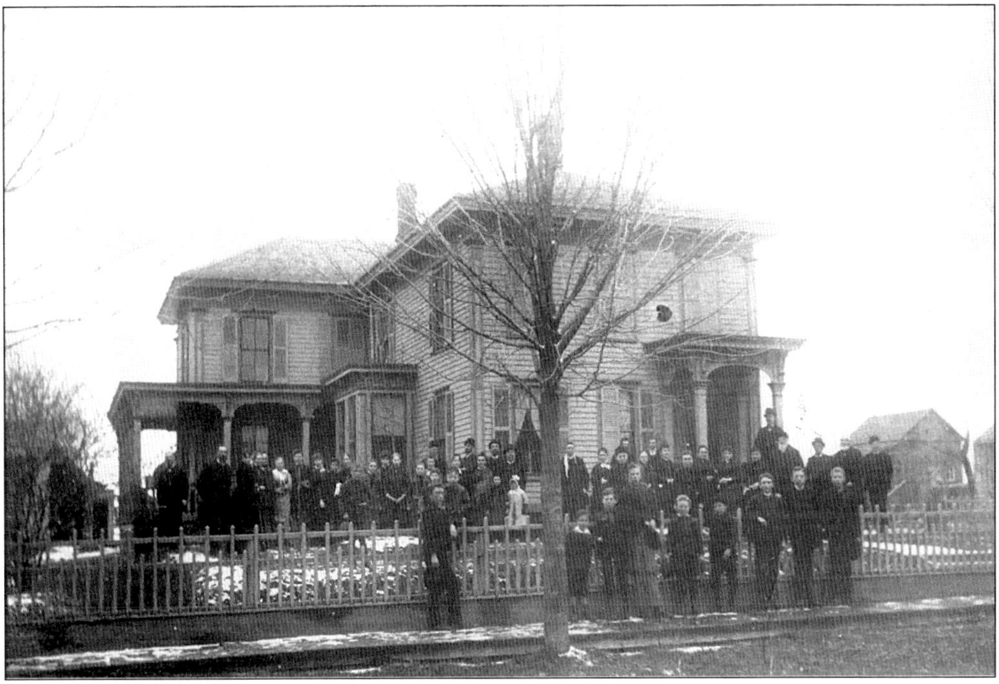

The George G. Tilden home, built in 1869, is seen here on Christmas Day, 1892. It was originally located on Douglas Avenue; later, half the house was moved to Kellogg.

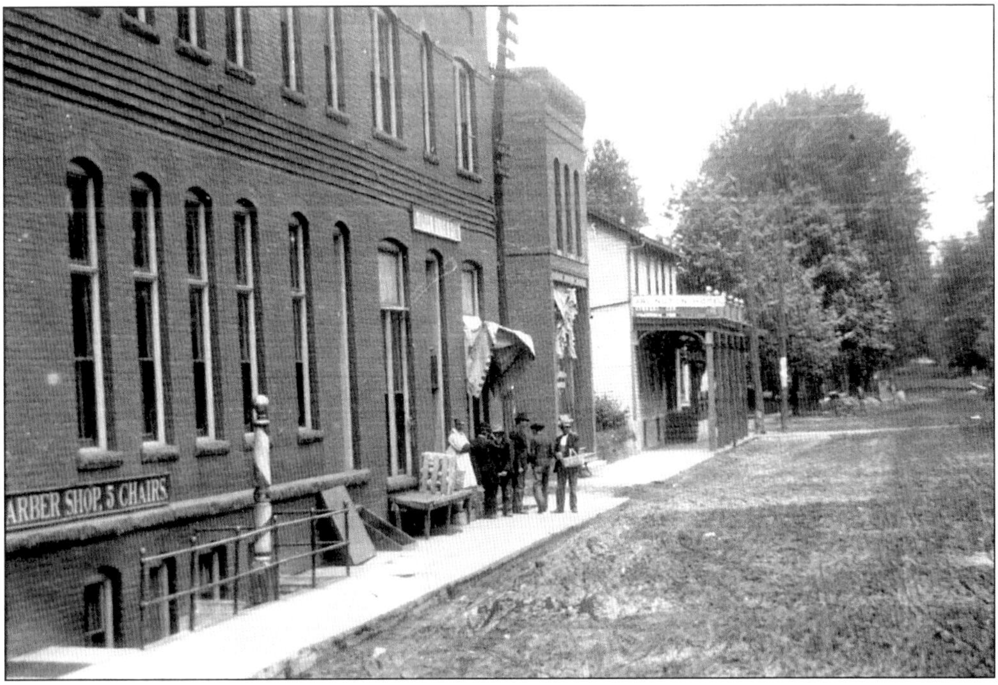

Looking north on Douglas Avenue, one could see on the left the O.K. Barbershop, Tilden Grocery, the newspaper office, and the Arlington Hotel, c. 1907.

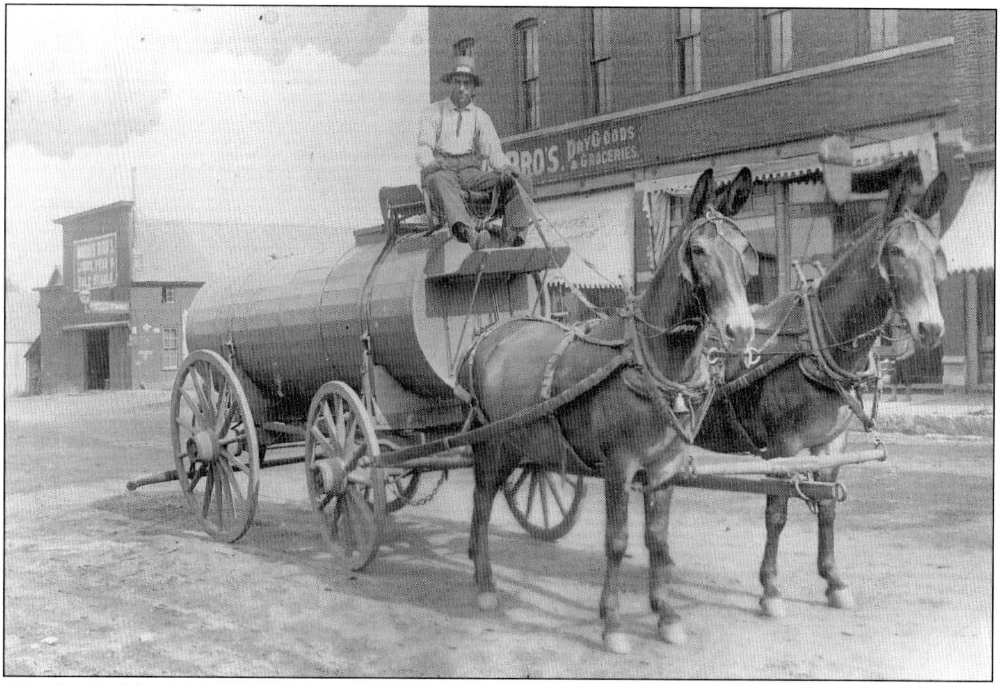

Charlie Holdredge, in 1895, contracted with the city to keep the dust settled in the business district with this sprinkler wagon, shown at the corner of Kellogg and Main.

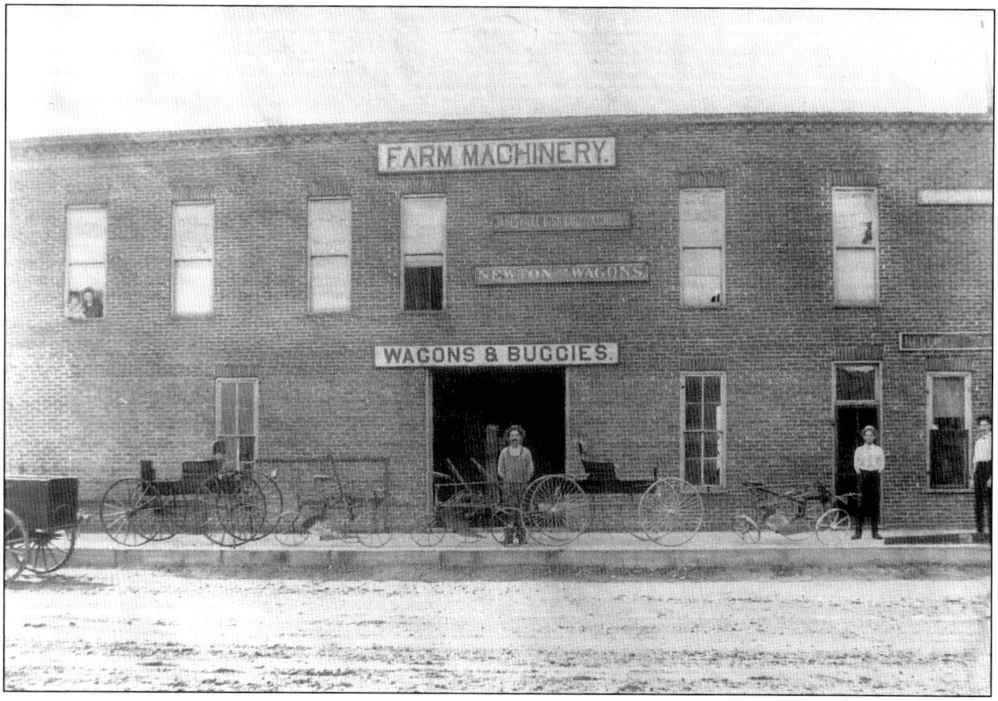

The Loughran Machine Company building, on the east end of Main Street, later became a part of the Munn Lumber Company. Stephen L. Loughran stands on the far right next to his brother-in-law, Harry Brown.

William West (1821–1919) was Ames' first mayor and proprietor of the West House, the first hotel in Ames, from 1869 to 1892. The hotel was located on the site of today's Octagon Art Center.

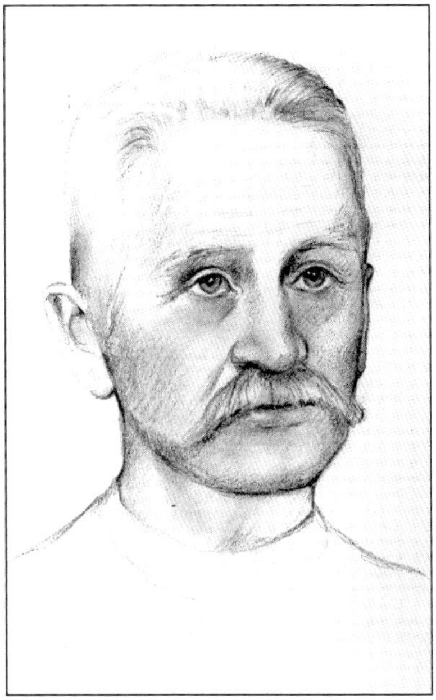

The City Drug Store stood opposite the "pocketwatch" clock on Onondaga (Main) Street, c. 1890.

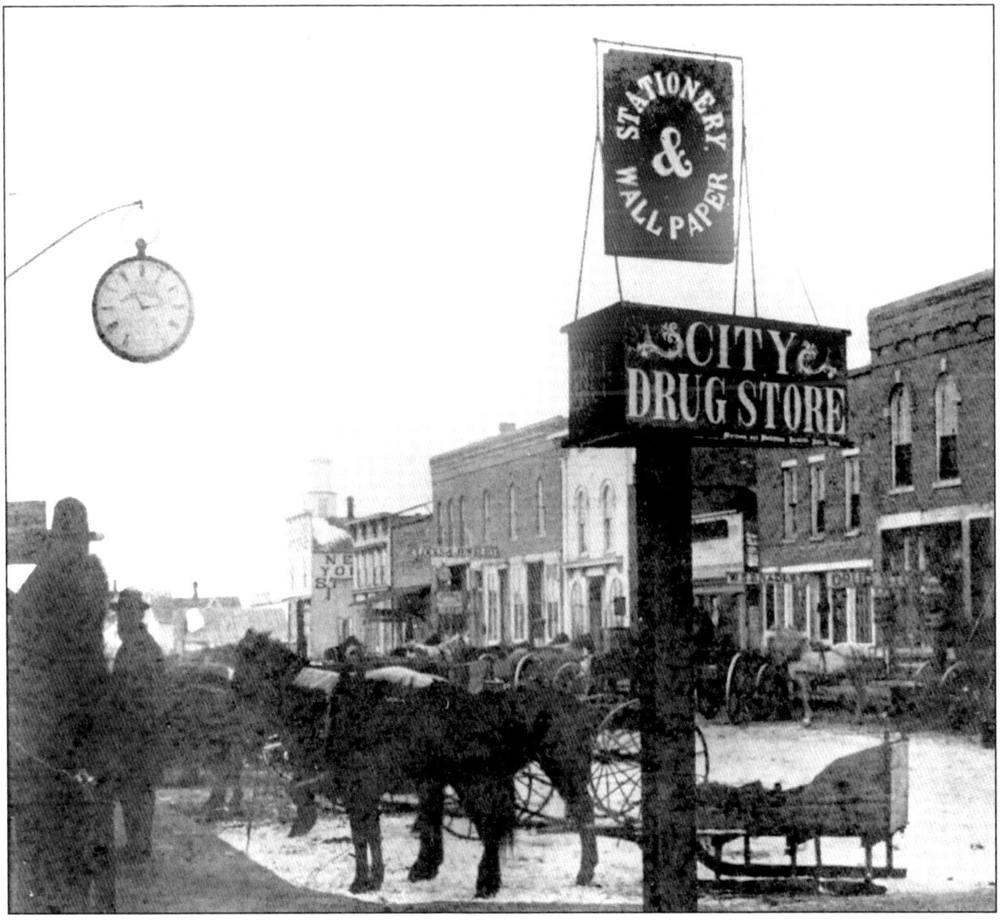

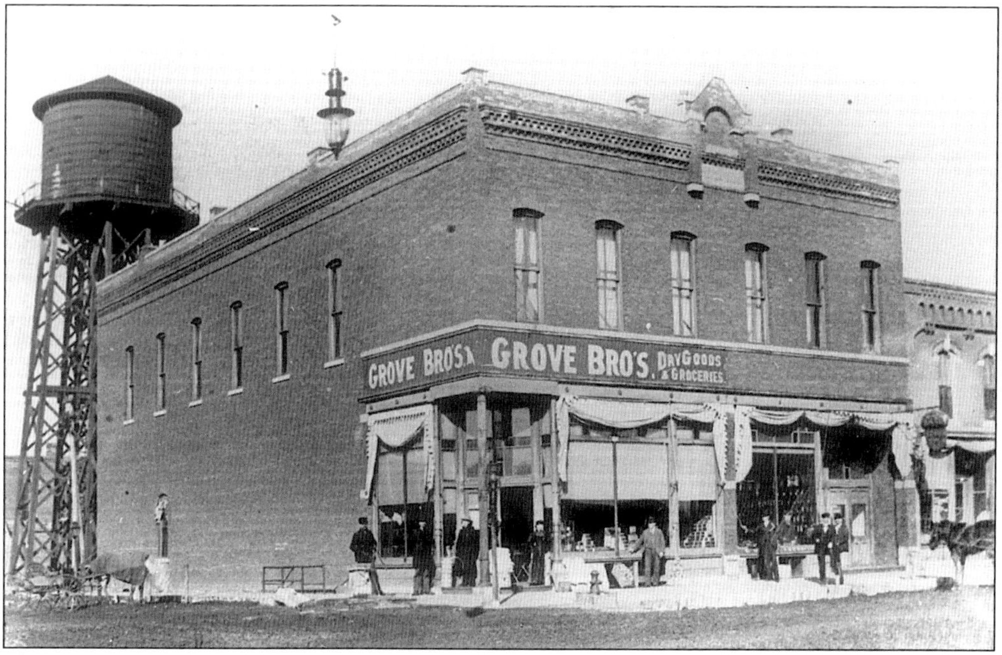

The Grove brothers' general store was on the northeast corner of Onondaga (Main) and Kellogg in 1897. The water tower was built in 1891.

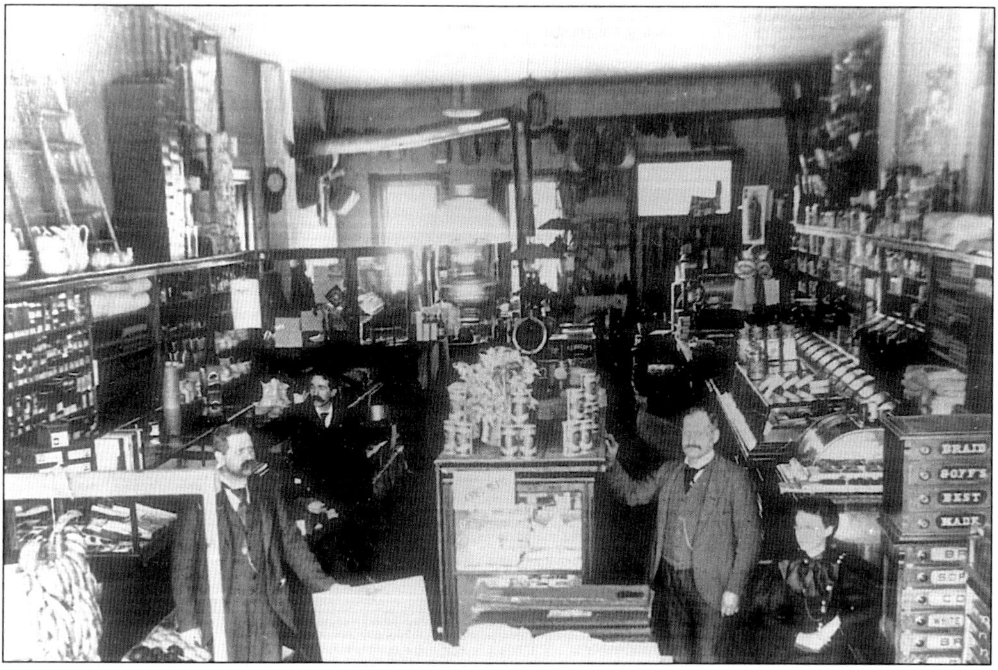

The interior of Grove Brothers Dry Goods and Groceries is seen c. 1892. The two men in front are probably A.J. and Jasper Grove.

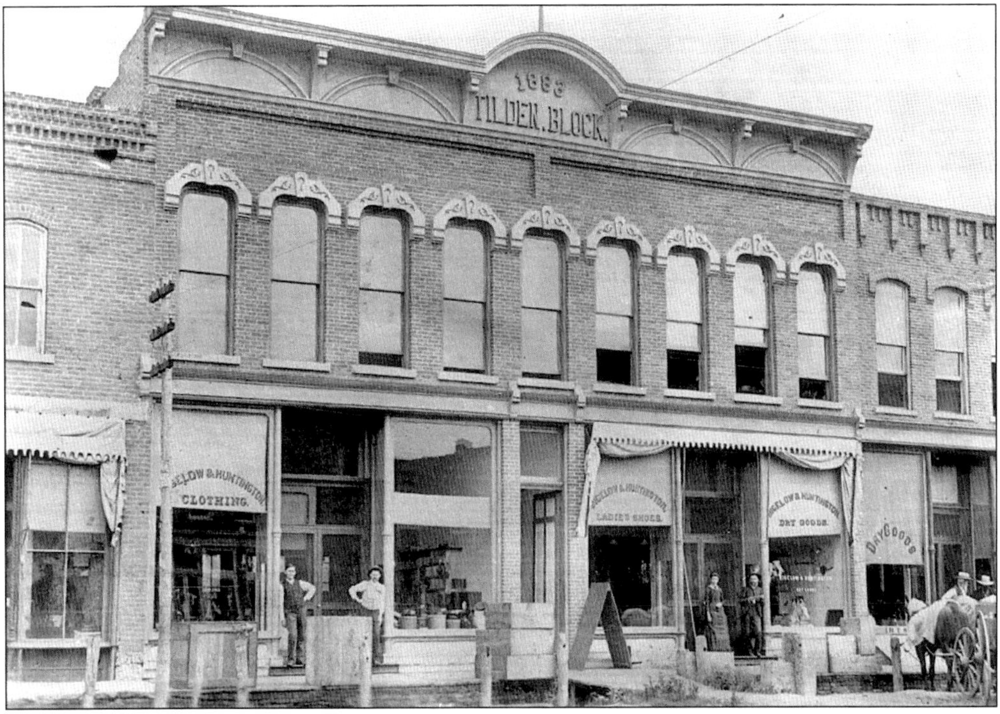

The Tilden Block on Onondaga (Main), built in 1883, housed Bigelow and Huntington, a clothing and dry goods store, until 1900. Shown in the west doorway are M.K. Smith and J.J. Grove. Shown in the east doorway are Margaret Mitchell and B.A. Bigelow.

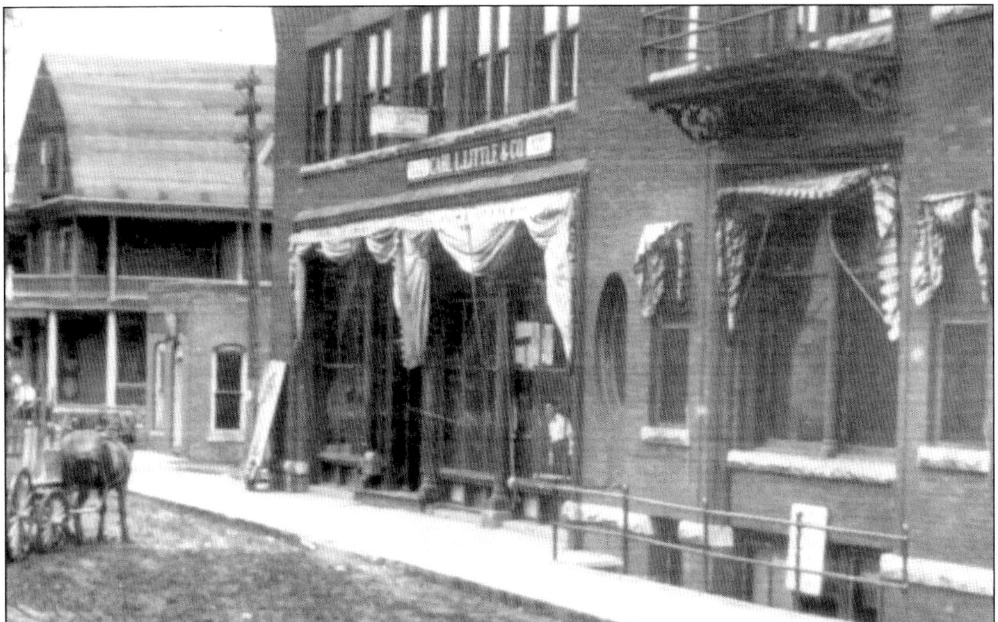

The Carl Little and Company real estate and insurance offices was located on Douglas in 1907, occupying the second floor of the building above the post office.

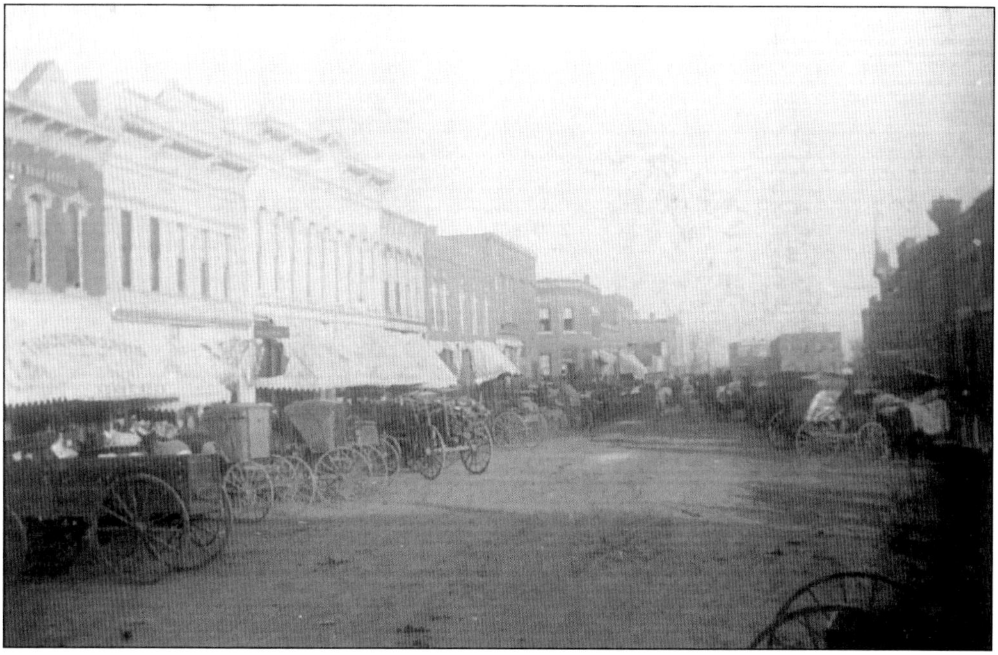

Buggies line Onondaga (Main) Street during Christmas week, 1895.

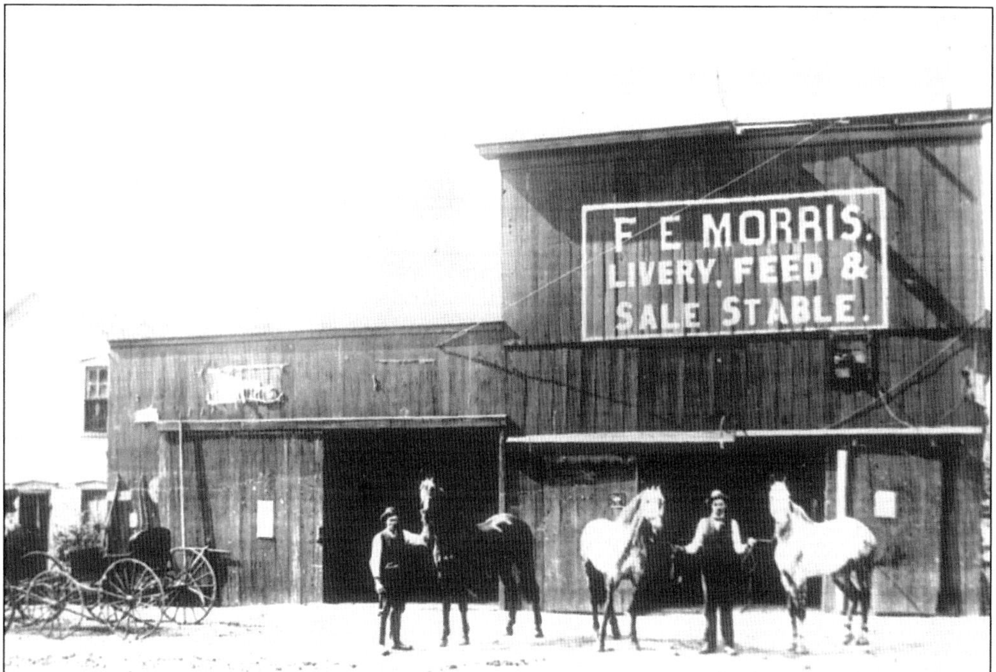

The Frank Morris livery barn on Onondaga (Main) Street (seen here *c.* 1900) was later the site of the Sheldon-Munn Hotel.

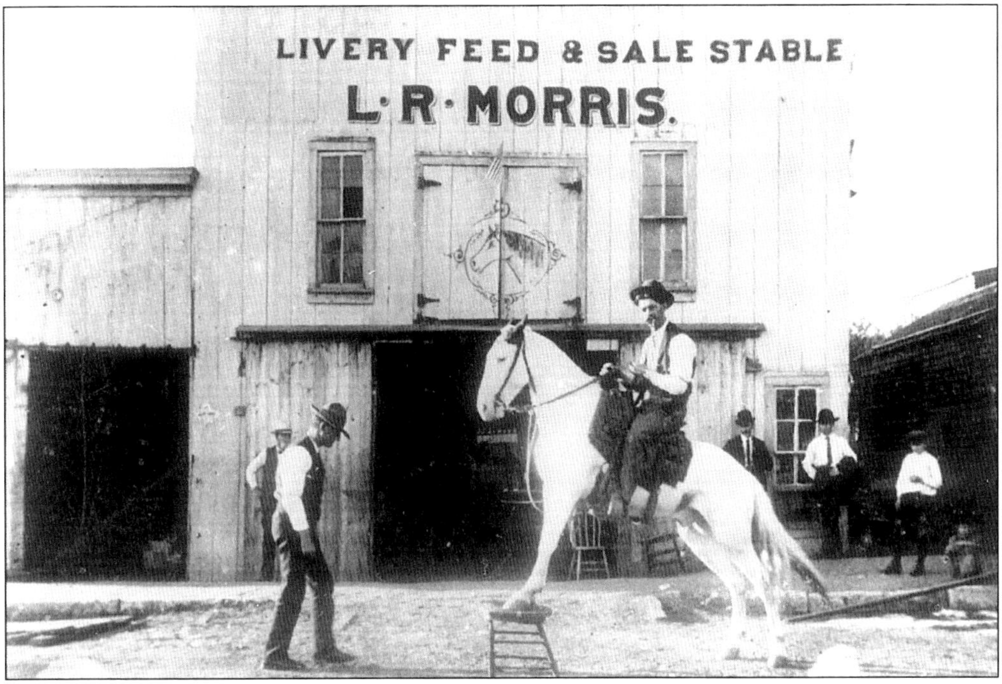

Some good-natured "horsing around" was occurring at the Lynn Morris livery on Main Street in 1910. Frank Morris operated a separate stable, also on Main Street.

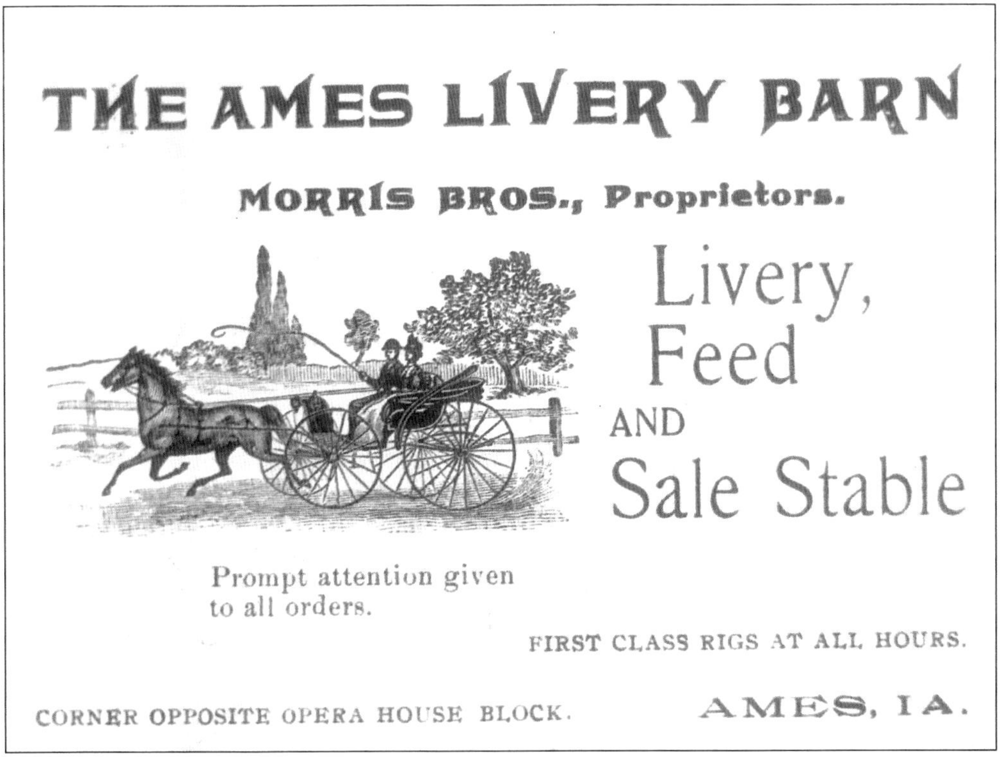

This ad for the Ames Livery Barn ran in the *Ames Intelligencer*, c. 1895.

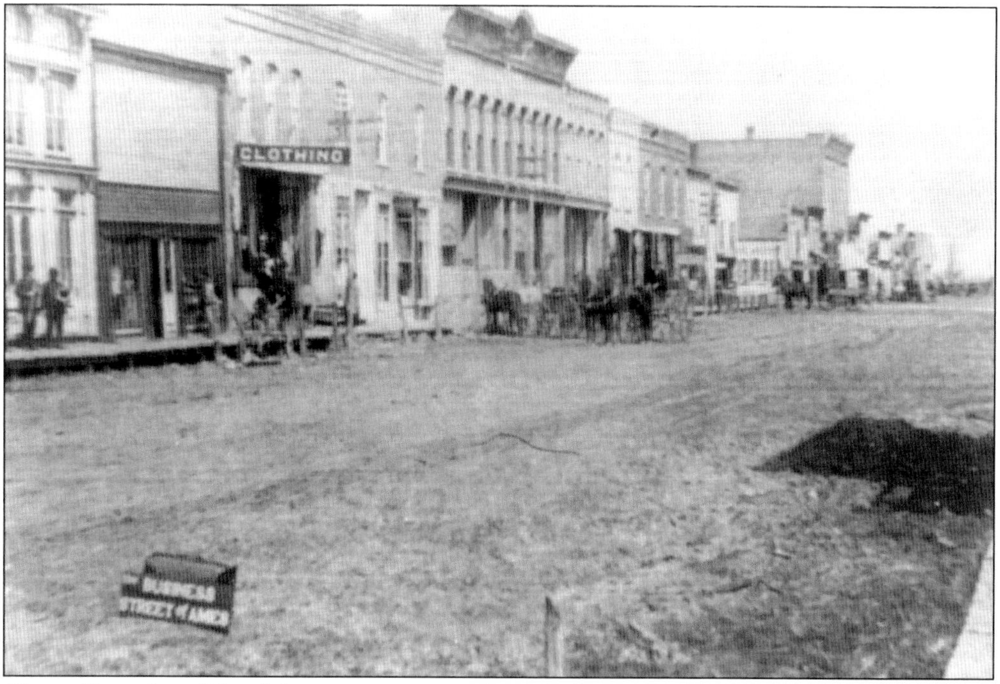

This is Onondaga (Main) Street as it appeared in 1885.

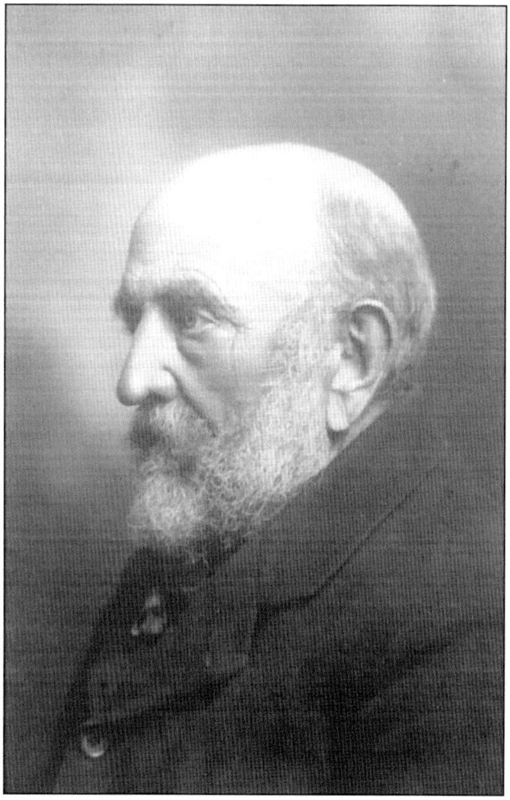

Henry May was the first teacher to work for the Ames school district. The photo is from c. 1866.

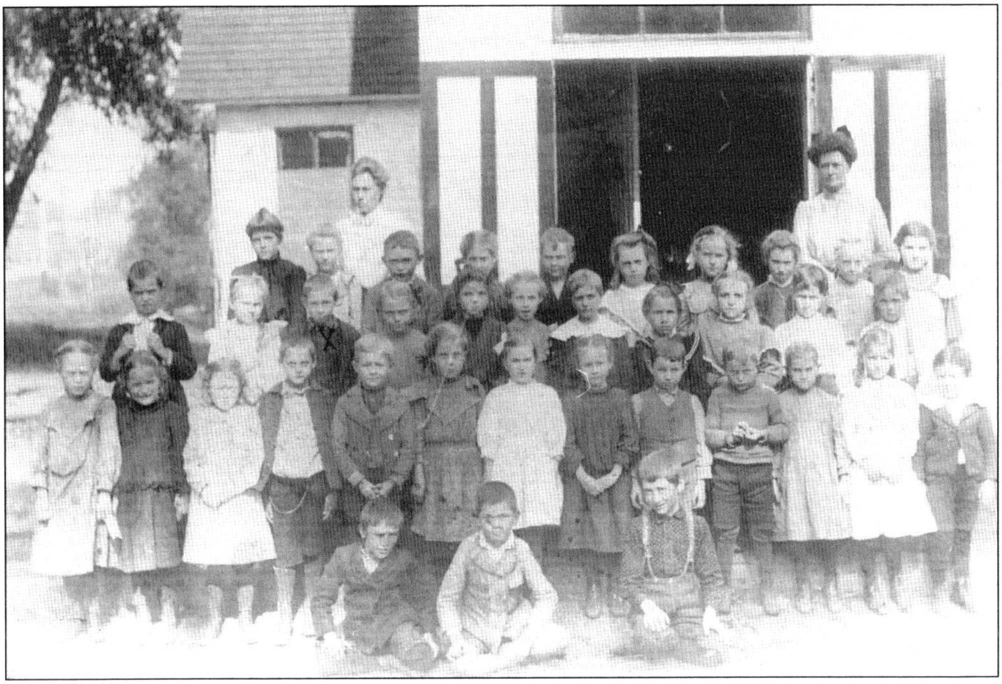

The second school built in 1868 in Ames was known as South School. In this photograph from c. 1905, Mearl Brown, an Ames RR crossing guard for 35 years, is believed to be third from left in the back row; Myrtle Lanning is believed to be the teacher at the left; Terra Gray Hytland is the teacher at the right. South School was sold at an auction in 1912 in order to build Lincoln School.

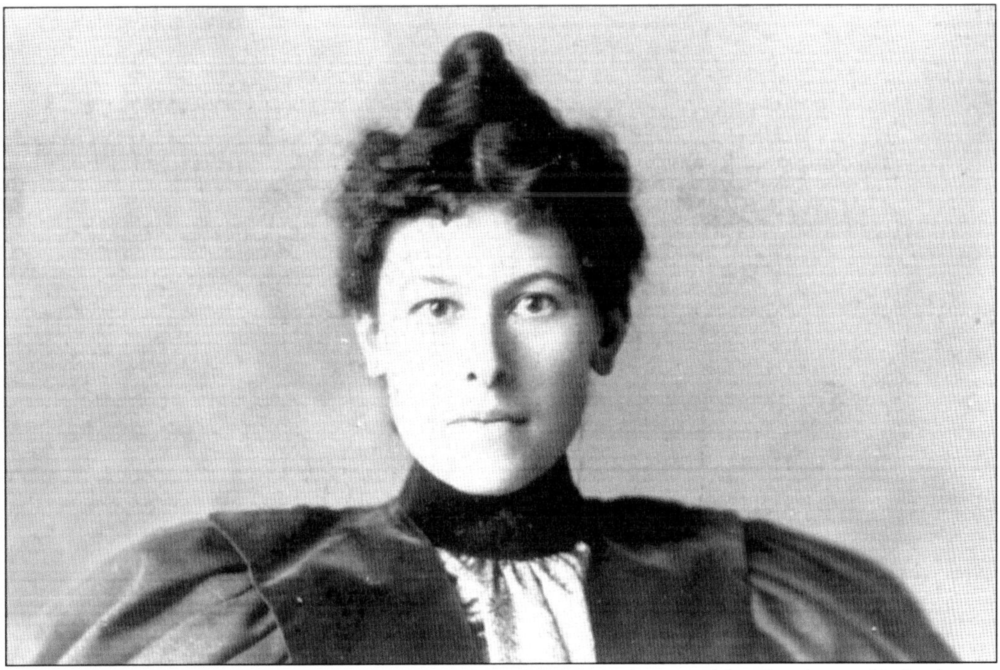

Myrtle Lanning, an 1887 Ames High School graduate, was honored by the Ames High alumni in 1954 for her 50 years of teaching in the Ames schools.

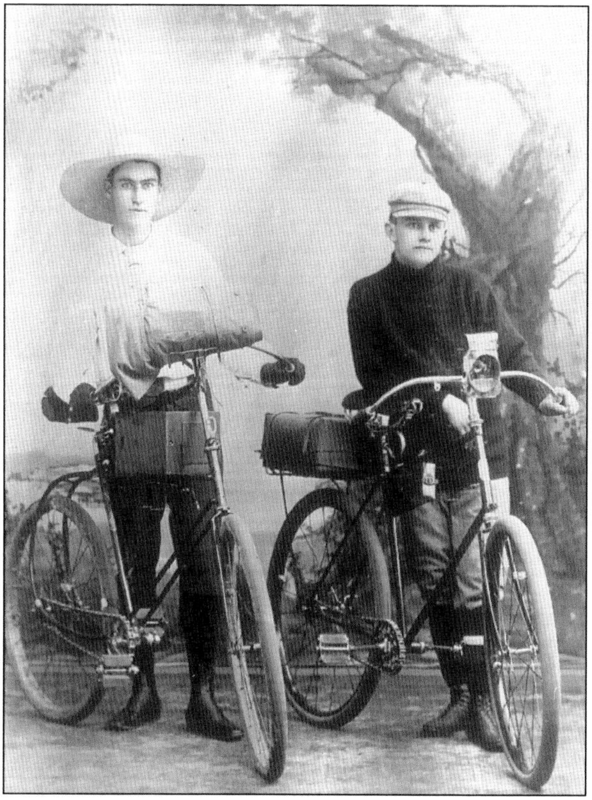

A few days after graduating from Ames High School, classmates Stuart Hutchinson (left) and Gates Brown rode their "safety" bicycles to Minneapolis and back, well before the days of continuous roadways and bridges.

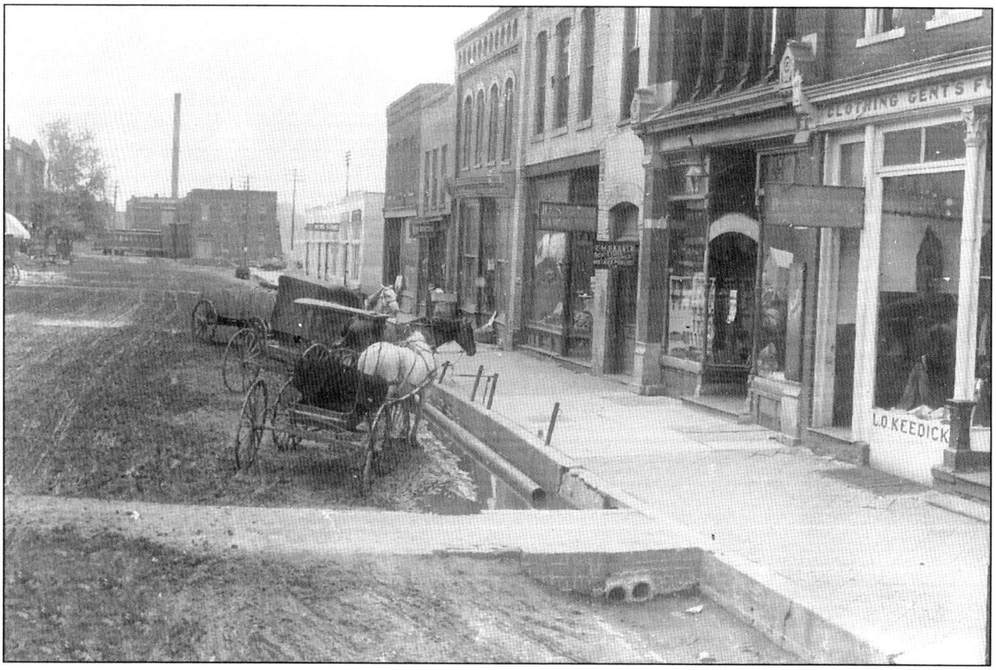

This is the southeast end of Onondaga (Main) in 1907.

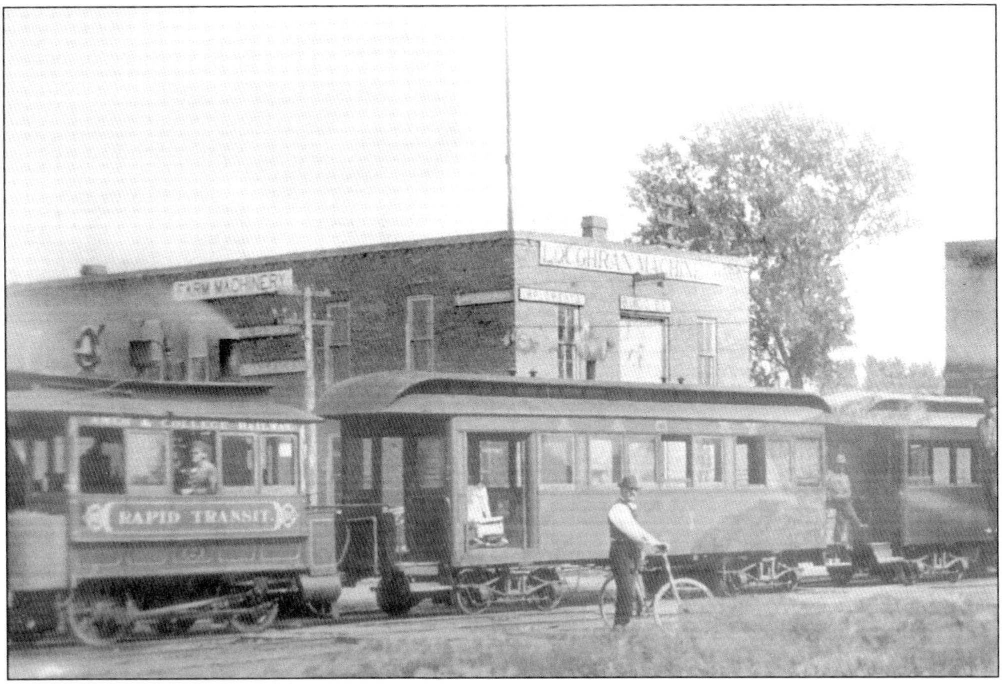

The Dinkey train is seen departing from the downtown terminal at the east end of Main Street, *c.* 1905.

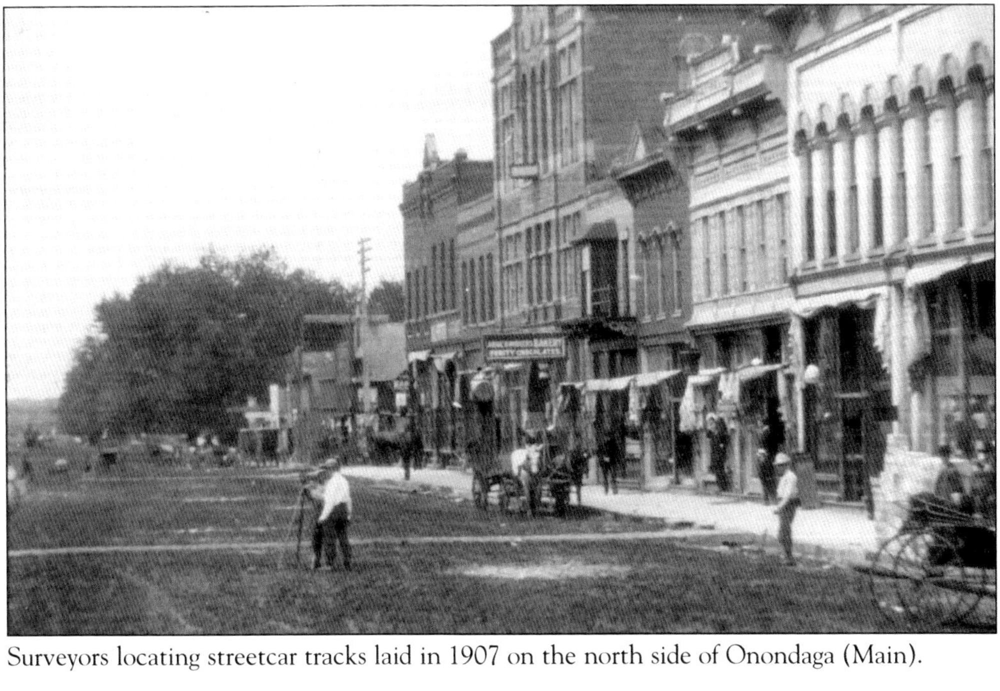

Surveyors locating streetcar tracks laid in 1907 on the north side of Onondaga (Main).

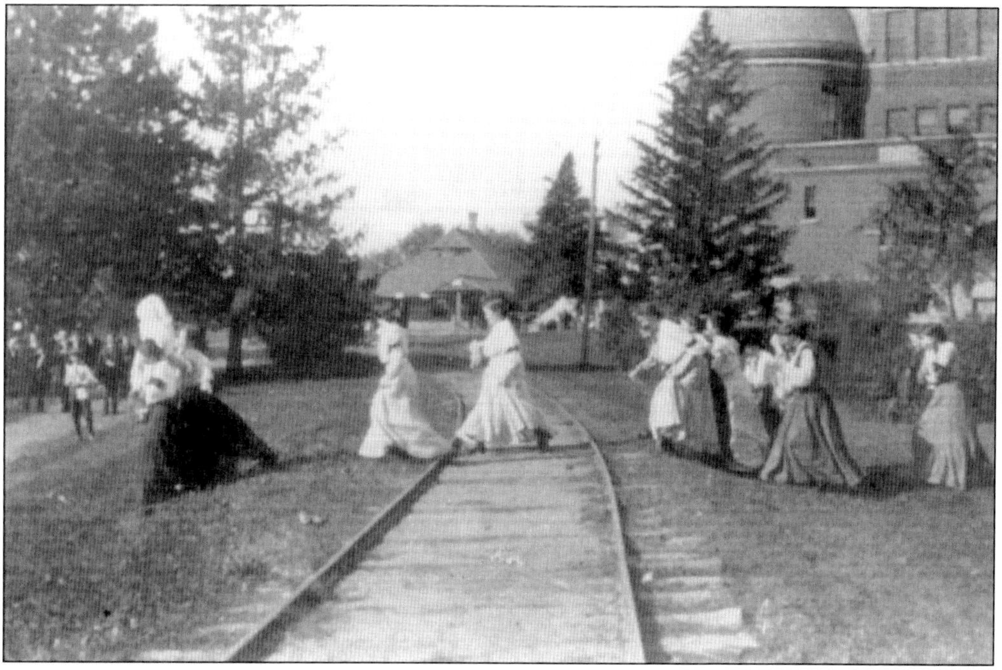

College women hurry across the tracks in front of the Dinkey in central campus, c. 1905.

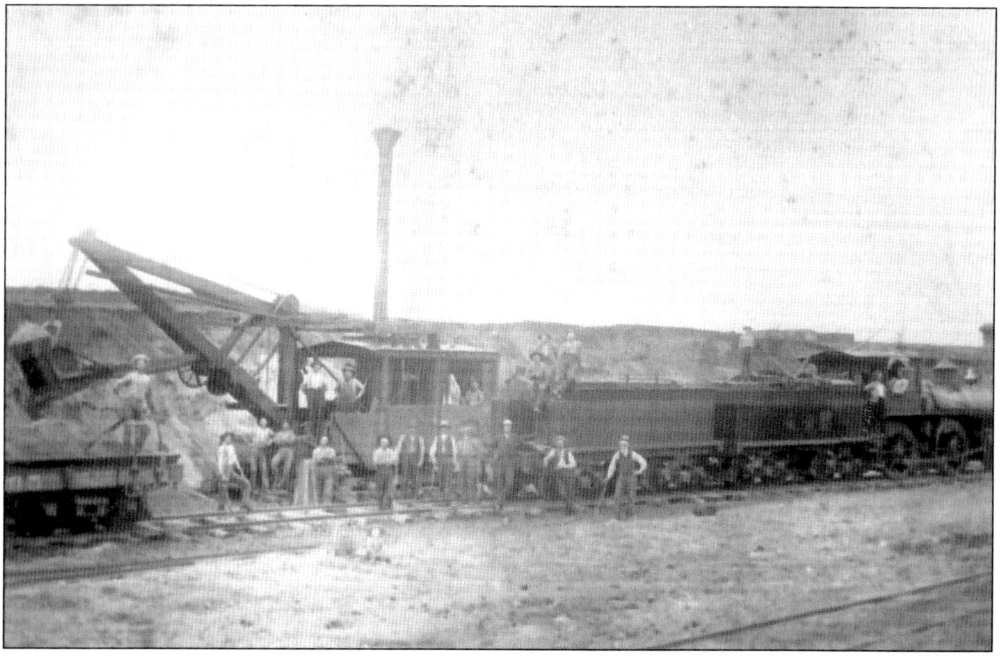

In 1900, these men were helping to dig a railroad on the west side of Brookridge Avenue. The hill at the east ridge of Brookridge Park was formed by material removed in order to lay track.

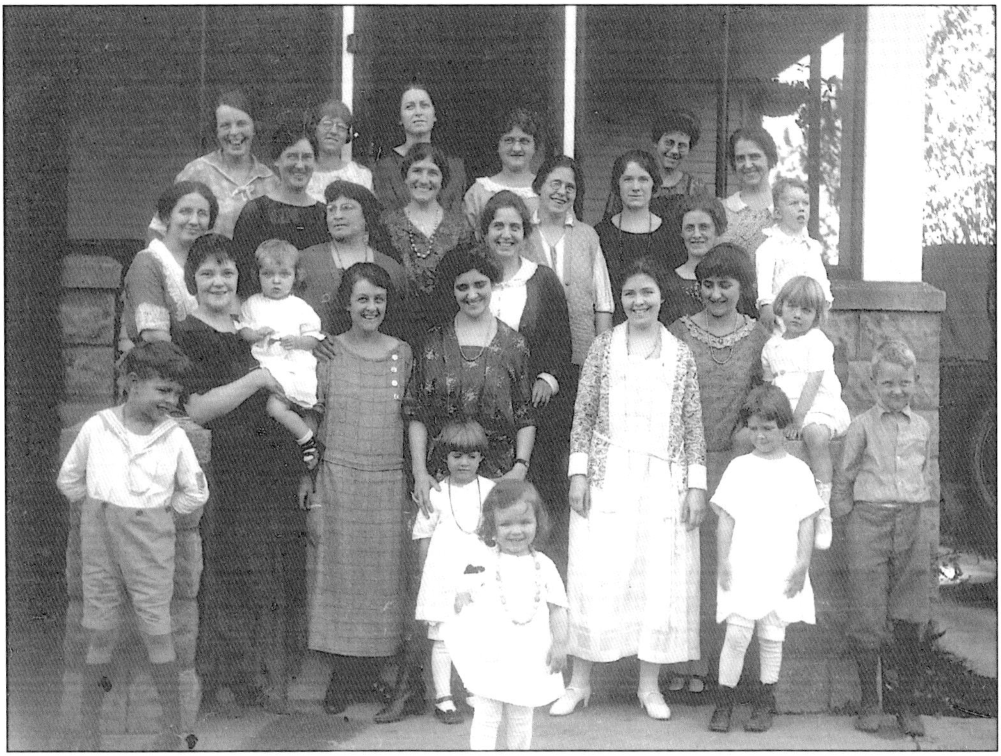

The Tuesday Club, with membership derived from the faculty wives, are seen here in 1923 with their children. They are, from left to right, as follows: (front row) Mrs. M.D. Helser holding daughter Peggy, Muriel Anderson, unidentified, Blyth Vance, Mrs. MacRae with daughter Jo; (middle row) Mrs. L.W. (Martha) Forman, Mrs. John Hug, others unidentified; (back row) unidentified, Helen Jeffers, Mrs. Clyde, unidentified, Mrs. G.B. MacDonald, Mrs. Paul Taff with son Jim. Virginia Vance Merrill is the little girl at center front and John MacRae is the boy at front far right. The remaining people are unidentified.

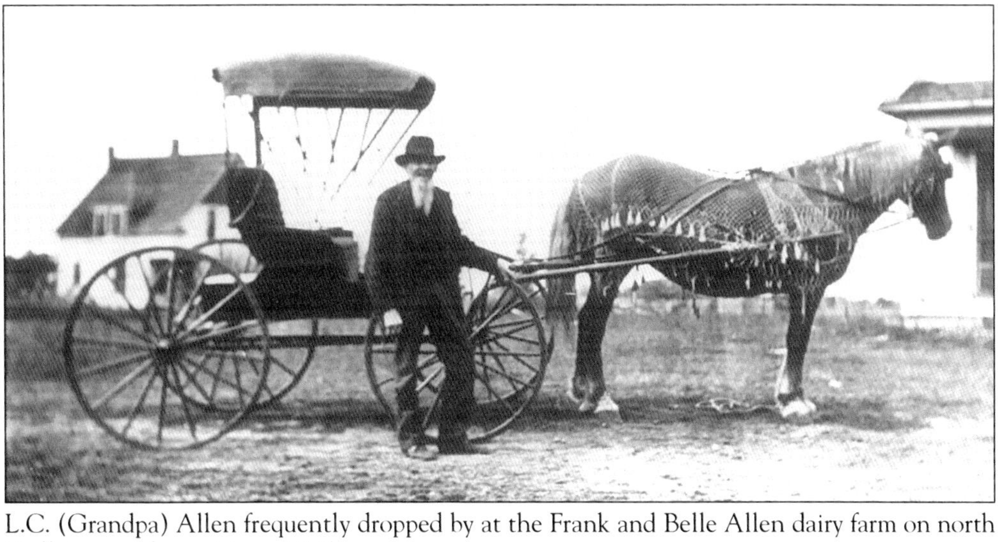

L.C. (Grandpa) Allen frequently dropped by at the Frank and Belle Allen dairy farm on north Duff Avenue for a visit, c. 1905.

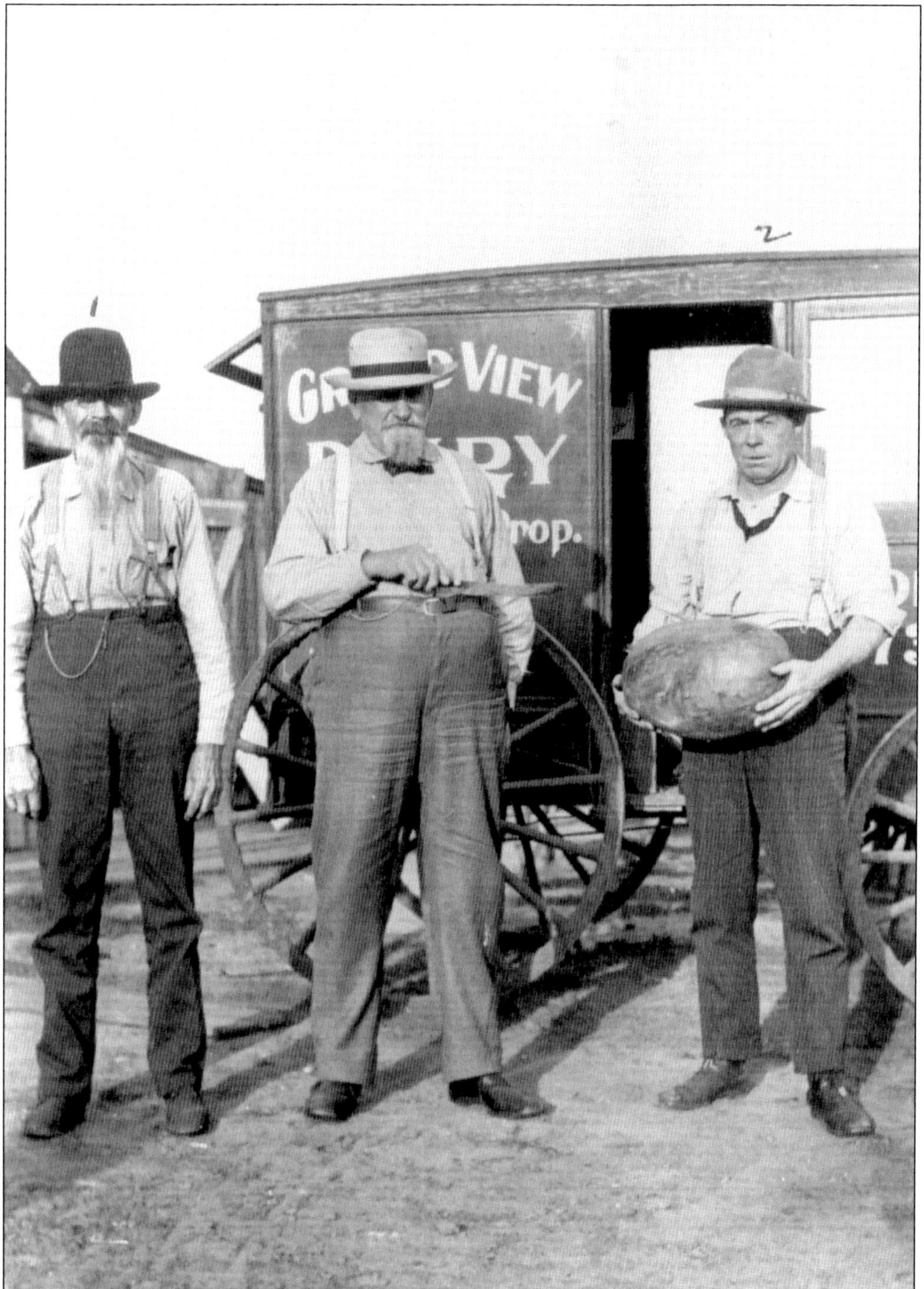

Frank Allen's farm on north Duff, *c.* 1905, shows L.C. Allen, left, and Frank, holding a watermelon, at right. Allen's Farm was on the east side of Duff about where O'Neil Drive is today. George Allen Avenue is named in memory of Frank and Belle's son, a casualty of World War II.

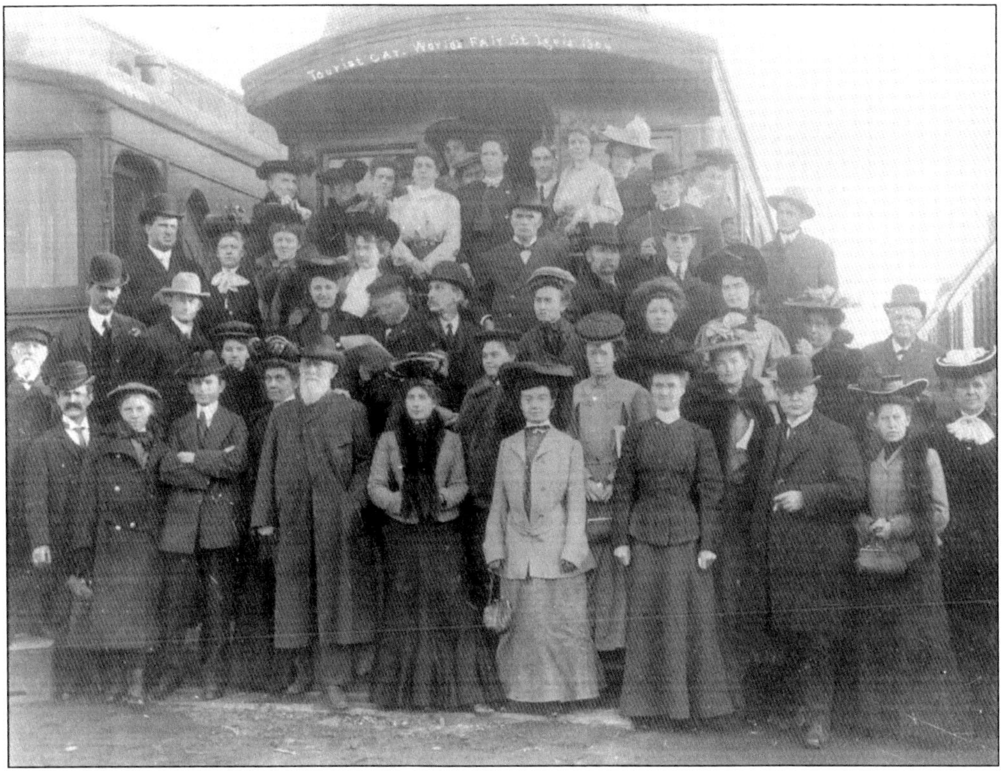

This is a group of Ames folks going to the 1904 World's Fair in St. Louis. They include, from left to right: Mr. and Mrs. C.M. McCaskey, Kate Maurice, Myrtle Lanning, Nell Cole, Jess Cole, Kate Sayles, Mrs. W. Grove, Mr. Tinsley, Mrs. Addison and daughter, and Miss Lida Bigelow. Others in the group are from Nevada and Des Moines.

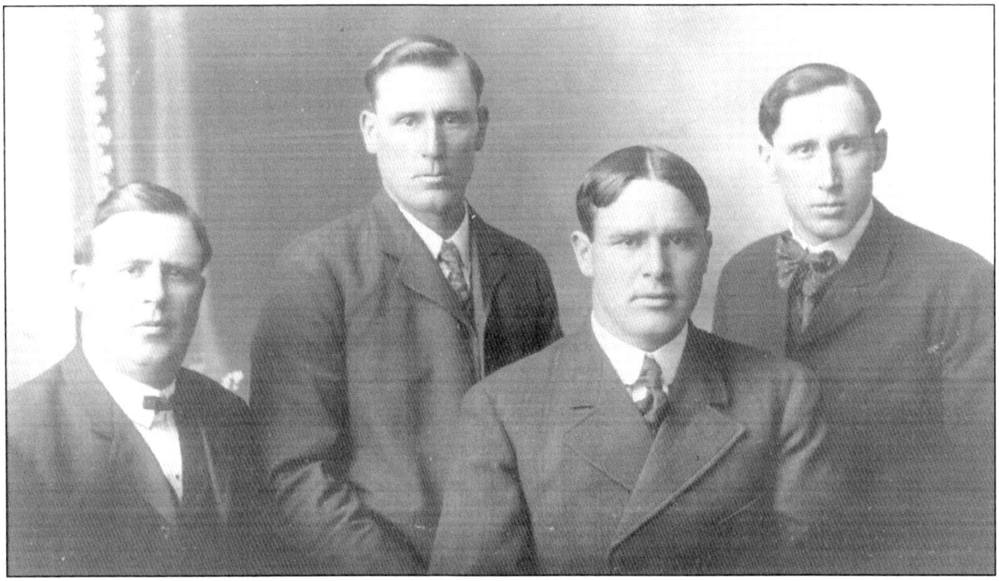

The Cole brothers pose for the camera, c. 1900. They are, from left to right, as follows: Ben, William, Lew, and Clarence.

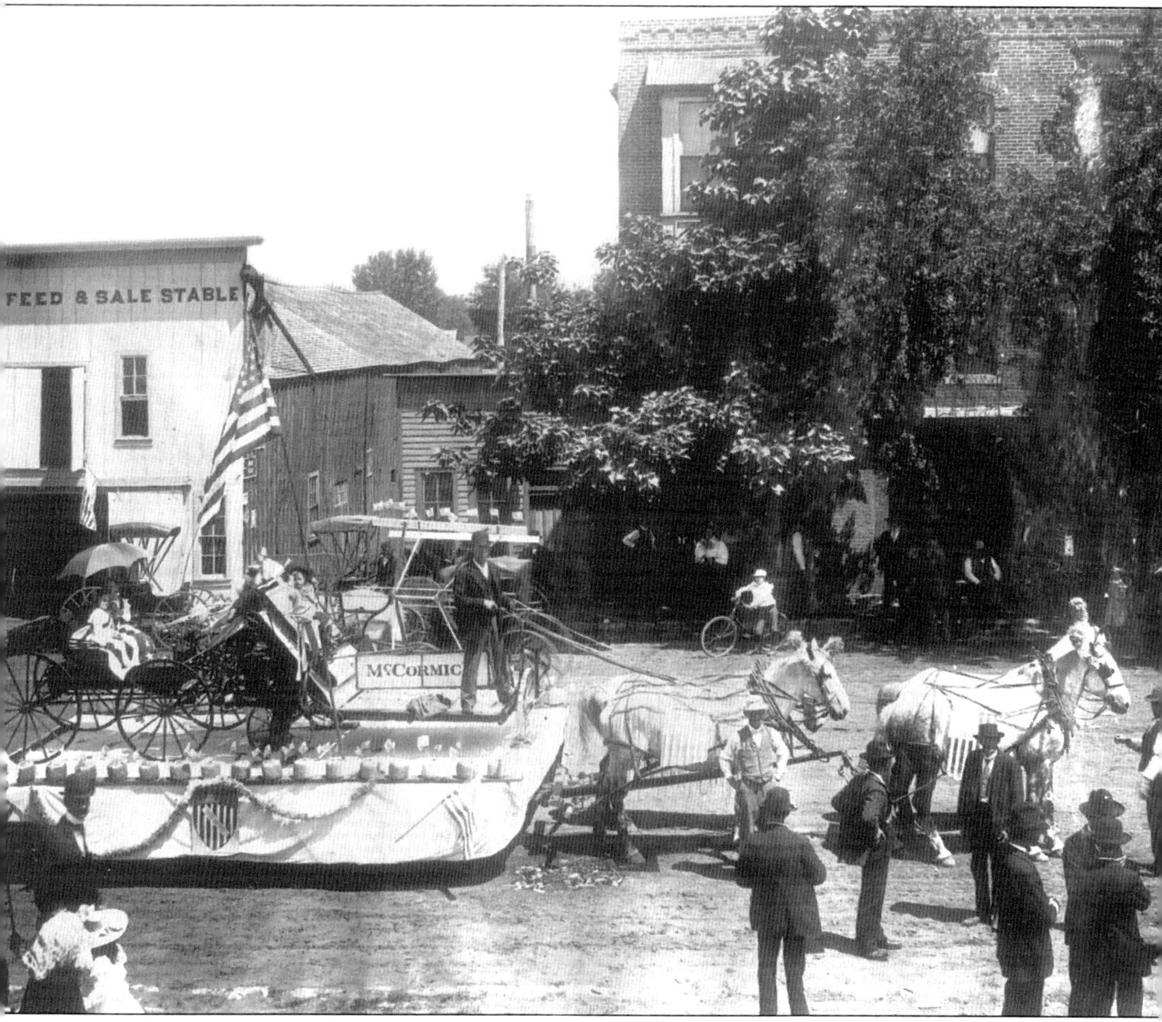

The Loughran Farm Machine Company's float in the 1905 Fourth of July parade heads down Onondaga (Main) Street. The boardwalk was used until the street was paved in 1910. The dignitaries on the right are believed to be Civil War veterans.

Three

The Dinkey is Electrified

In 1906, the Fort Dodge, Des Moines & Southern Railroad was organized, in part, through the purchase of the former Newton and Northwestern steam railroad that ran from Newton, through Colfax, Cambridge, and Midvale to Boone and Rockwell City. The line was then electrified and extended to Des Moines, Fort Dodge, and Ames—where the connection was made in 1907 after the purchase of the Ames & College Line. That year, electric streetcars were introduced into service in Ames and the steam Dinkey was retired. Interurban cars then started providing passenger and freight service between Ames and all points on the Fort Dodge Line. In Ames, the former Dinkey's tracks were moved from Fifth Street to Main Street in downtown Ames.

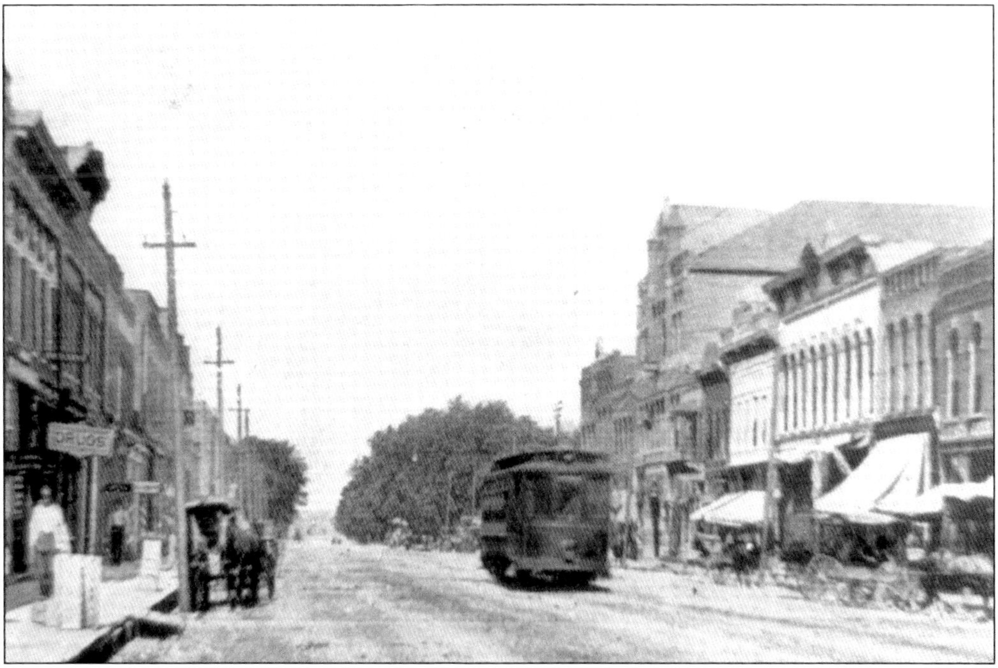

For a time, electric cars operating between downtown Ames and the campus continued to cross the central campus, as had the Dinkey. By 1916 however, the route had been extended around the entire campus to form a "loop." It went past the new veterinary and chemistry buildings, on west to what is now the west side of the Design College parking lot. From that point, the tracks ran south on the east side of Sheldon to Knapp Street, then east to merge with the interurban tracks on Knapp between Welch and Lynn. Local streetcars then took the interurban route north and easterly, crossing the campus about where the Memorial Union parking ramp is now located. From there, it traveled east to downtown Ames. Usually there were ten streetcars operating within Ames on that route on a frequent run schedule. Throughout the life of the former steam Dinkey, the fare had been 5¢. That same fare remained unchanged on the electric cars until 1926, when the fare was raised to 7¢.

By the late 1920s, buses had begun to compete with the electric trolley. The Hutchinson Bus line had obtained a license to operate on Ames streets. With the end of the college year in 1929, the Fort Dodge line petitioned the Commerce Commission for permission to cease service for the summer months. As it turned out, by September, the Fort Dodge Line introduced their own buses into service in Ames, and streetcars permanently ceased to run between downtown Ames and the ISC campus.

The era of bus transportation had begun. The Mid West Bus Company was the primary operator of buses in Ames after a few years. Buses were here to stay.

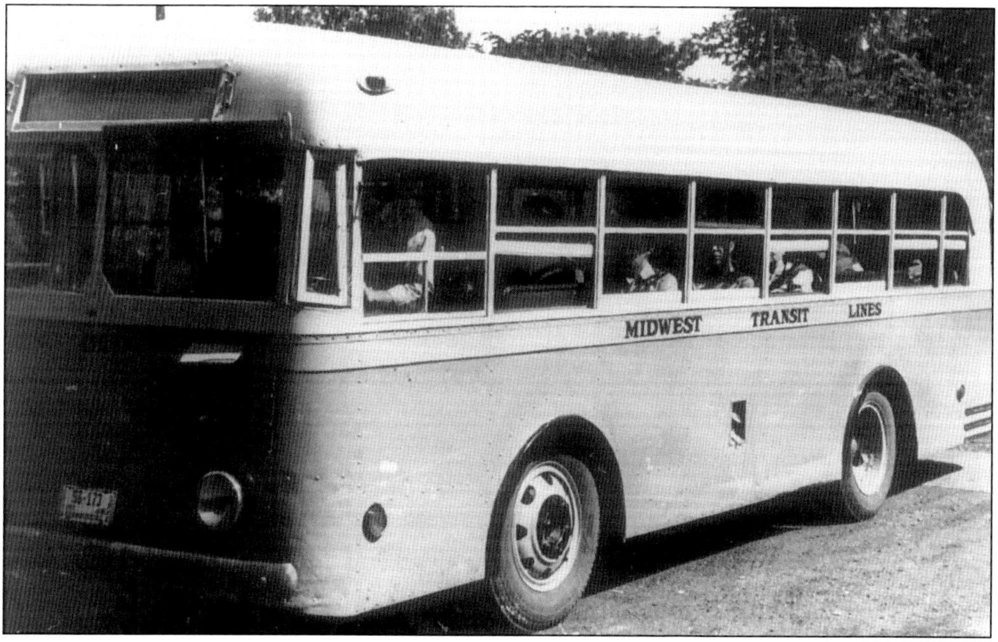

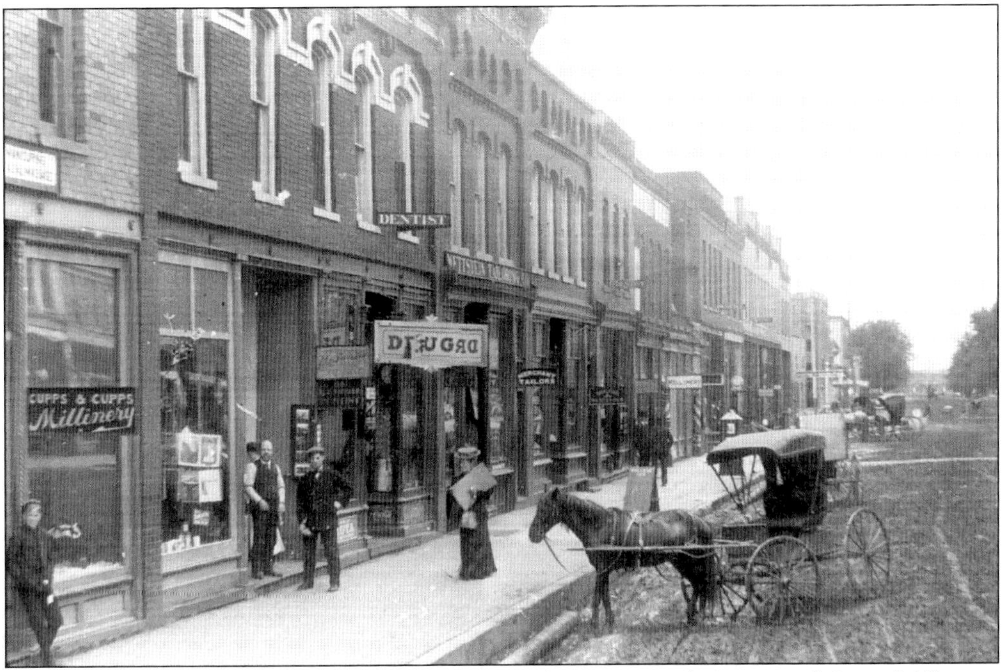

This is a view of the south side of Onondaga (Main) in 1907, with Cupps and Cupps Millinery, a drugstore, a dentist's office, and the Western Tailoring Company lining the street.

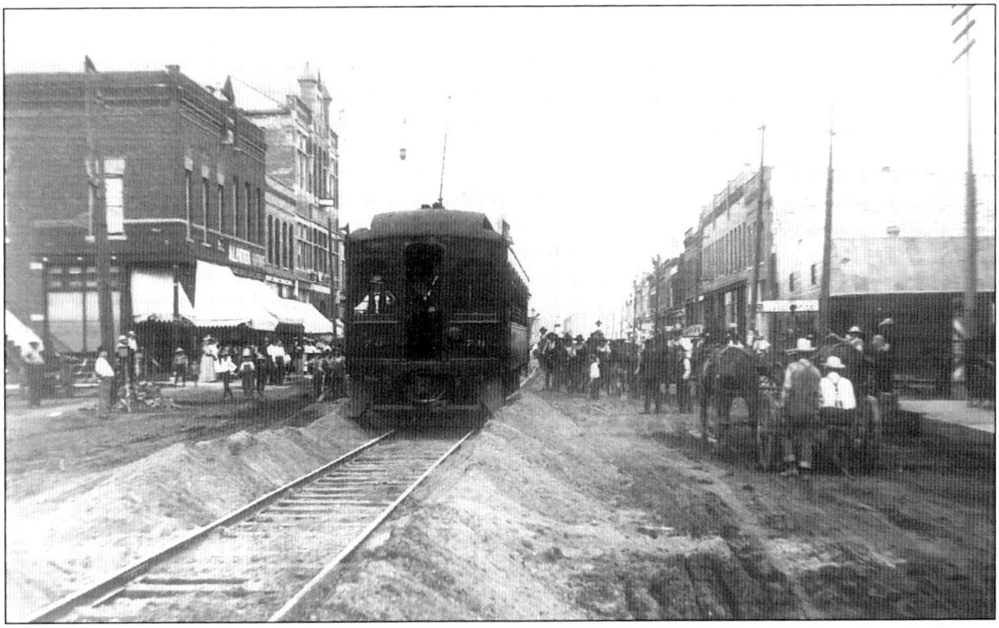

The first interurban railroad came up Onondaga (Main) in July, 1907. Grove's Store is shown on the corner of Kellogg Avenue.

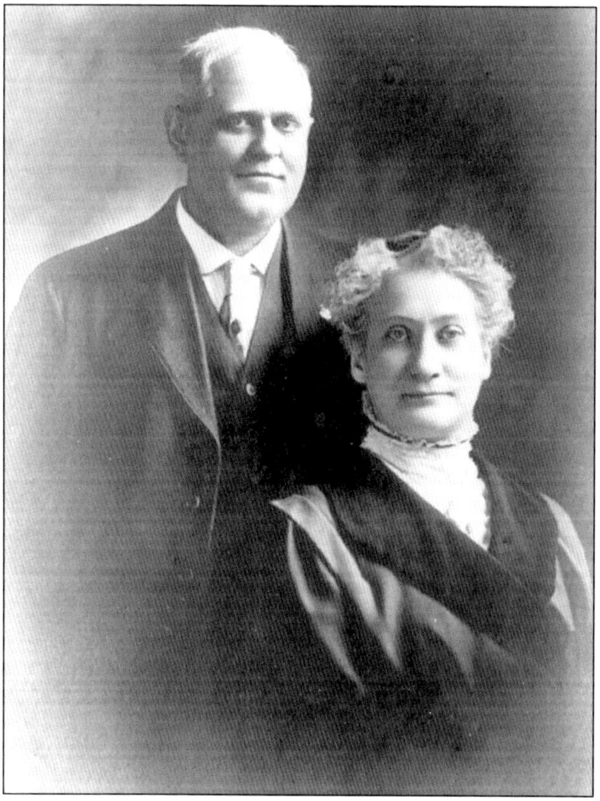

Jasper Grove and his wife, Mary Tamzen Grove, pose for the camera in this undated photograph. Jasper operated a grocery-general store on the corner of Main and Kellogg for many years.

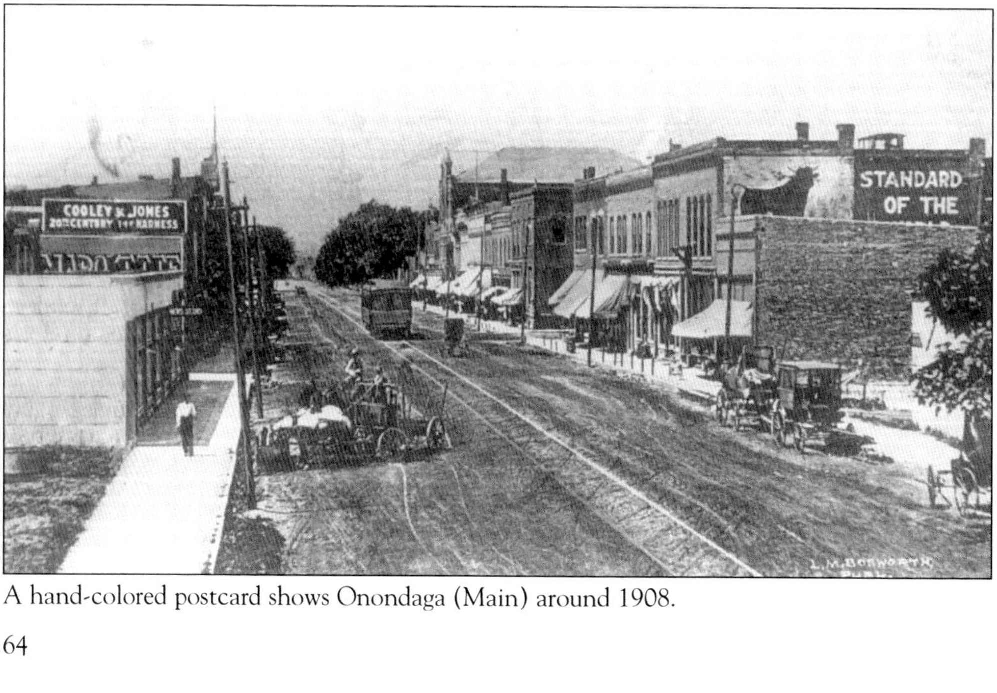

A hand-colored postcard shows Onondaga (Main) around 1908.

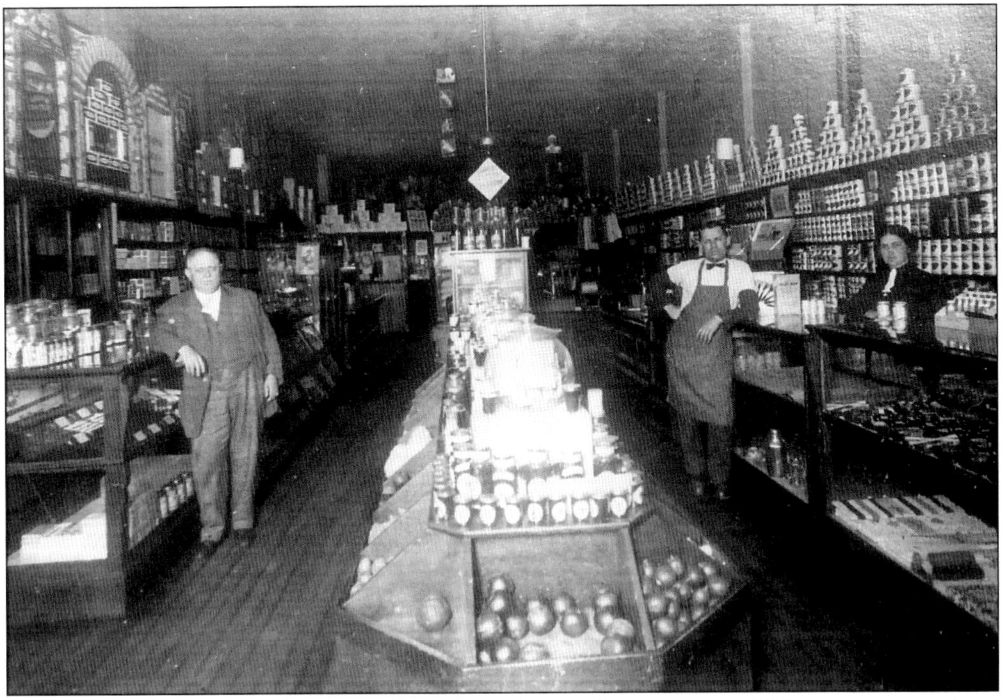

This is the inside of Jasper Grove's grocery and general store on its 25th anniversary, April 1914. Mr. Grove is shown on the left.

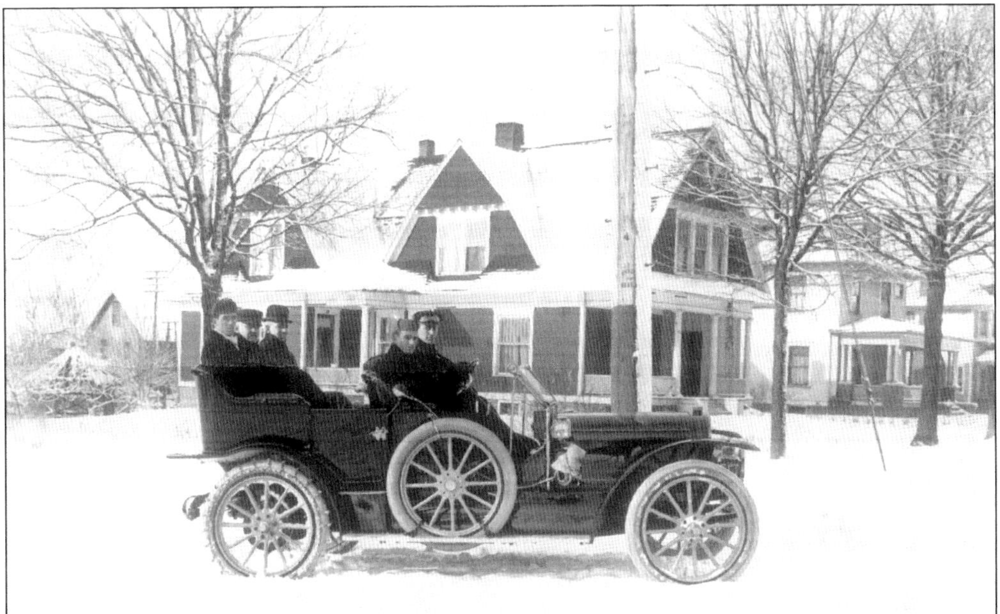

Lou Tilden, a merchant and former mayor (seated in far rear), and Fred Munn of Munn Lumber Company (driver), stop with friends for a photo in front of the Tilden home in 1908.

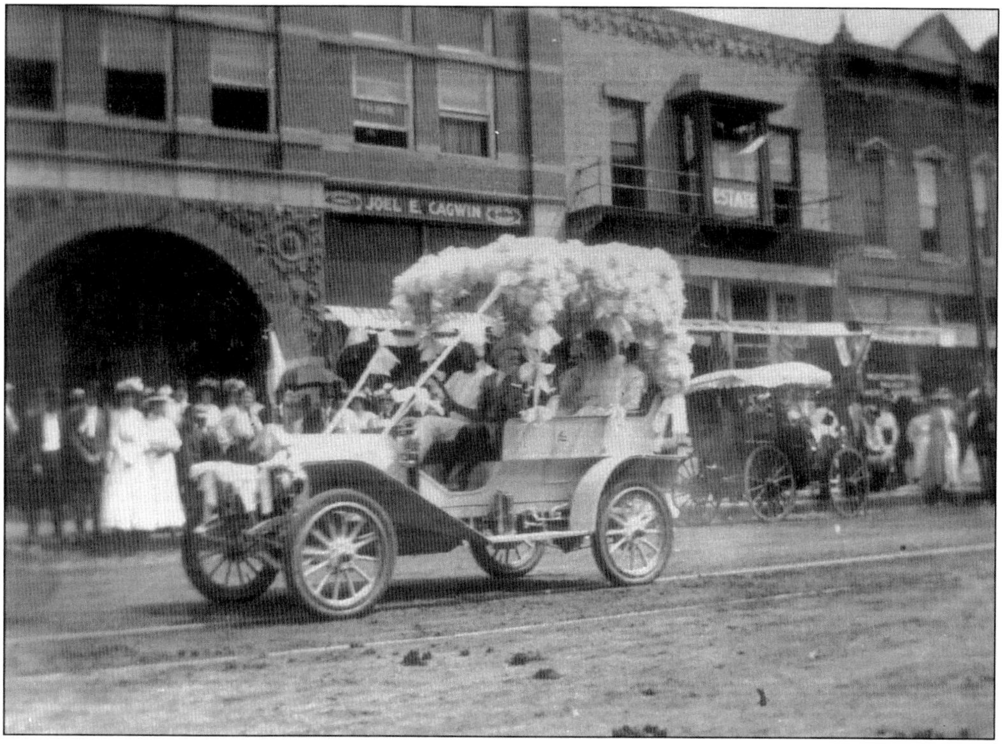

A parade on July 3, 1909, to celebrate the 50th anniversary of the founding of Iowa State College shows the Munn Lumber Company car with Fred Munn driving. His father Hiram L. Munn, founder of Munn Lumber, is in the front seat next to him.

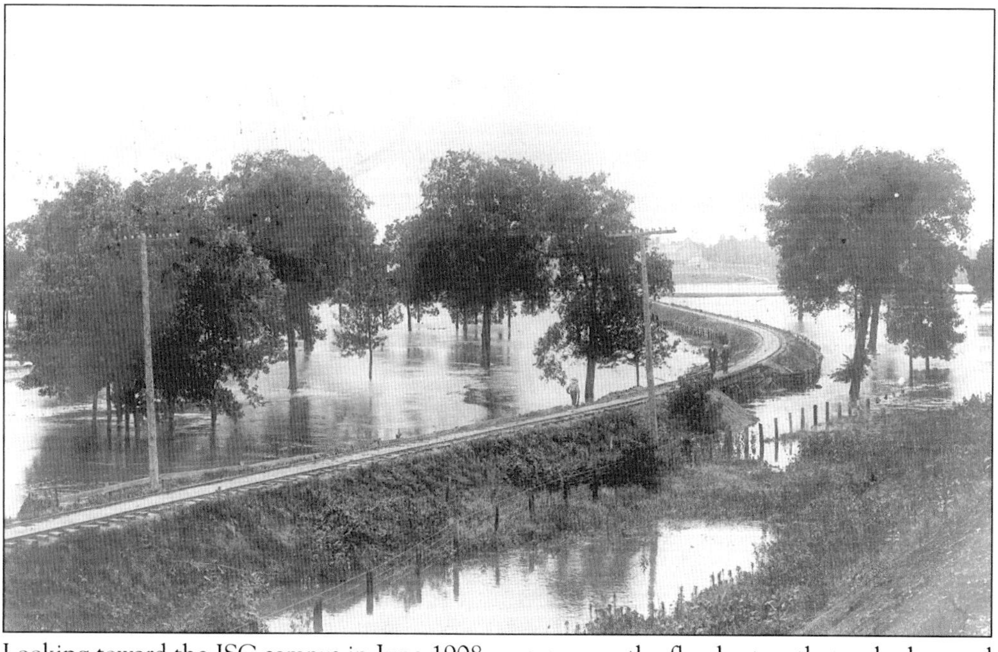

Looking toward the ISC campus in June 1908, one can see the floodwaters that only damaged crops that year. Streetcar tracks can be seen in the center of the photo.

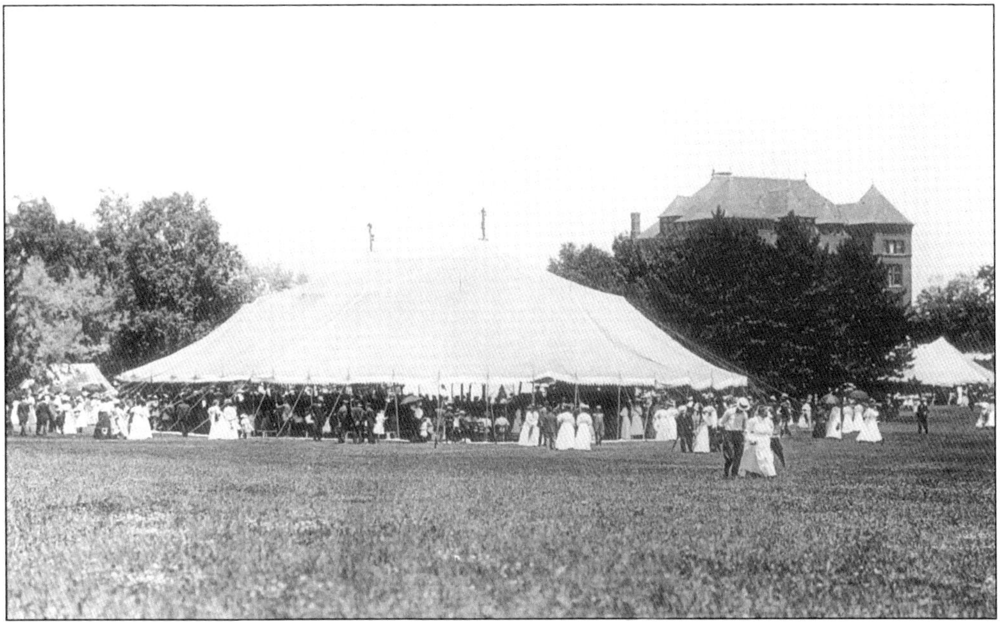

Twenty-thousand people were reported to have attended the 50th anniversary of Iowa State College on July 3, 1908. Kate Shelley, the railroad heroine from Boone, was the special guest.

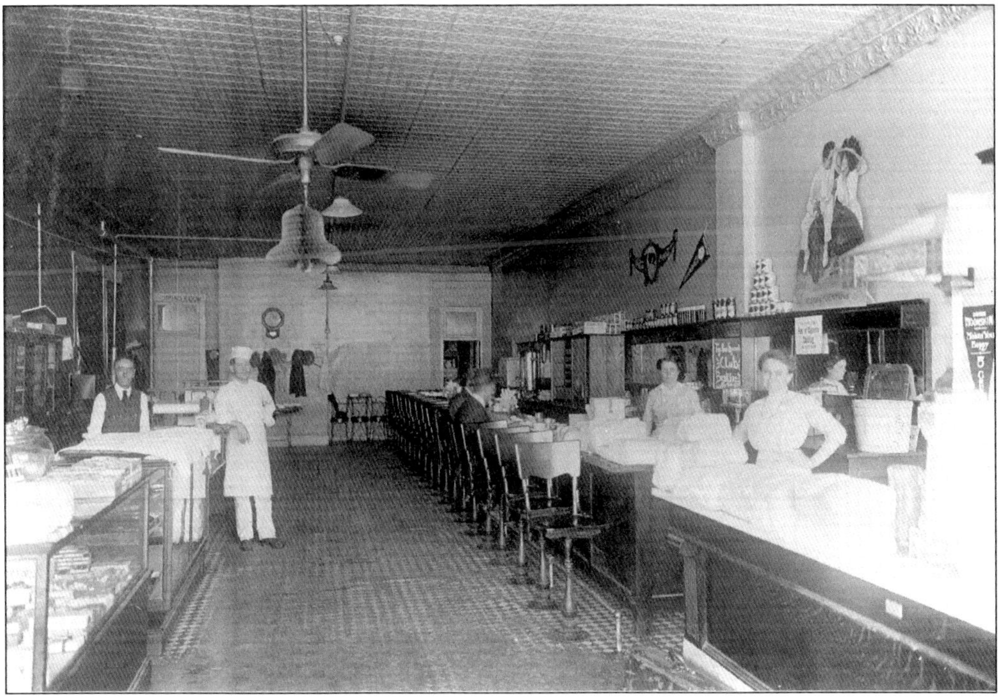

This is an interior view of Kegley's Restaurant and Bakery at the southwest corner of Main and Kellogg, c. 1911.

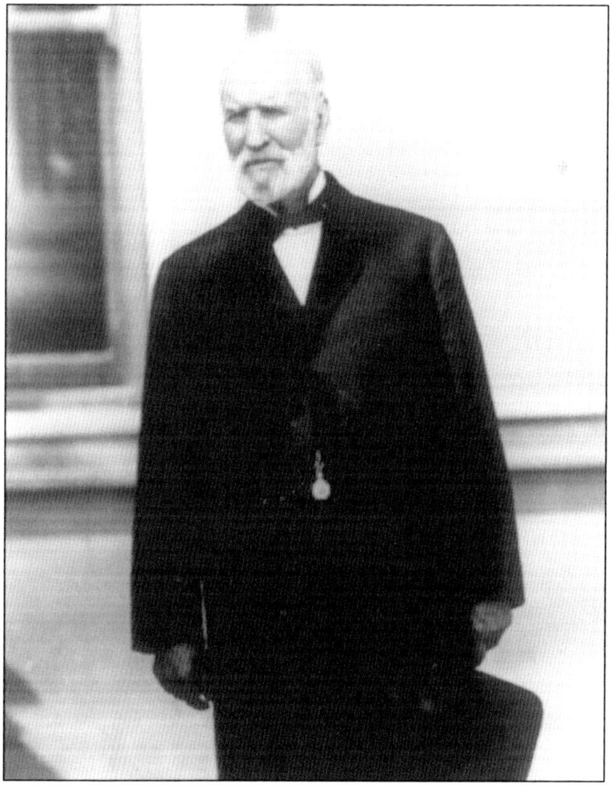

James "Tama Jim" Wilson, once head of ISC's agricultural division, was granted official leave in 1897 to become the nation's first Secretary of Agriculture, a position that he held for 16 years. During his homecoming on March 12, 1913, Wilson received recognition from ISC President Pearson.

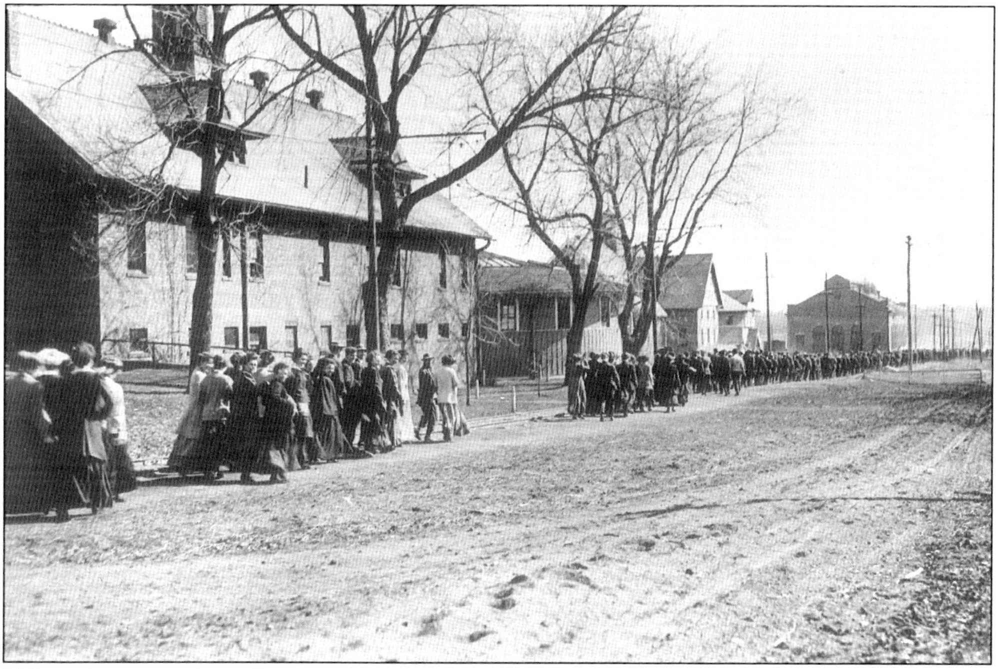

ISC students march to downtown Ames on St. Patrick's Day in 1910. Here they are near the old horse barn on campus.

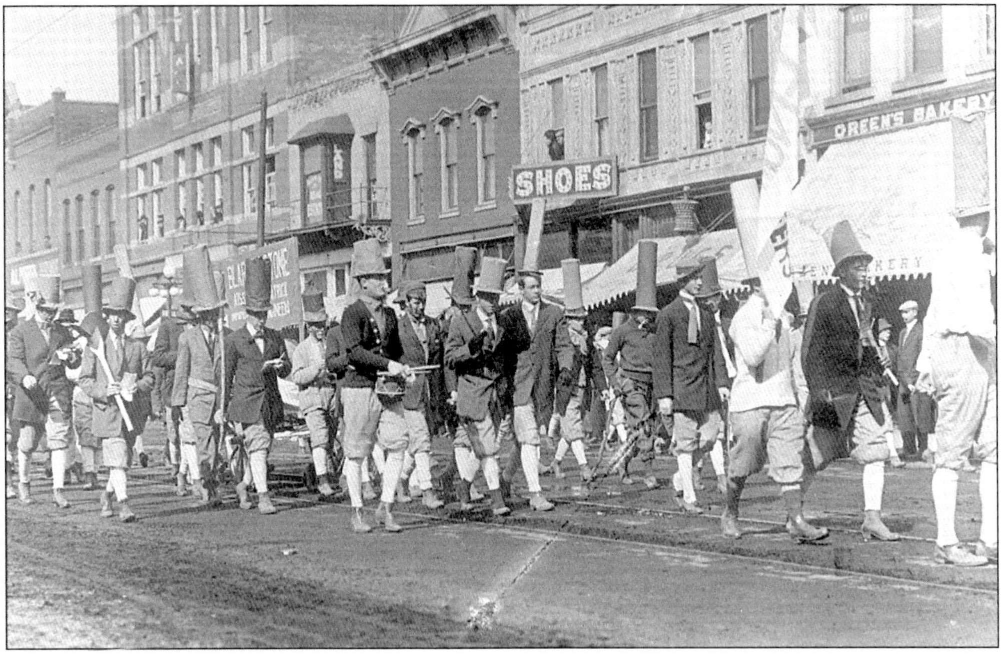

ISC engineering students march down Main Street during the St. Patrick's Day parade of 1910.

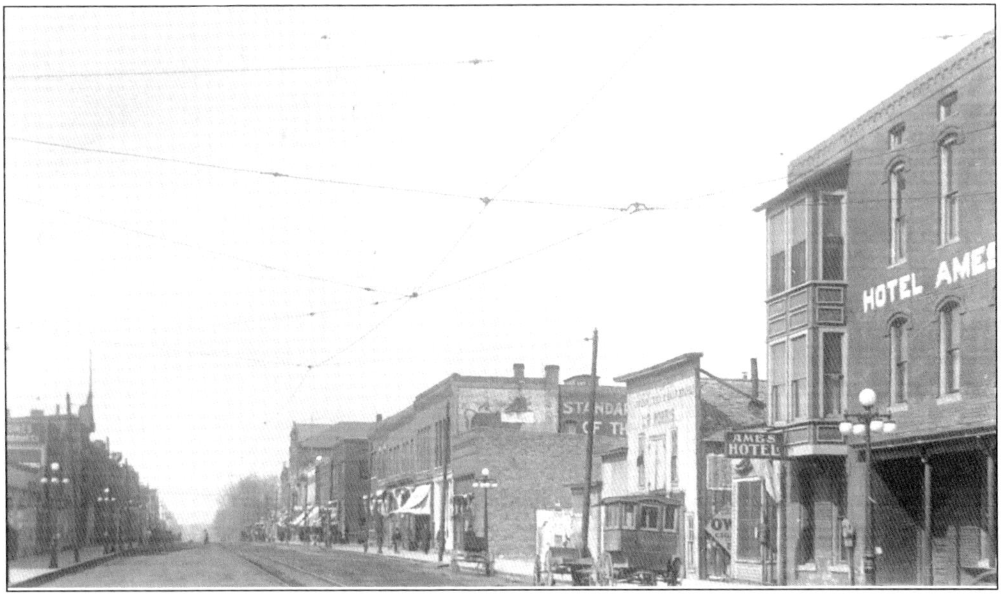

Looking west of Onondaga (Main), one can see the horse-drawn hack, known as the "College Bus," c. 1908.

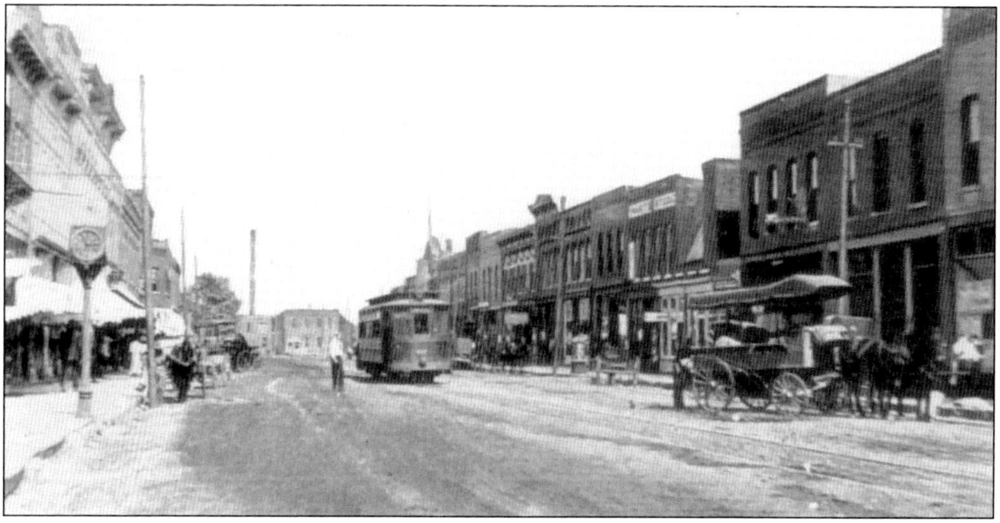

A horse-drawn, double-decked grocery wagon and a streetcar share Onondaga (Main) Street around 1908.

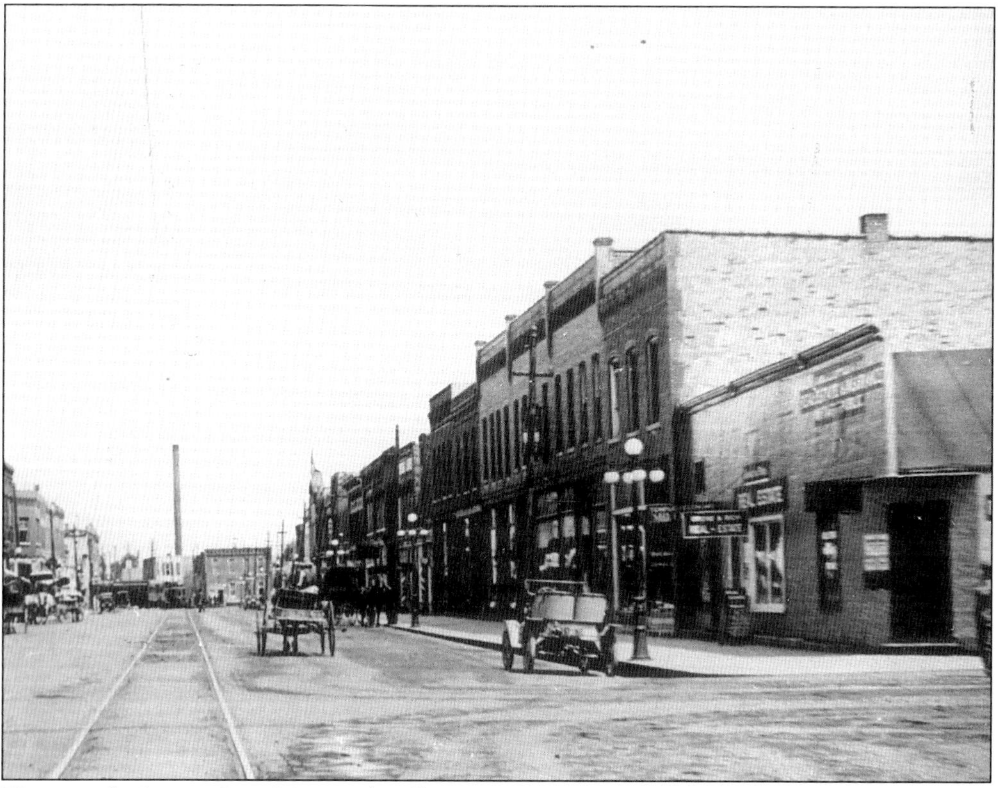

This view looks east from Main and Kellogg, c. 1911.

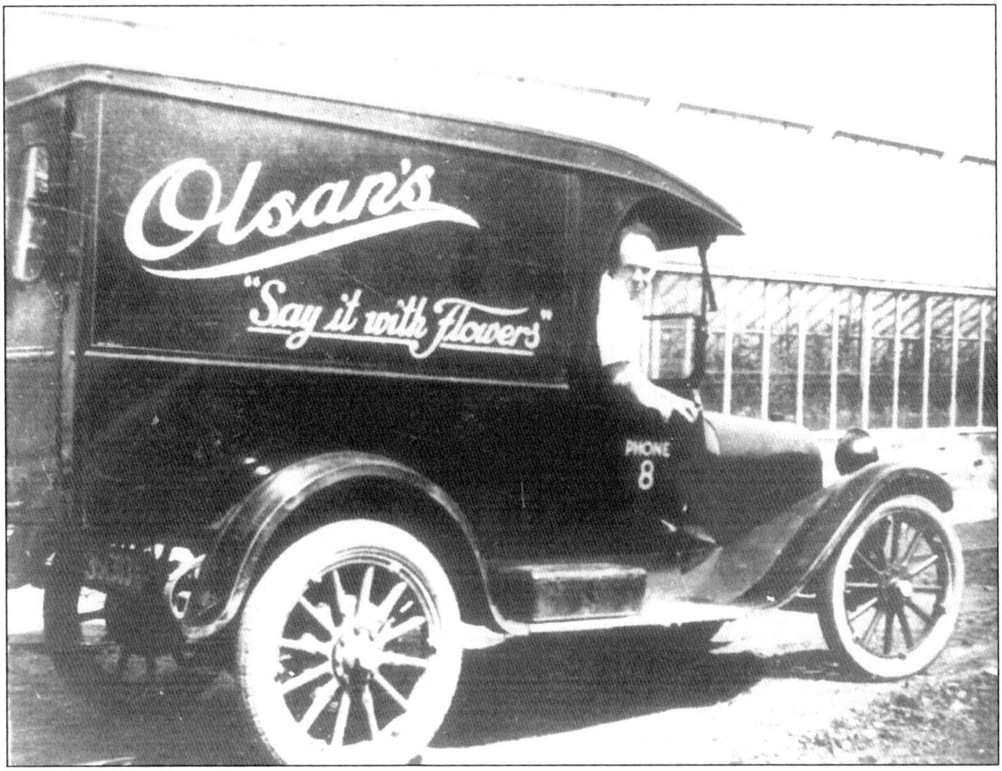

Olsan's Flowers, the first large-scale greenhouse, occupied Ames' first all-concrete building on the corner of Burnett and Main, in 1915.

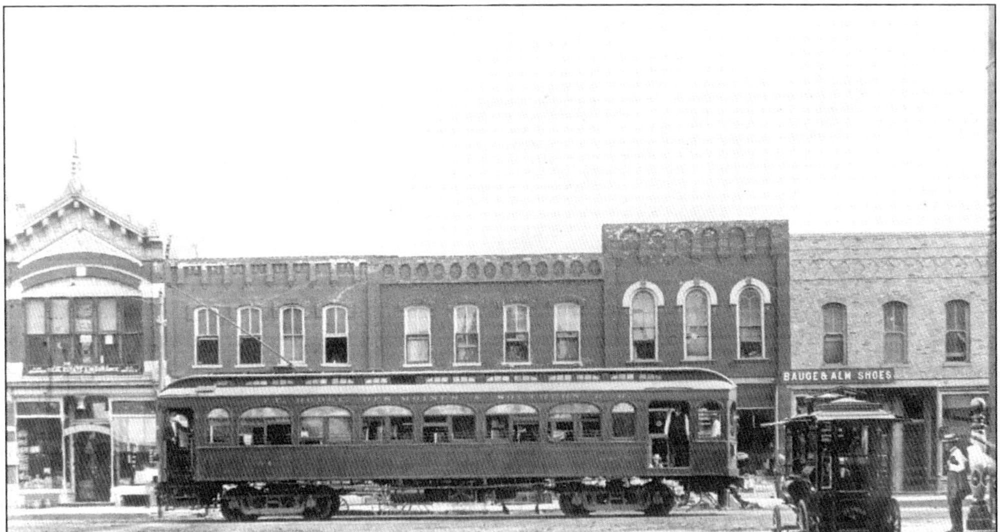

This popcorn wagon dispensed hot-buttered popcorn on the corner of Douglas and Main from 1905–1939 until the town council outlawed "in the street" business locations because of increased auto traffic. Ben Young owned the wagon for 24 of the years it was in operation.

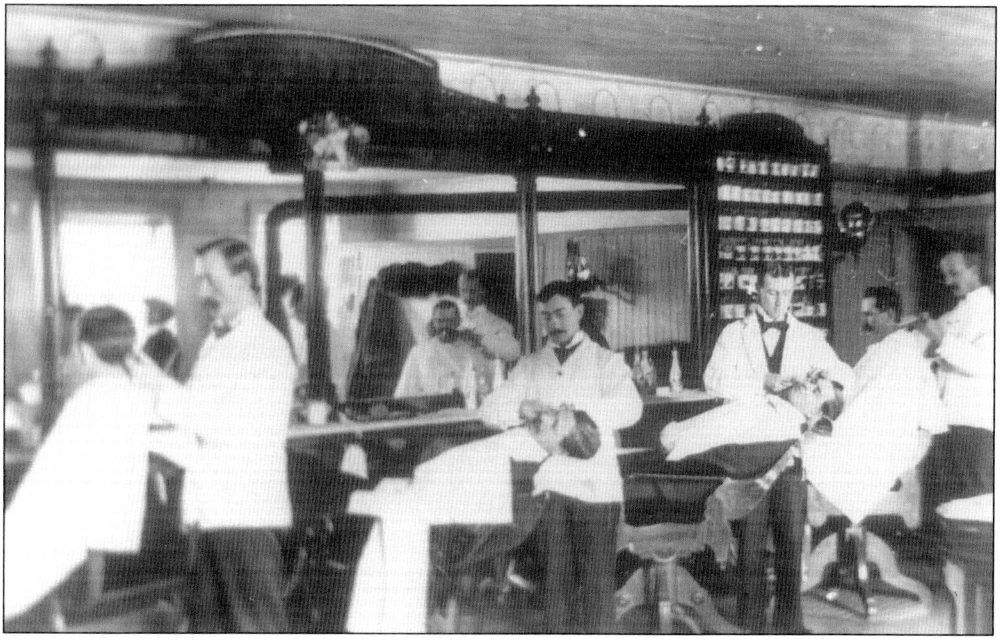

George Kintzley's O.K. Barbershop, located under the Union National Bank on the corner of Main and Douglas, contained a rack full of personalized shaving mugs for the many businessmen shaved there daily. In 1913, haircuts were 15¢ and a shave was 10¢.

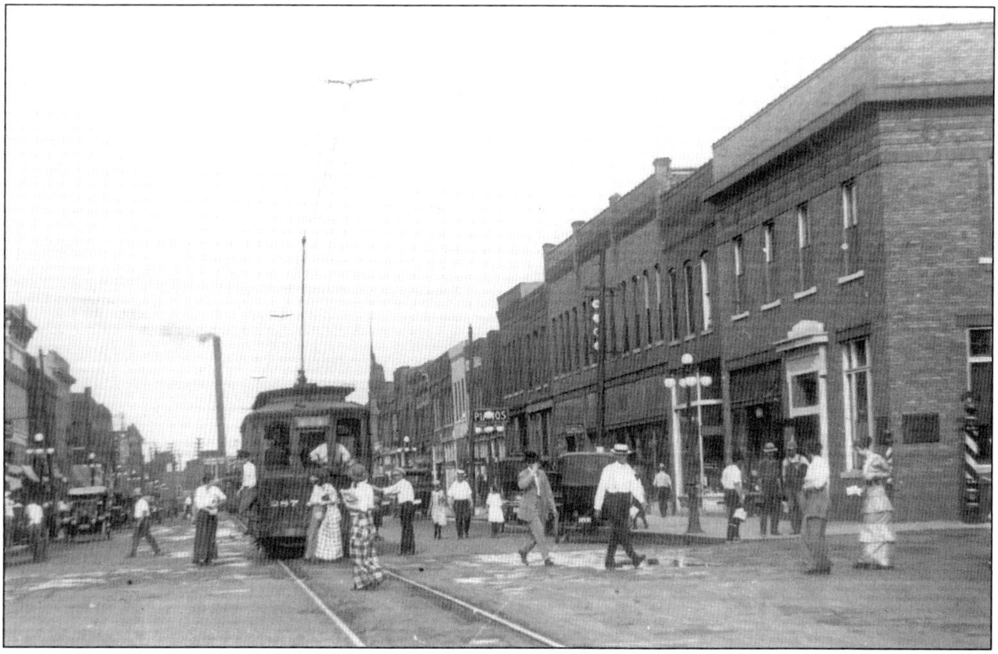

Ames Trust and Savings Bank, Ames Stationers, Tallmon Jewelers, and the Fair Store were located on this block of Main Street in 1916.

Here is Mary Victoria Greeley (1847–1914), in whose memory the hospital was named.

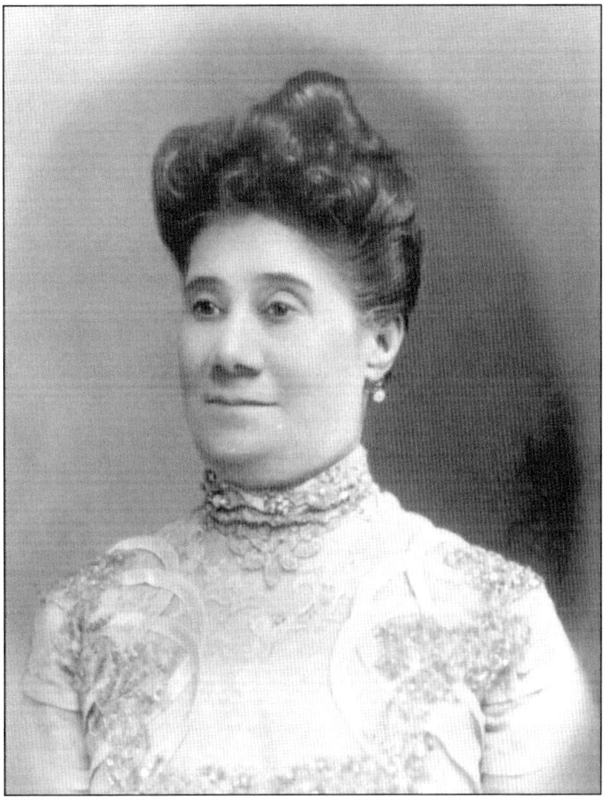

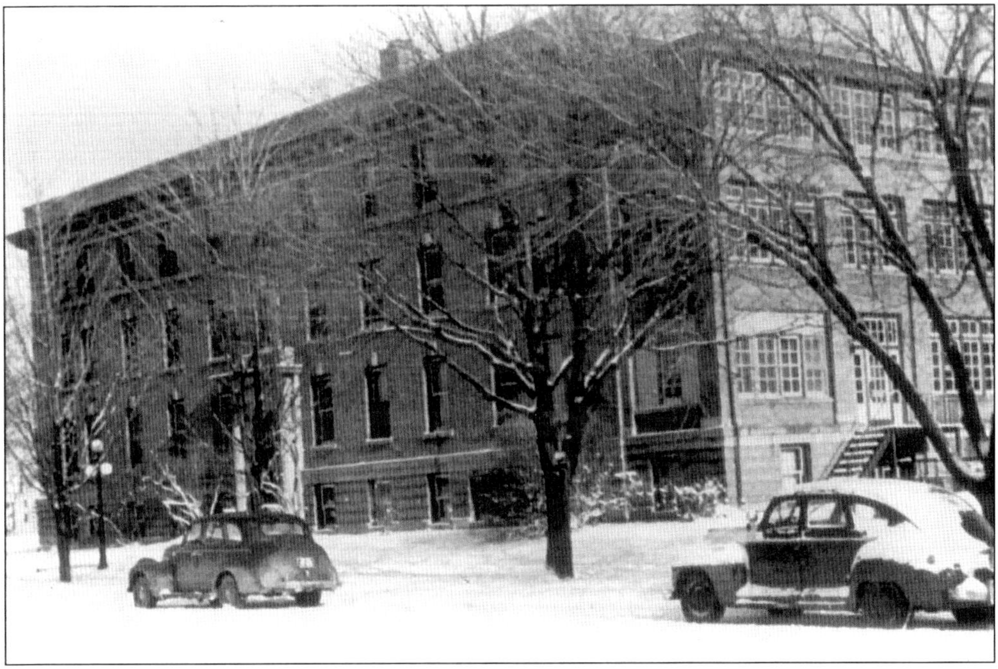

The Mary Greeley Hospital was dedicated in 1916.

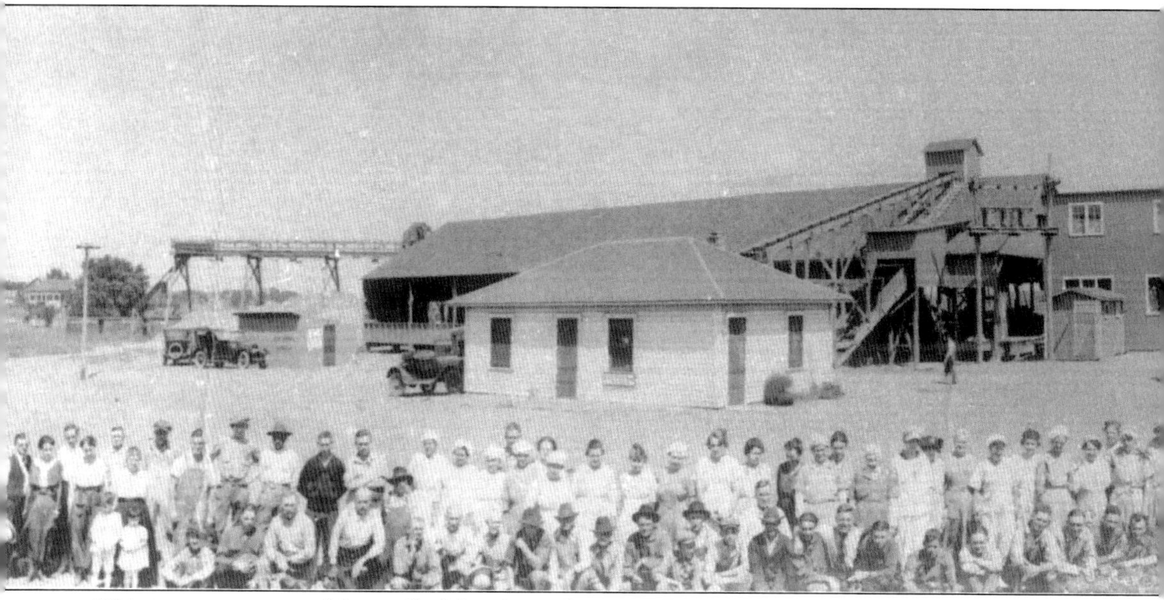

This is a panoramic of the staff of the Ames Canning Factory in 1919. The factory was located at east Third and Boone, and was in operation until some time in the 1940s. Canned sweet corn was marketed under two brand names, "Pride of Ames" and "Iowana," as well as under

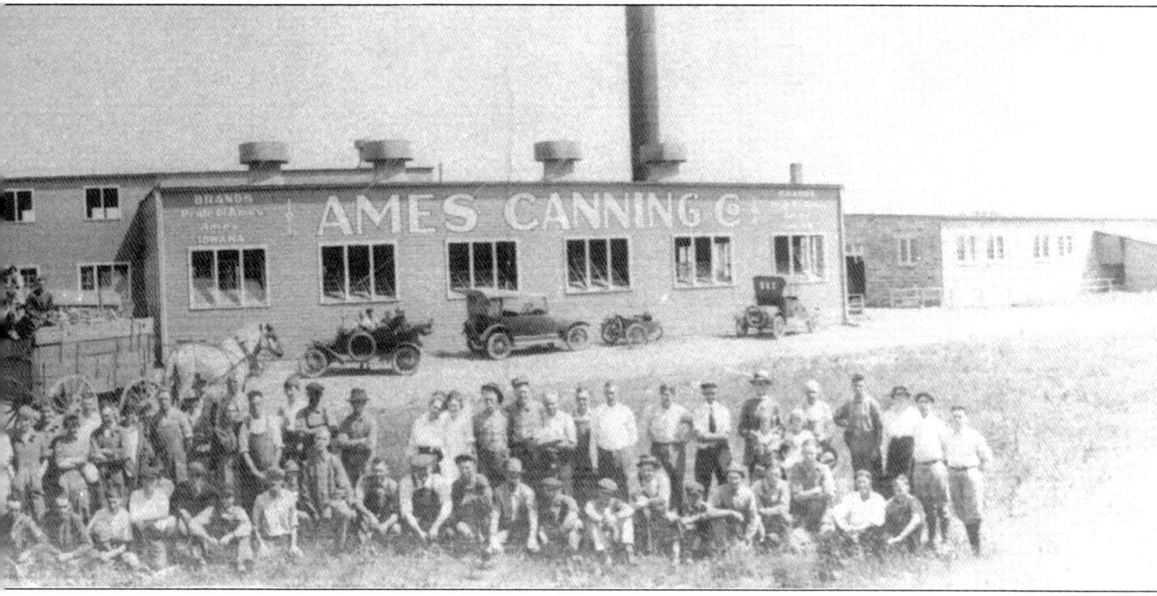

independent grocery company names. The government was sent 25 percent of the 1918 production for troop rations during World War I.

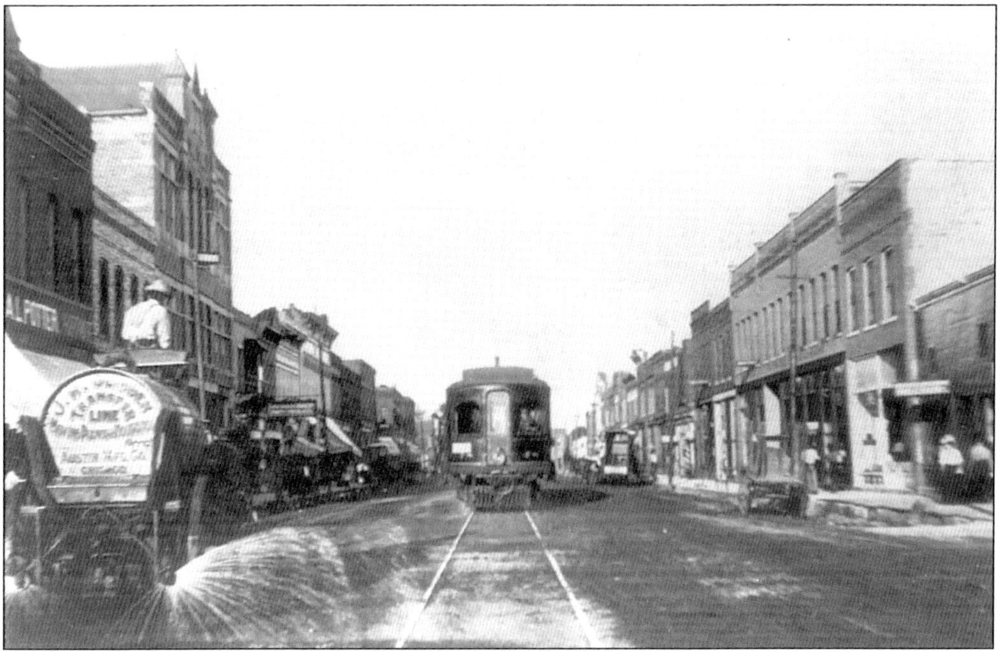

The interurban railroad travels down Onondaga Street, c. 1909. The sprinkler truck is shown keeping down the street's dust. Onondaga was paved in 1910 and renamed Main Street.

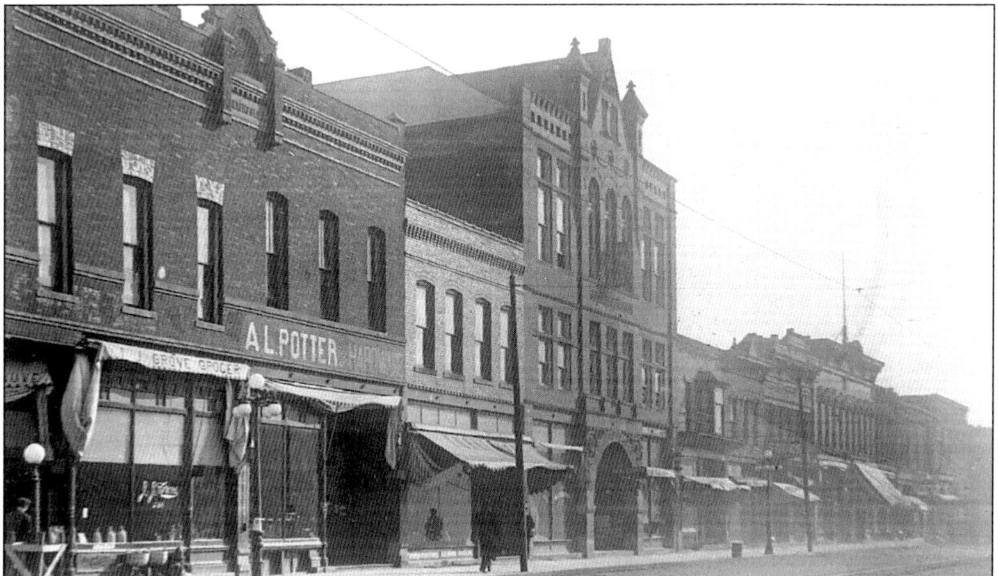

This is another view of Onondaga Street, taken nine years earlier.

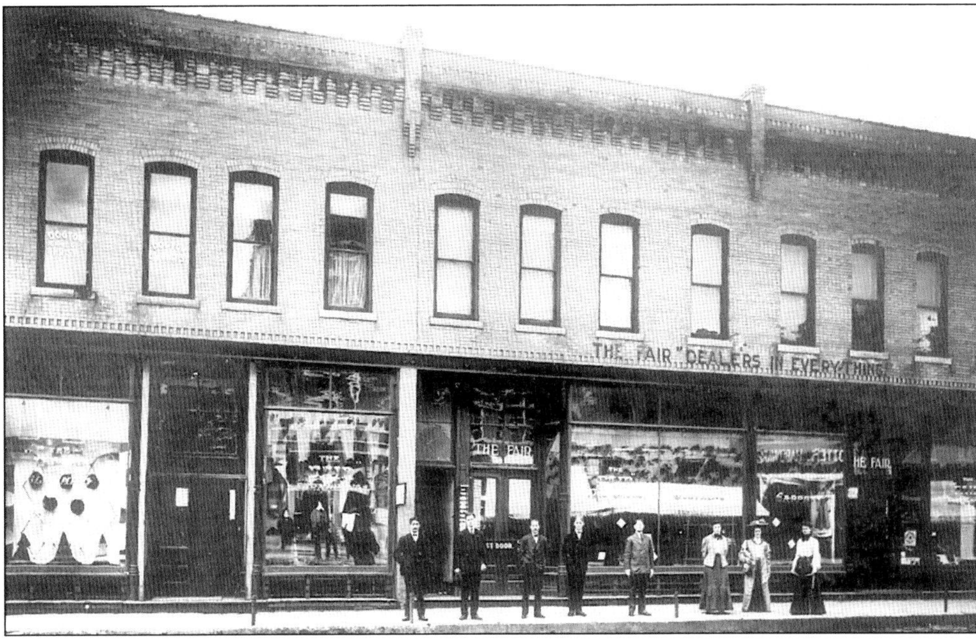

The Fair Store on Main Street was founded by J. Jacobs in 1895, and was a complete department store—featuring a men's store and grocery department.

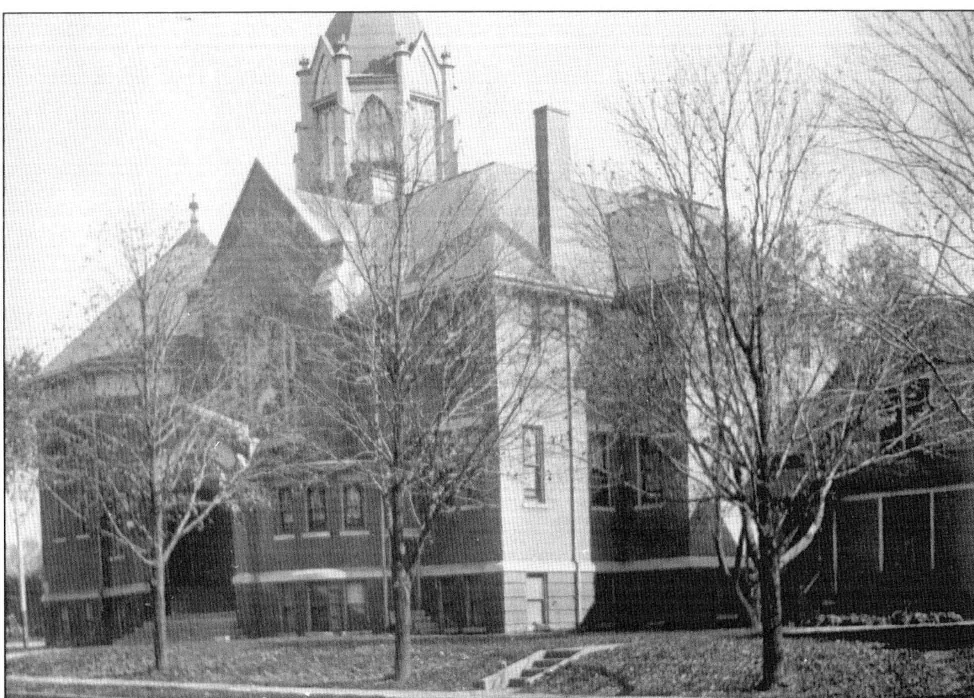

The First Methodist Church, on the corner of Kellogg and Sixth streets, was built in 1907.

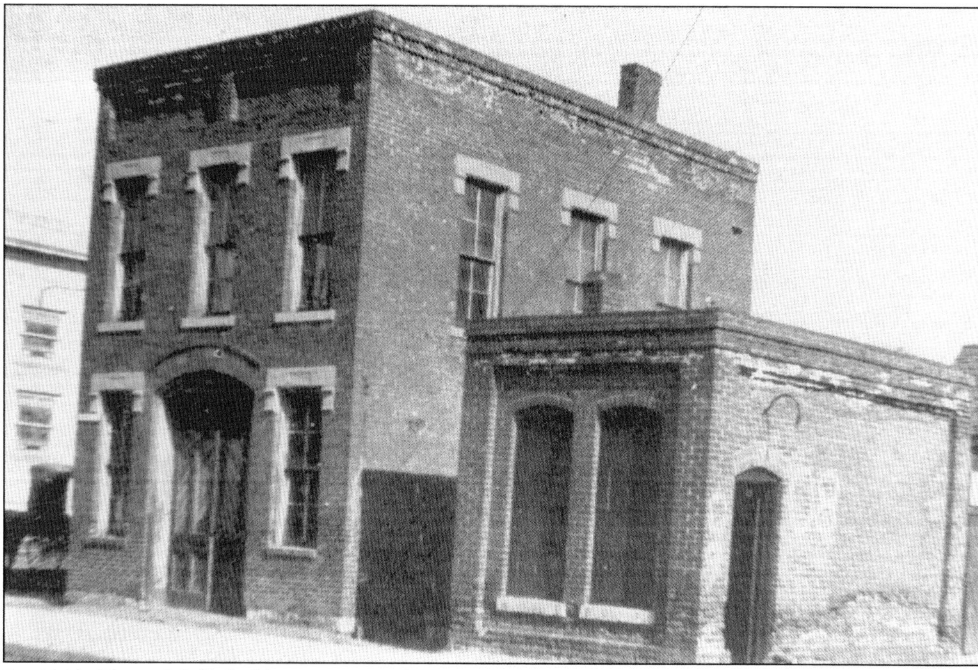

In 1910, Town Hall (left), constructed in 1886, housed the fire wagon in the ground level of the building. The jail (right) was equipped with two cells.

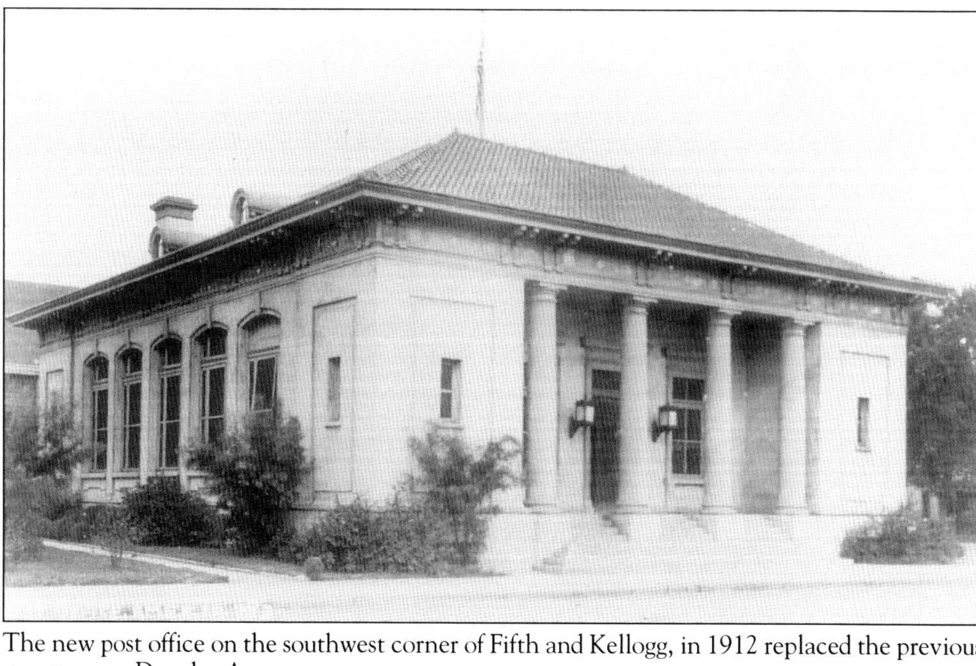

The new post office on the southwest corner of Fifth and Kellogg, in 1912 replaced the previous structure on Douglas Avenue.

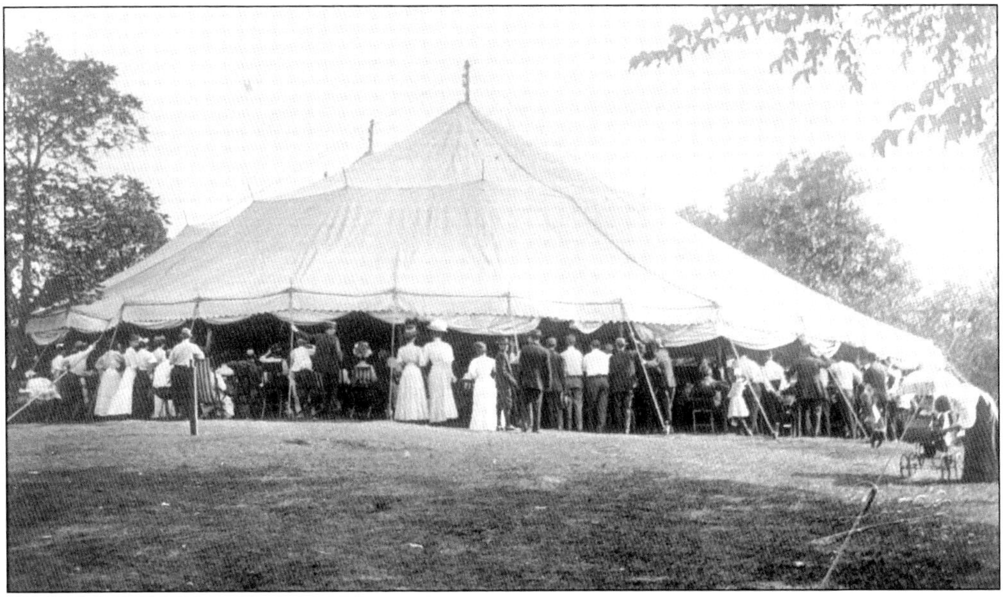

Booker T. Washington was among the Chautauqua headliners in Ames during August 1906. This large tent, pitched adjacent to the future Brookridge Avenue, was the auditorium facility for this weeklong family cultural program.

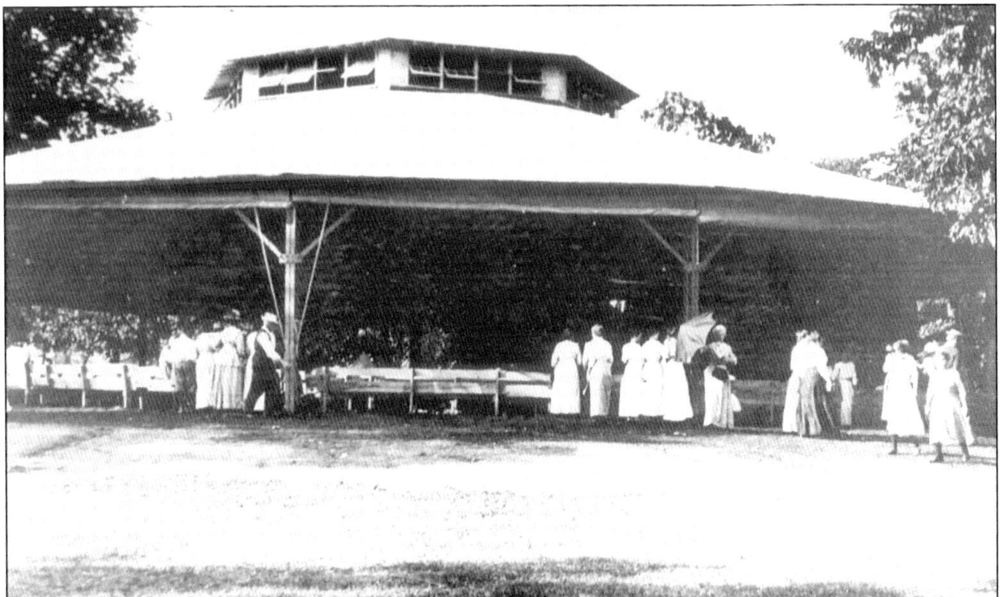

Chautauqua, the annual summer family cultural program in Ames, moved from a field to a permanent auditorium in the north part of what was later to be the Municipal Cemetery.

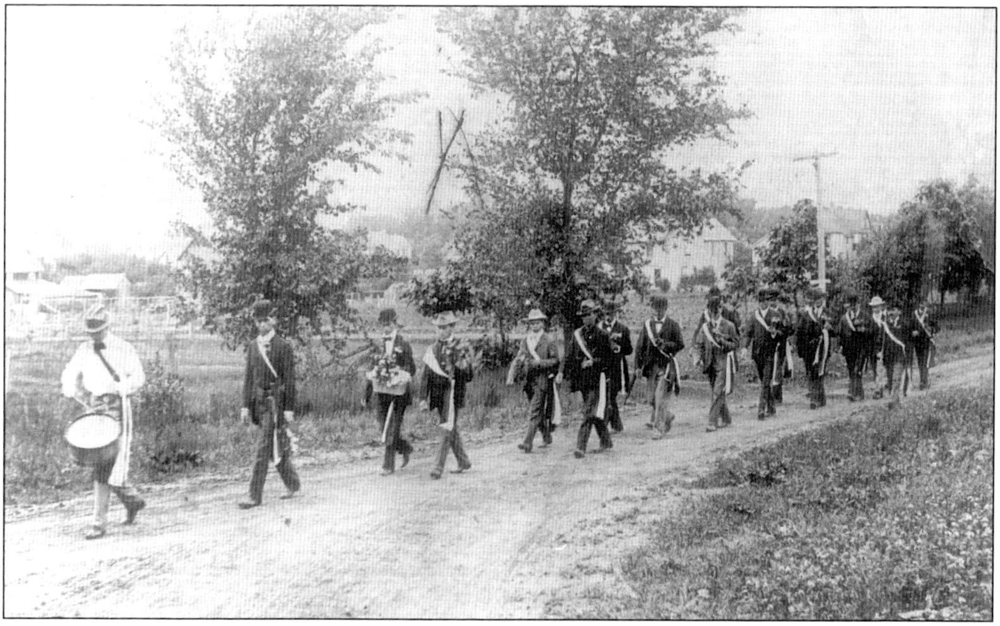

The 1875 Memorial Day Parade was captured on film as it wound its way through Ninth Street.

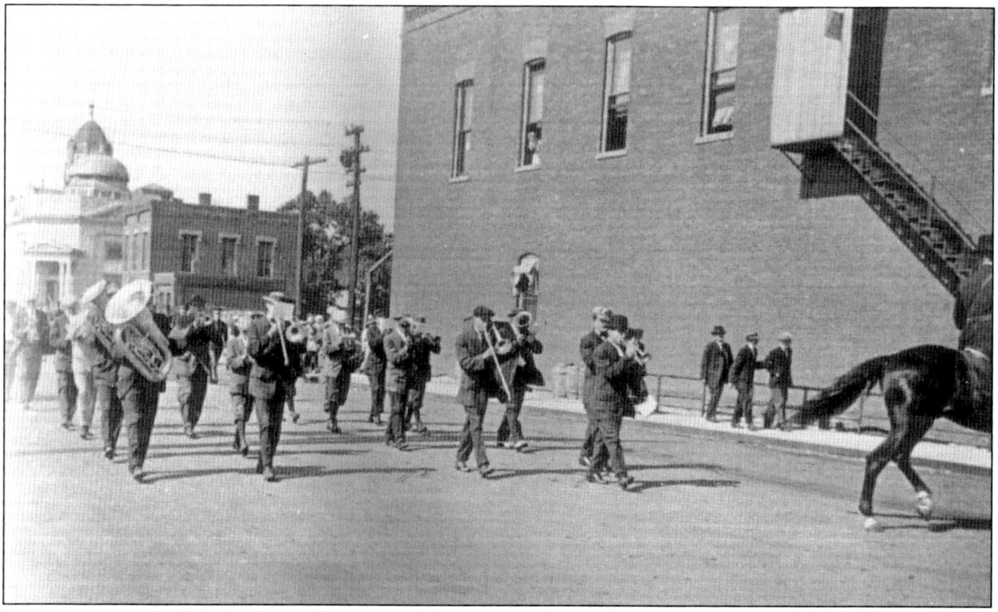

Harvey Stearns, playing a coronet, leads the Municipal Band in the 1913 Memorial Day Parade down Kellogg Avenue in downtown Ames.

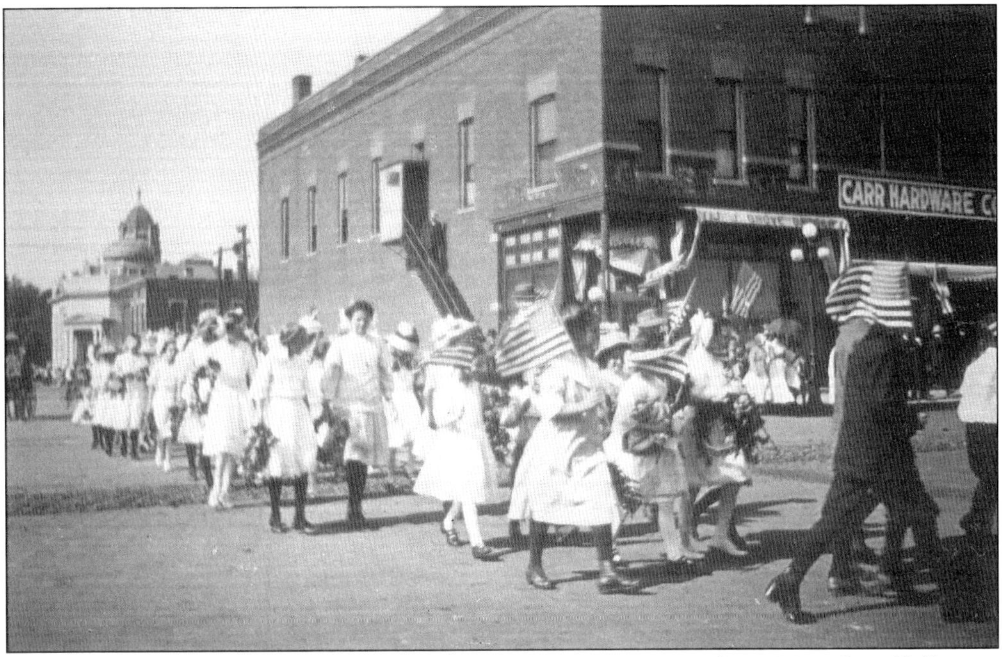

Another portion of the 1913 Memorial Day Parade is seen turning down Main from Kellogg at J.J. Grove's corner grocery.

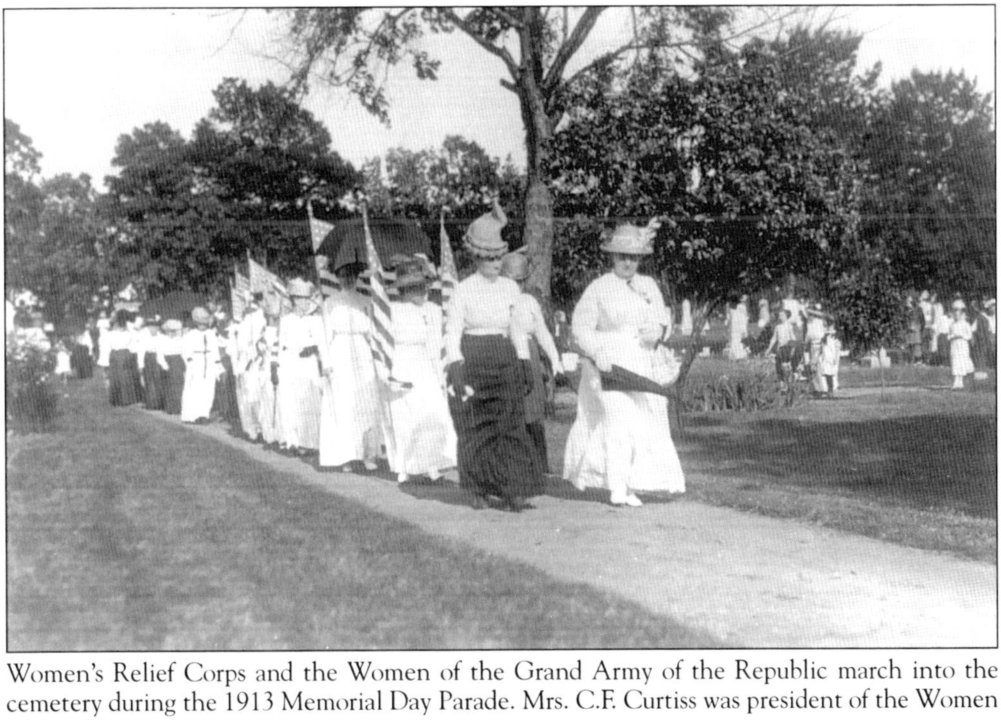

Women's Relief Corps and the Women of the Grand Army of the Republic march into the cemetery during the 1913 Memorial Day Parade. Mrs. C.F. Curtiss was president of the Women of the G.A.R. that year.

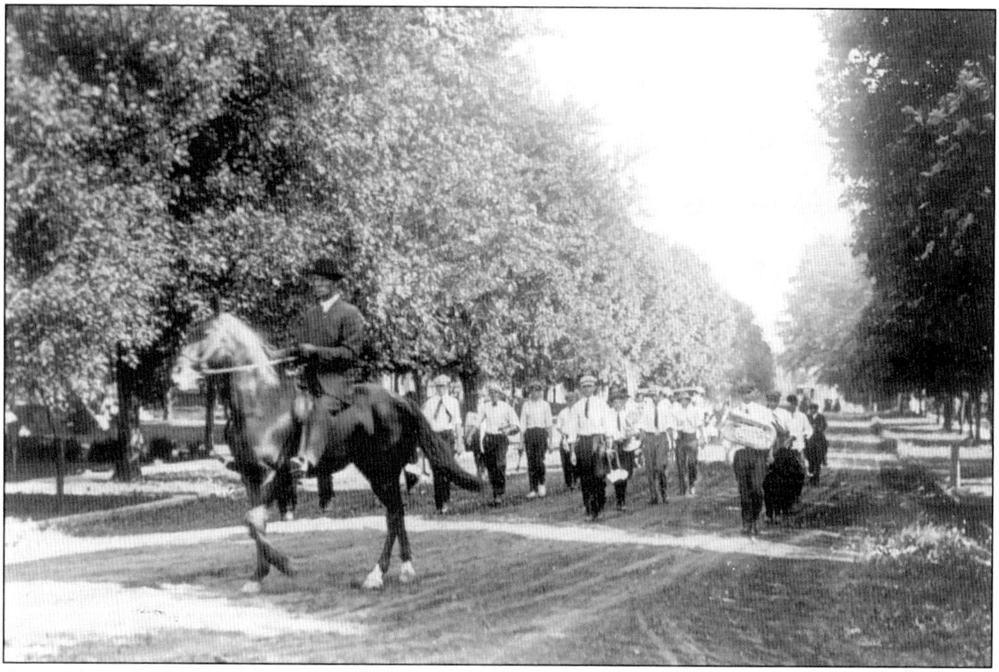

General Rush D. Lincoln, head of military tactics at ISC, was parade marshal of the 1913 Memorial Day Parade.

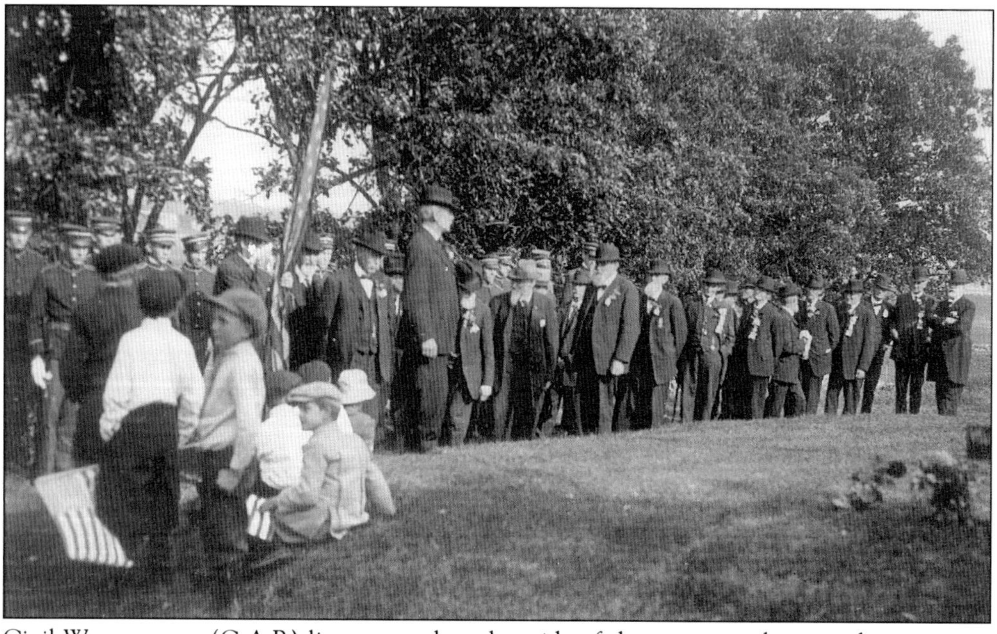

Civil War veterans (G.A.R) line up on the other side of the ceremonial site at the cemetery. The raising of the flag and the firing of the 21-gun salute followed.

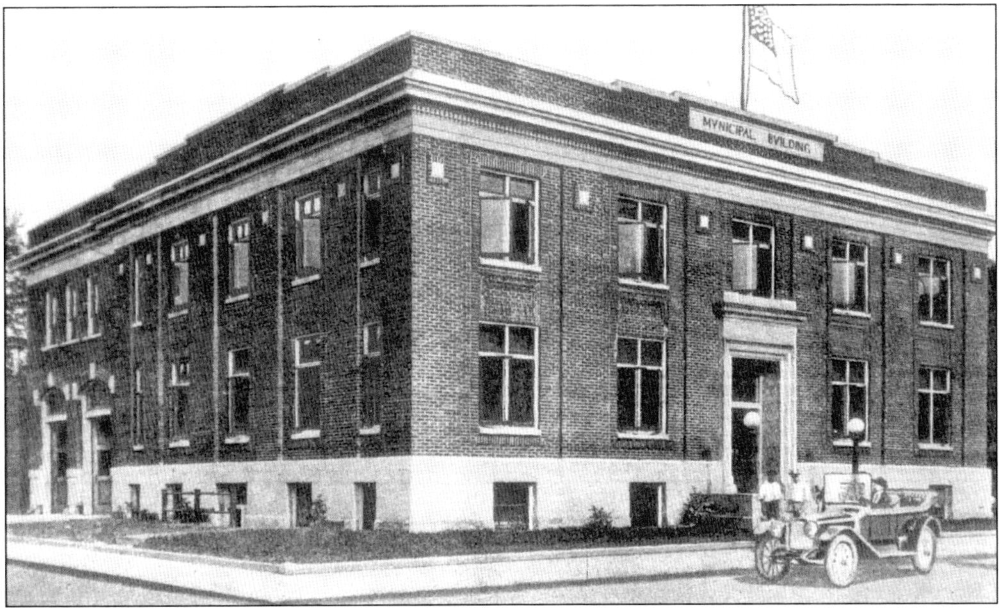

This postcard of the Municipal Building (City Hall) was taken not long after its completion in 1915.

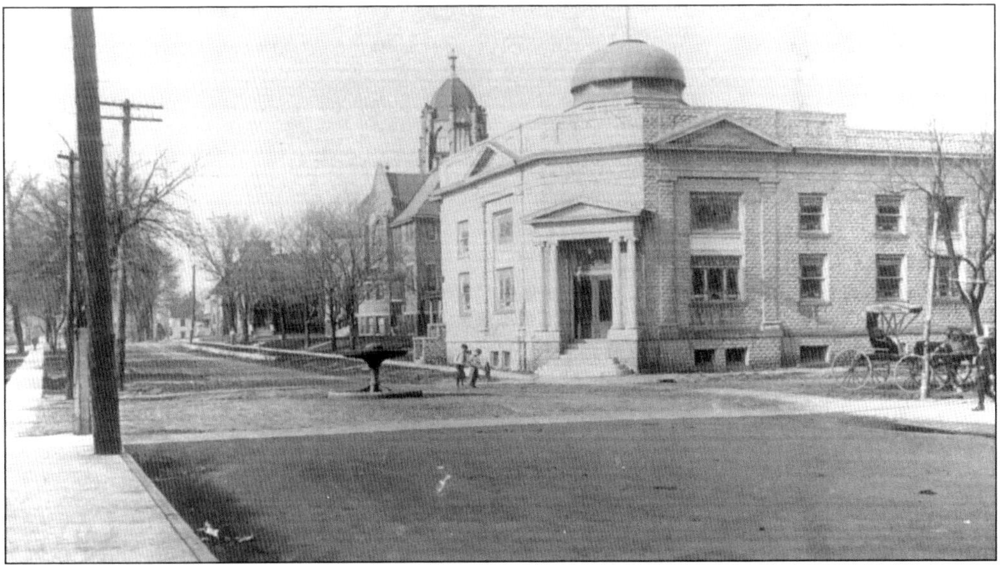

The First Baptist Church on the corner of Kellogg and Fifth still has the cast iron watering trough and hitching posts in 1915. The Methodist and Congregational churches can be seen further up the street.

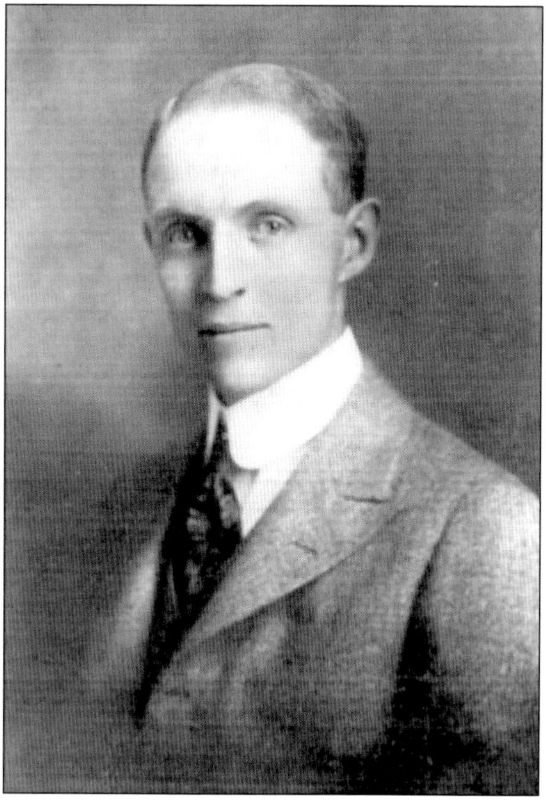

Albert Caldwell, Ames High School principal from 1914 to 1916, was a survivor of the *Titanic* disaster of 1912.

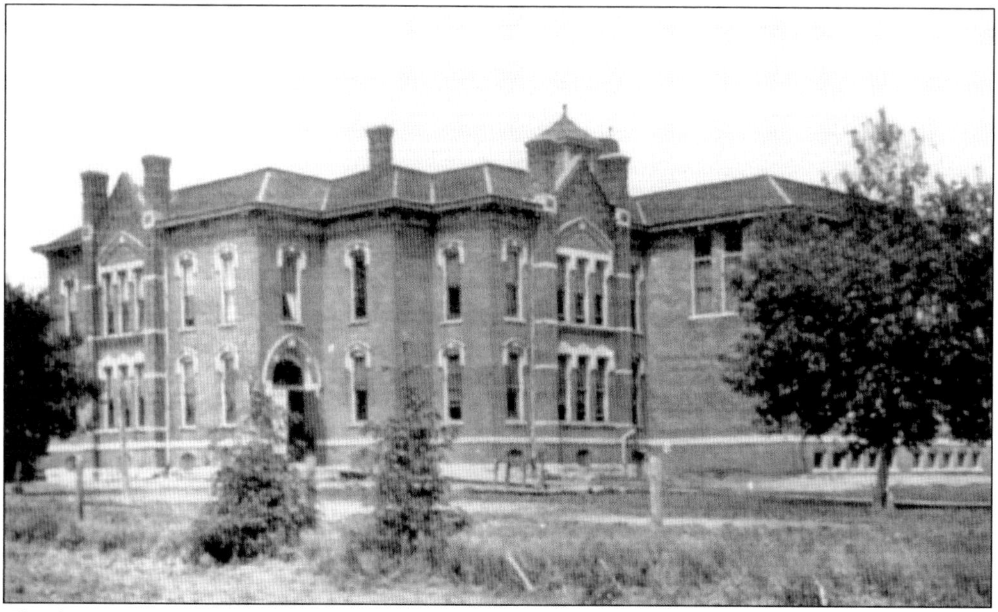

The first Ames High School, built in 1881 as the Union School for all grades, was added onto in 1900. It was the first brick schoolhouse in Ames and stood on the west side of Clark between Fifth and Sixth streets.

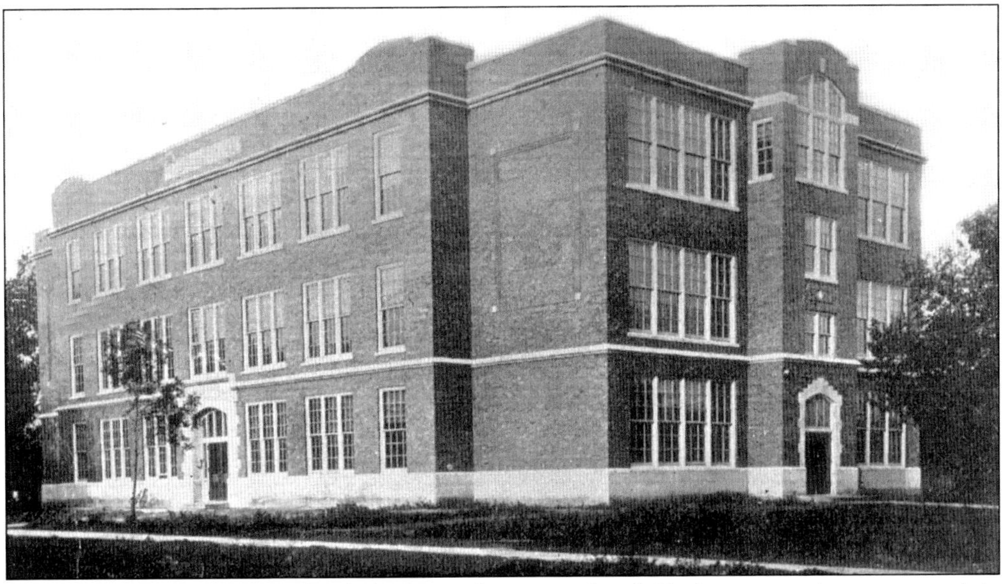

The second Ames High School, built on the east side of Clark, was newly constructed in 1917. By 1939, it had been replaced by the new building in the block to its west. This newer building served as both grade school and junior high facilities until razed in 1981 for needed parking lot use.

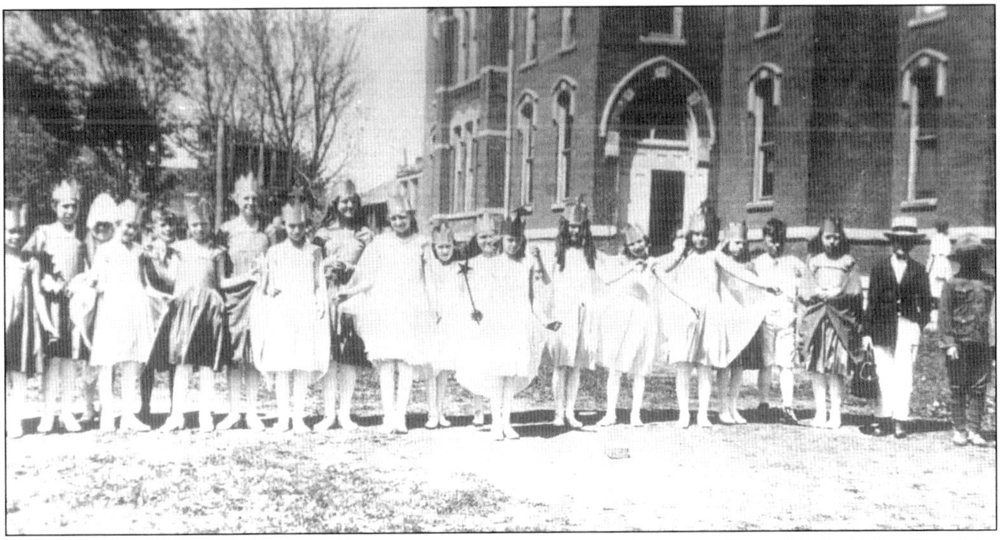

Central School's fifth grade class in costumes for their production of the "Milk Fairy Play," in 1921. From left to right, they are as follows: Mabel Langford, four unidentified children, Irene McCarthy, unidentified, Lucile Wood, two unidentified children, Ruth Aplin, unidentified, Lola Aplin, Adeline Morrissey, Margaret McCleod, five unidentified children, and David Griffith.

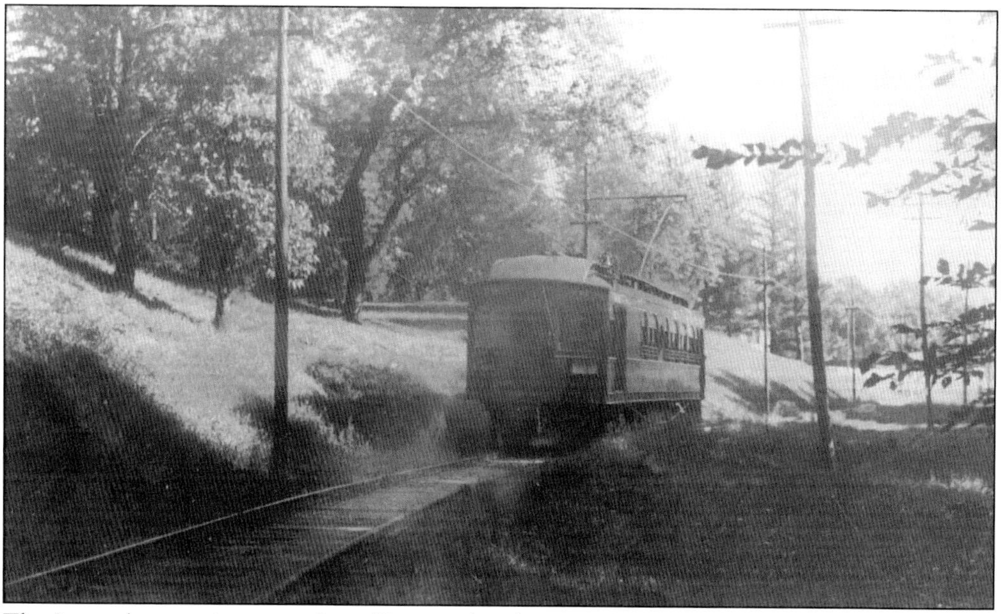

The Interurban car is captured on film as it heads out to Des Moines in 1916. The Memorial Union exit ramp stands at this location today.

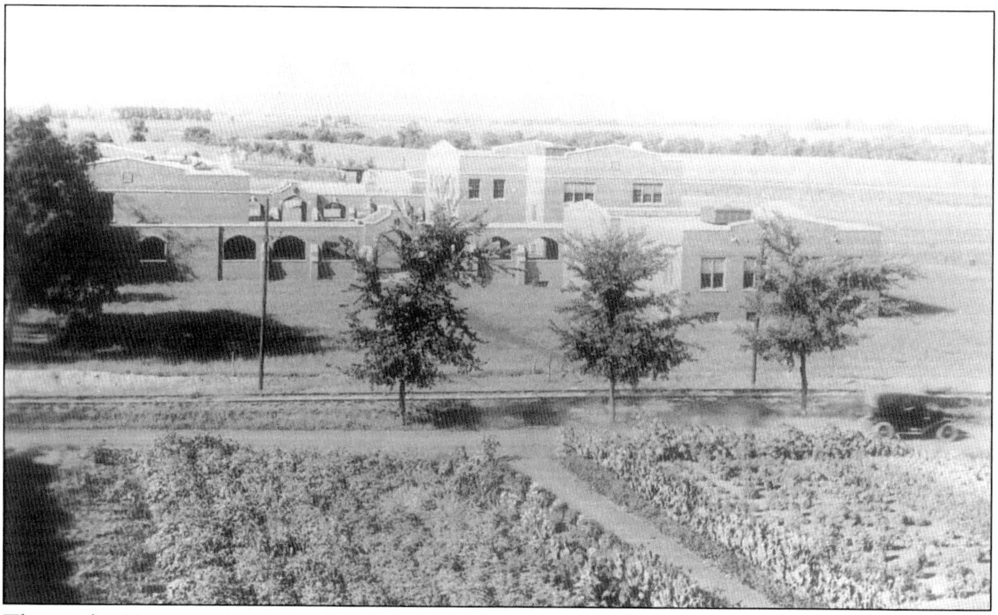

This is the Veterinary Quadrangle after 1916, when the streetcar "loop" was first used. Tracks are on the north side of what is now Osborn Drive.

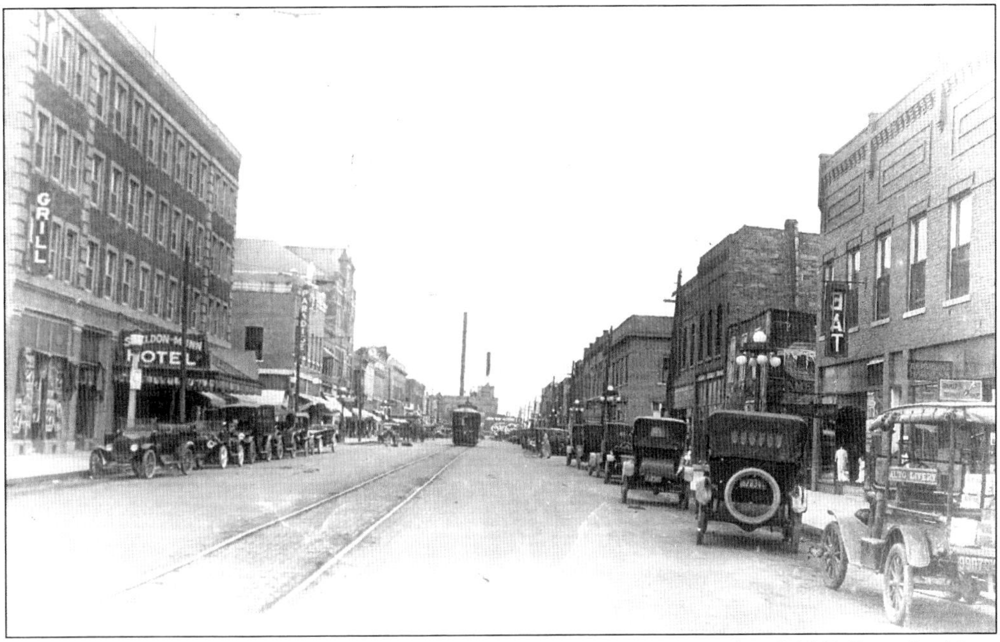

This view is looking east toward Kellogg on Main Street in 1917. The Odd Fellows Building beyond Kellogg, on the left, burned later that year.

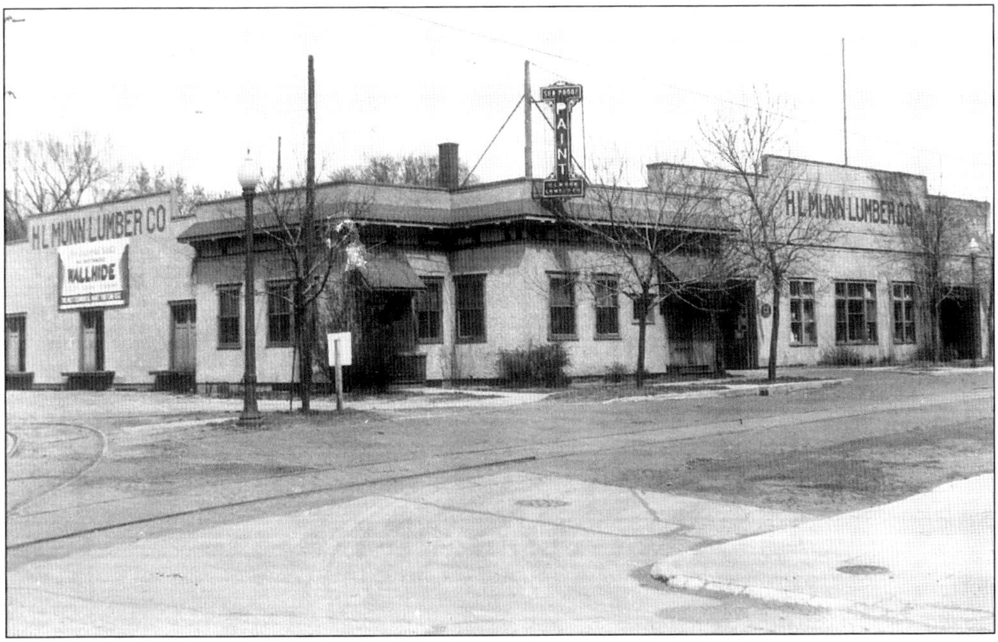

Munn Lumber Company as it looked c. 1925, at the east end of Main Street.

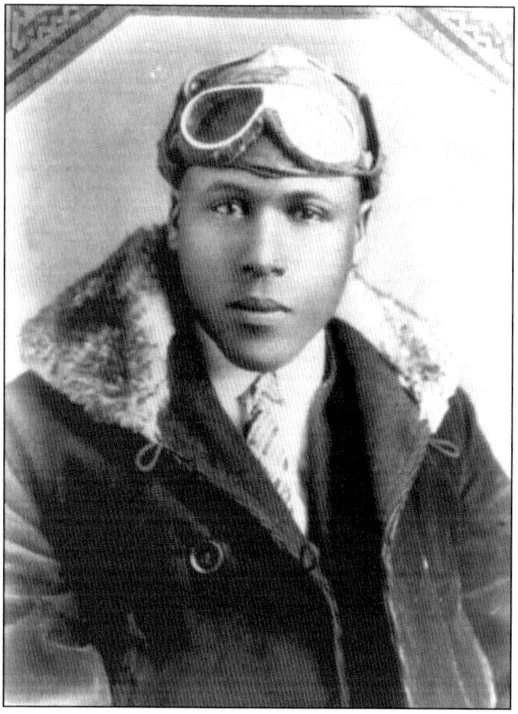

Born in 1899 in Oklahoma, J. Herman Banning and his family moved to Ames in 1919, where he studied electrical engineering at Iowa State College for little more than a year. He later became the first African-American aviator to obtain a license from the U.S. Department of Commerce.

J. Herman Banning performed in his plane, *Miss Ames*, in air circuses and flew politicians during their campaigns, including Illinois Representative Oscar Depriest, the first African American elected to serve in the U.S. Congress since the Civil War. This photograph is from c. 1928.

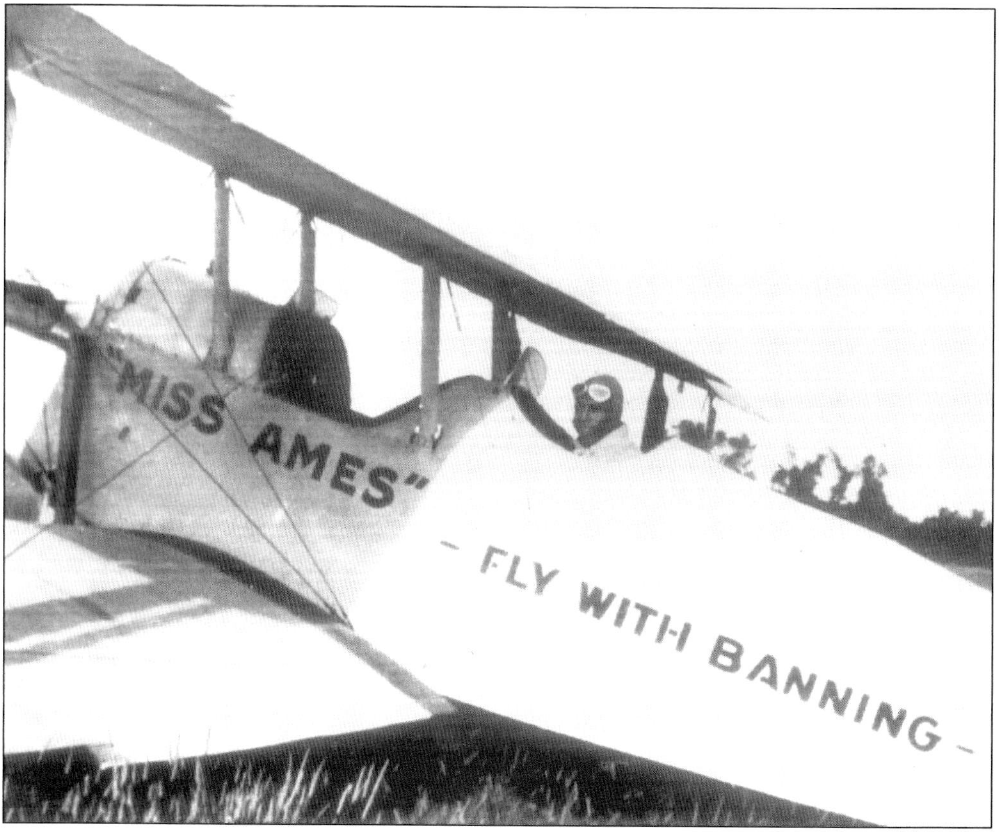

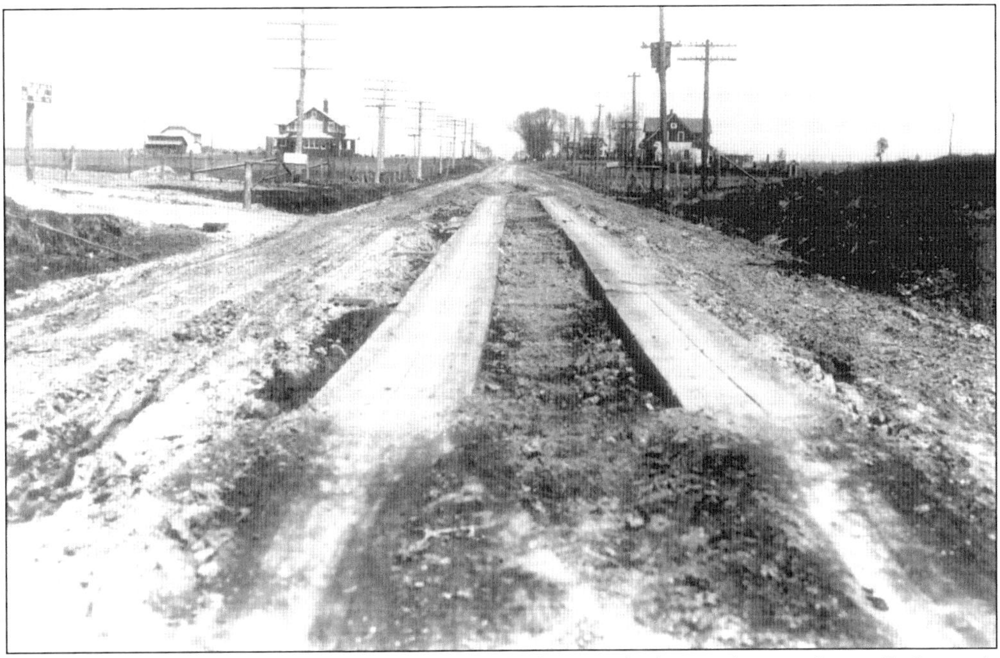

North Grand Avenue before it was paved shows planking about where Eighteenth Street is today.

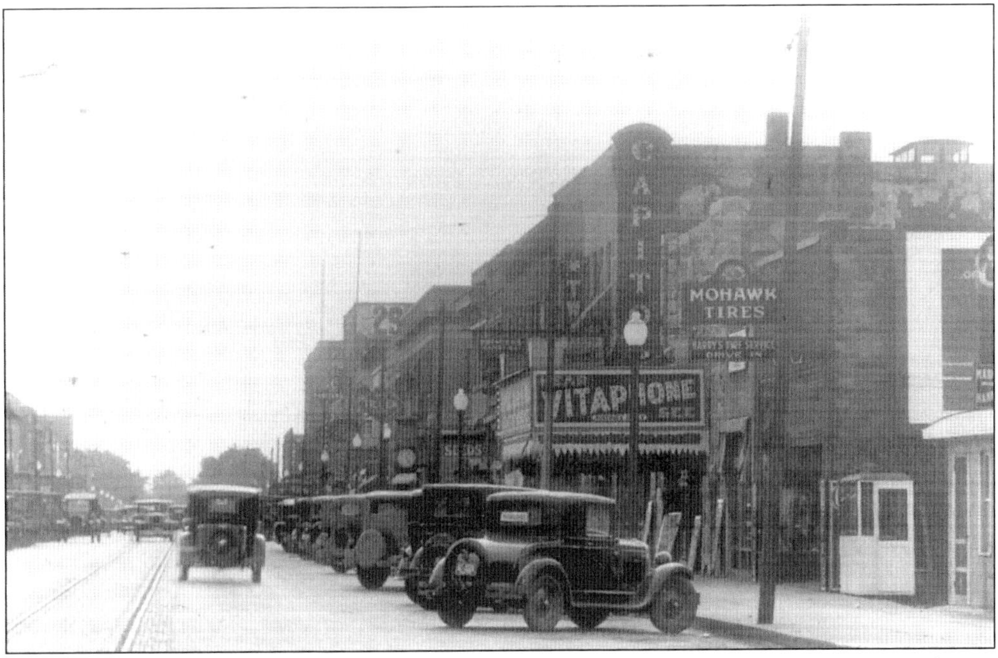

The Capitol Theatre on Main Street is shown in this image around 1930. The movie house was built in 1911 and was acquired by Joseph Gerbracht in 1920, who then changed the name from the Princess Theater.

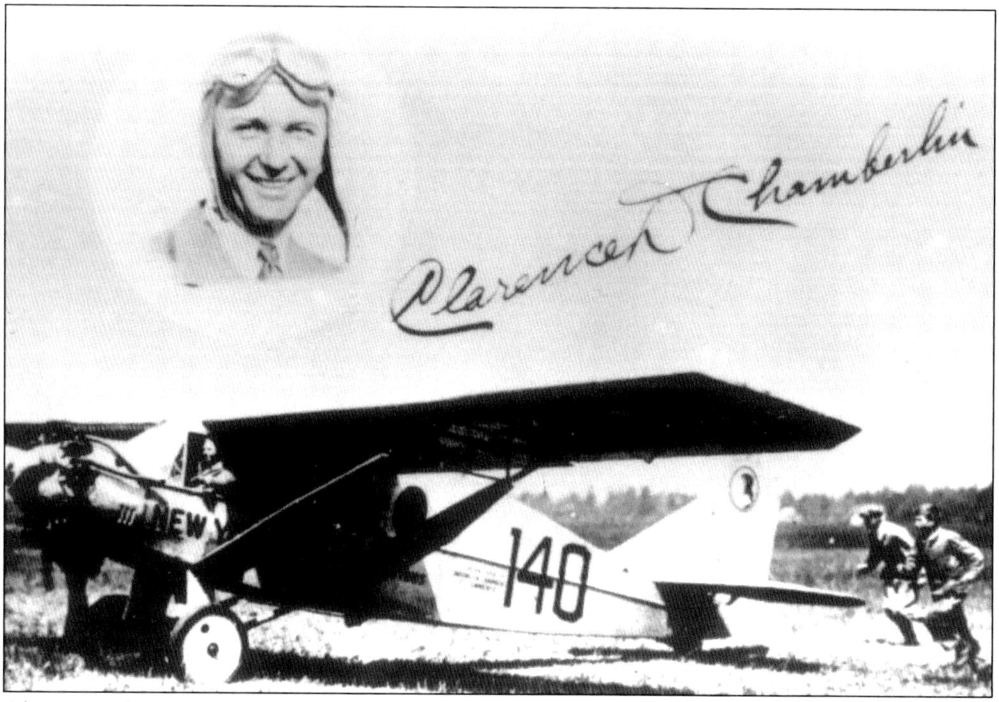

Clarence Chamberlin, a former student at Iowa State College, was honored in Ames a few weeks following his transcontinental flight from New York to Berlin in 1927. His plane, the *Miss Columbia*, was the first to fly across the Atlantic with a passenger.

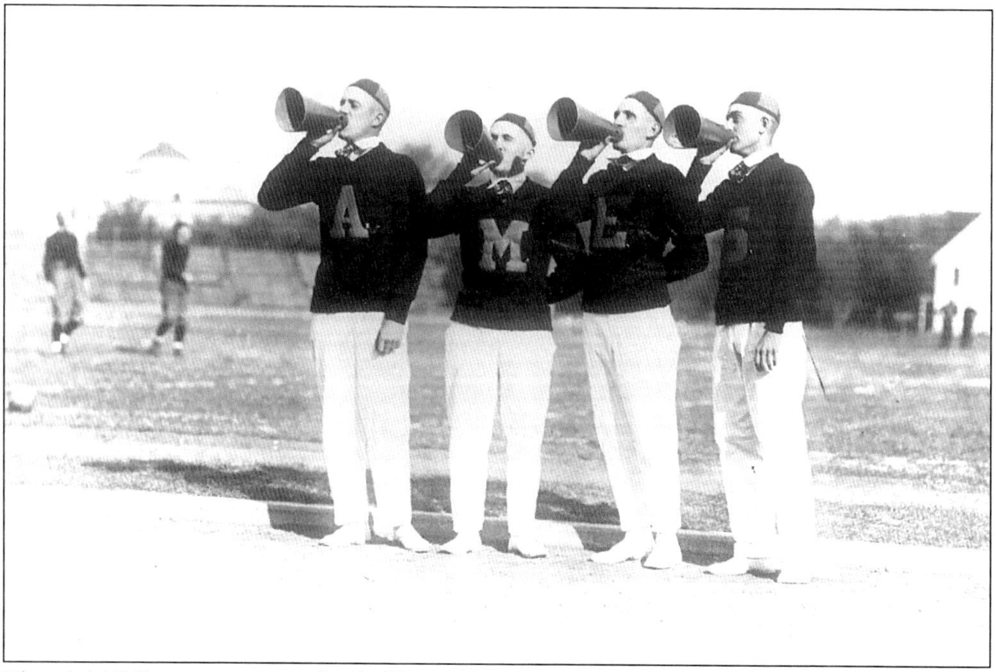

The A.M.E.S. quartet provides halftime entertainment during a football game at State Field in 1915.

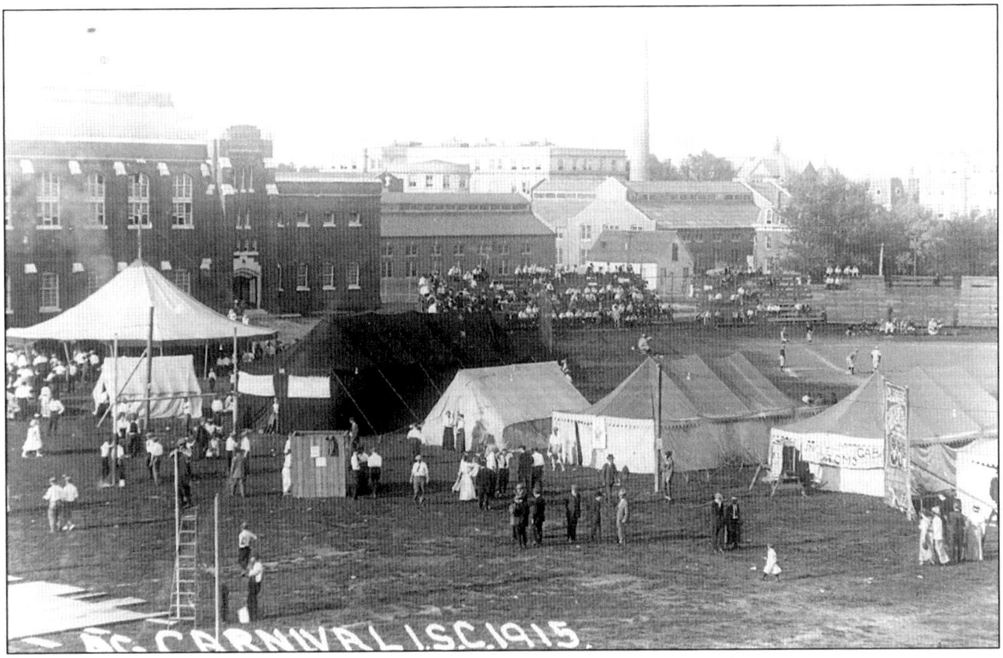

The crowds in this photograph are visiting the Agricultural Carnival in 1915.

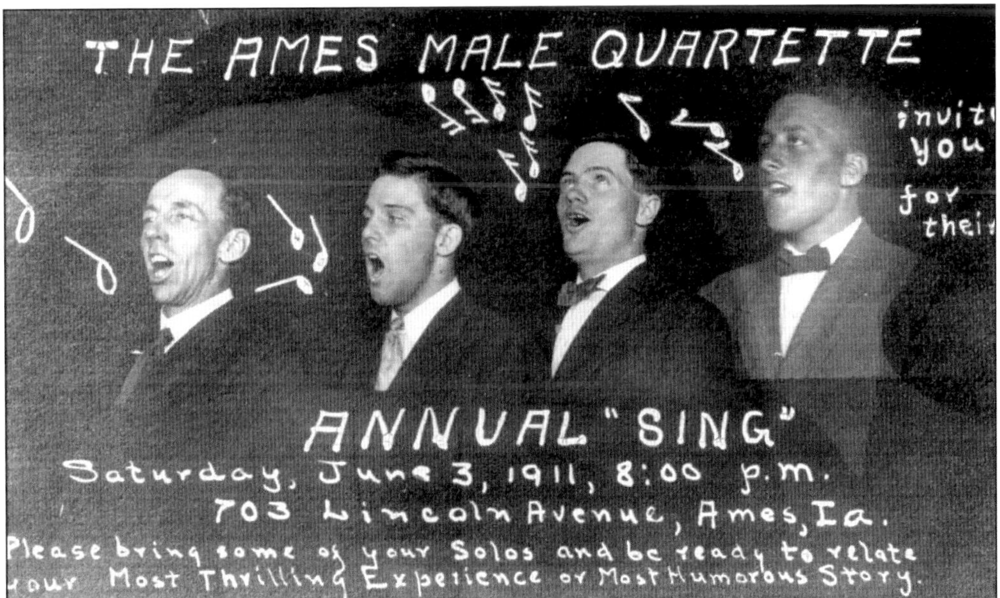

The Ames Male Quartette holds its annual "SING" on June 3, 1911. Harvey Stearns, who later became Ames Municipal Band director and a teacher at Ames High School, is second from the left.

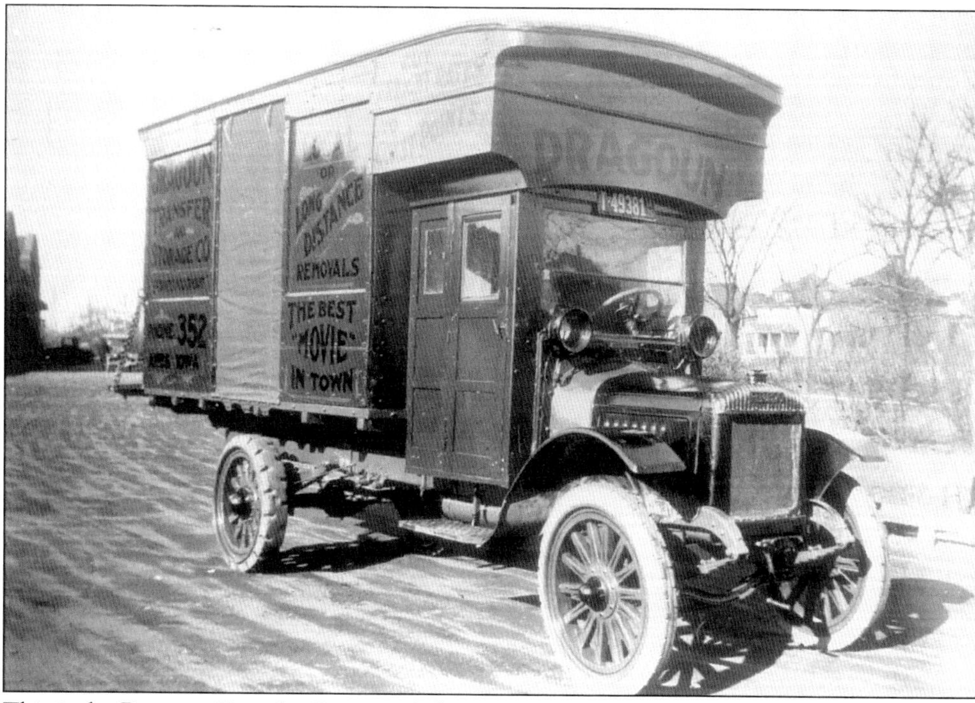

This is the Dragoun Transfer Company's first motorized truck, *c.* 1917.

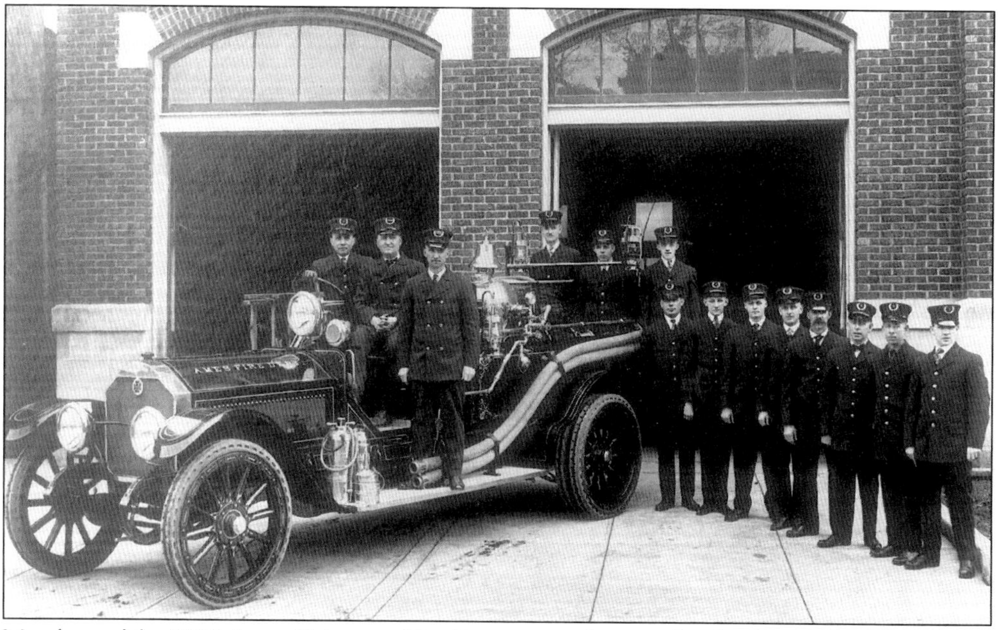

Members of the 1917 Ames Volunteer Fire Department (except for the driver who was the first paid firefighter) pose around their first motorized truck. They are, from left to right, as follows: Sam Long, driver; Lynn Morris, chief; Art McCoy, assistant chief; W.L. (Bill) McCoy; Bernice J. (Gravy) Graves; H. Clyde (Gabby) Nible; J. Kenneth (Doc) Kelso; Glenn (Newt) Morris; Harold (Heavy McDowell; W.L. (Hop) Hoppins; Oscar McCoy; Howard Adams; Henry N. (Hank) Valline; and Charles Foster.

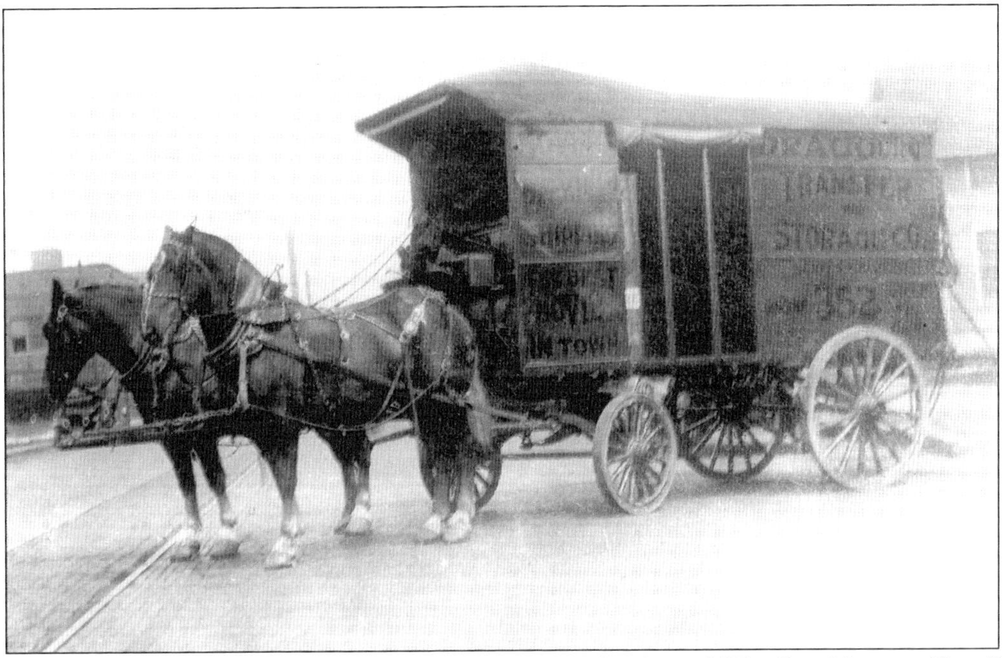

Proud of their horse-drawn moving vans, Dragoun Transfer claimed "The Best Movie in Town" on the side of their vans, c. 1915.

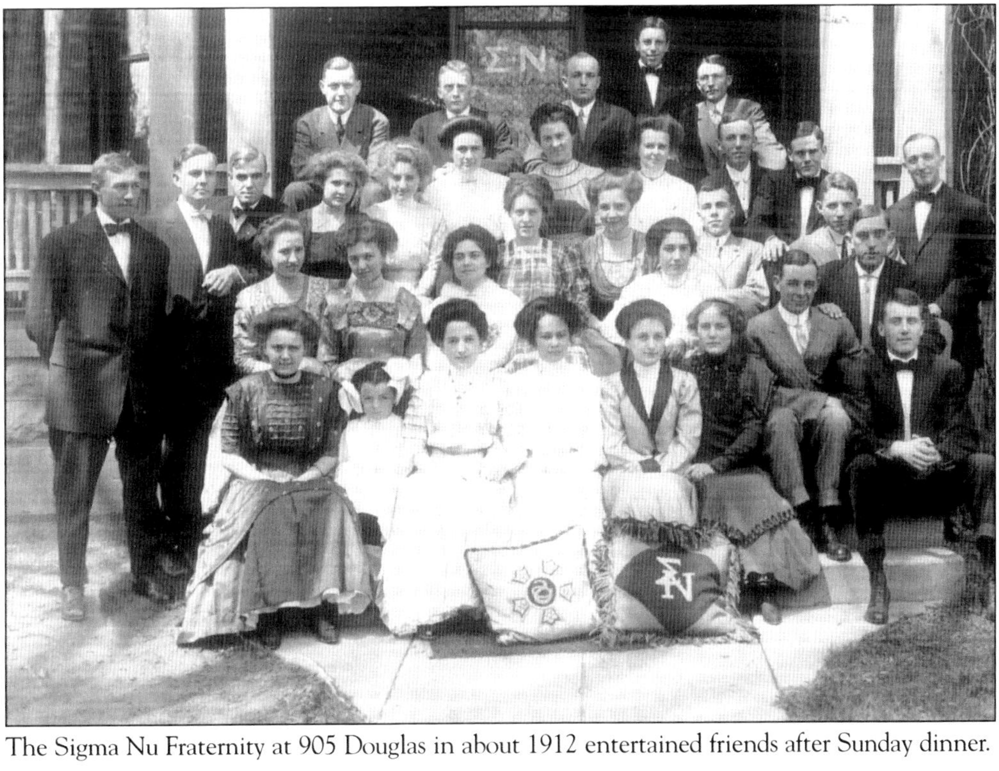

The Sigma Nu Fraternity at 905 Douglas in about 1912 entertained friends after Sunday dinner.

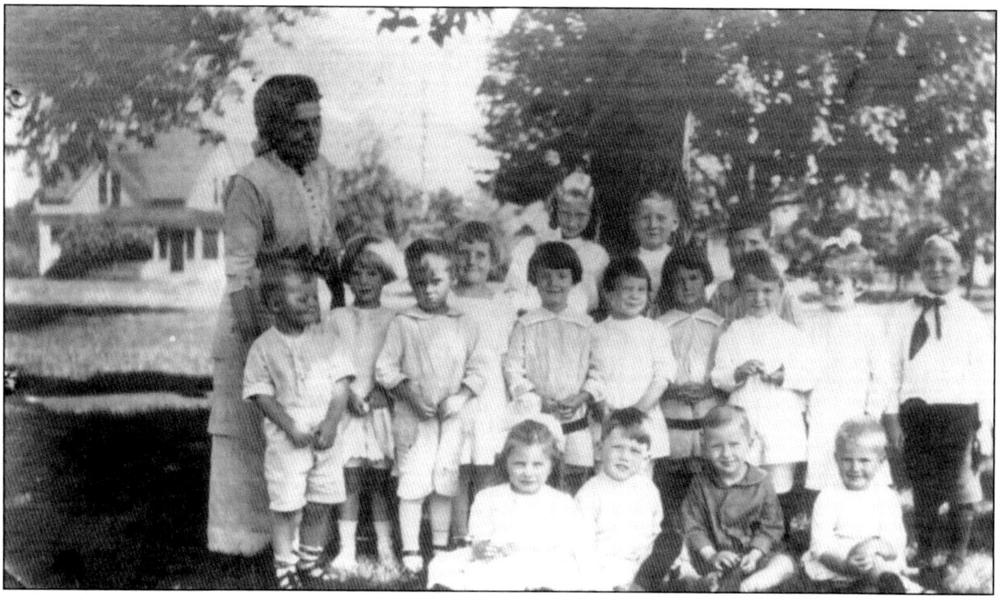

Louise Crawford, Ames' first kindergarten teacher, watches over her summer school class on the old Central School grounds in 1916.

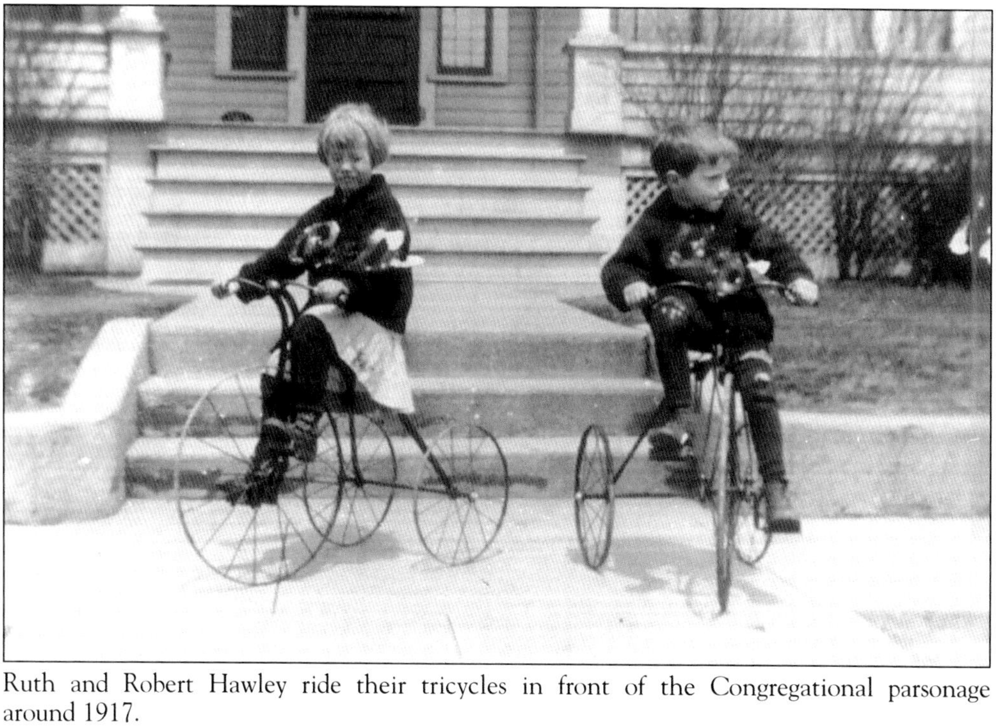

Ruth and Robert Hawley ride their tricycles in front of the Congregational parsonage around 1917.

The second location of Bethesda Lutheran Church on the corner of Seventh and Kellogg was dedicated in 1928. Today, the Ascension Lutheran Church occupies this building, and Bethesda Lutheran is located on Northwestern Avenue.

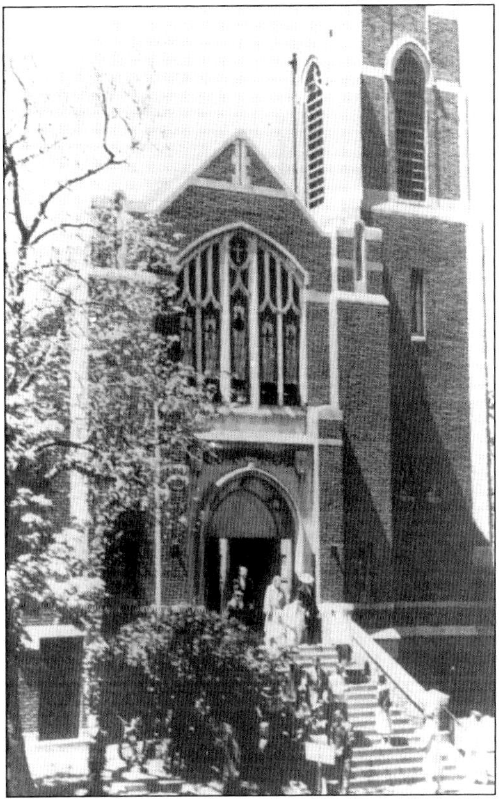

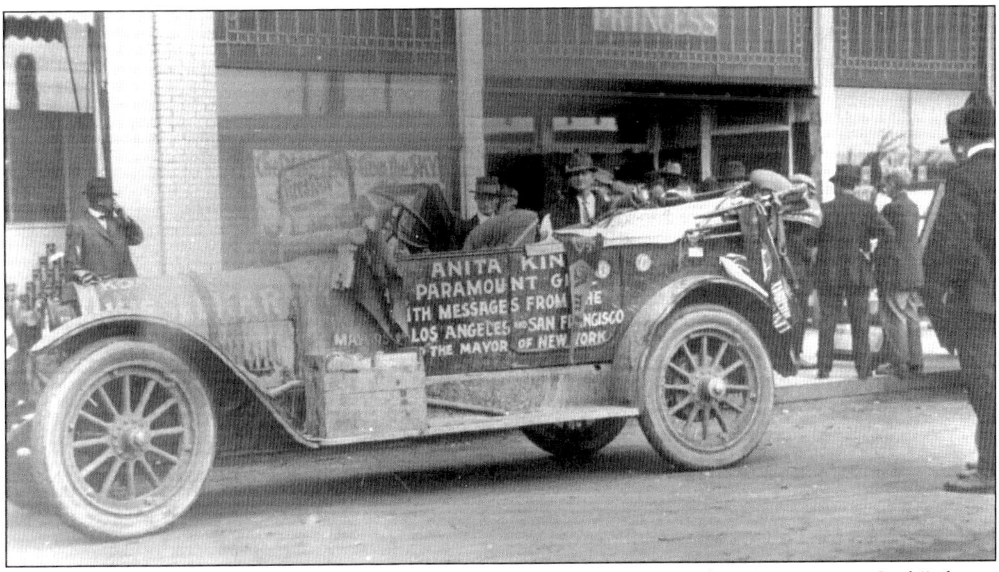

Soon after the completion of the Lincoln Highway, Anita King, the "Paramount Girl," drove her Kissell Kar from San Francisco to New York, stopping in Ames in September of 1915.

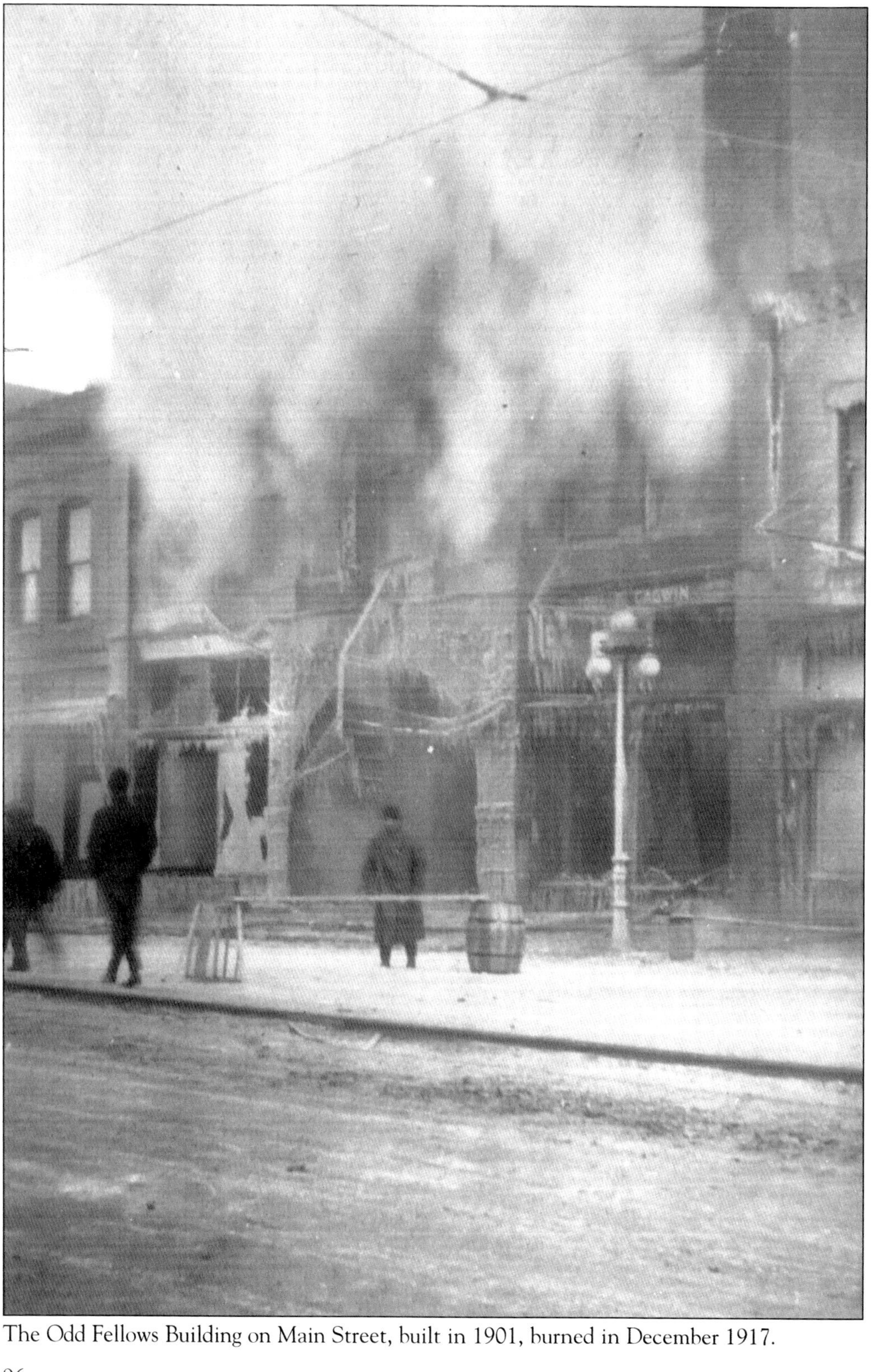

The Odd Fellows Building on Main Street, built in 1901, burned in December 1917.

Four

Railroads, People, and Events

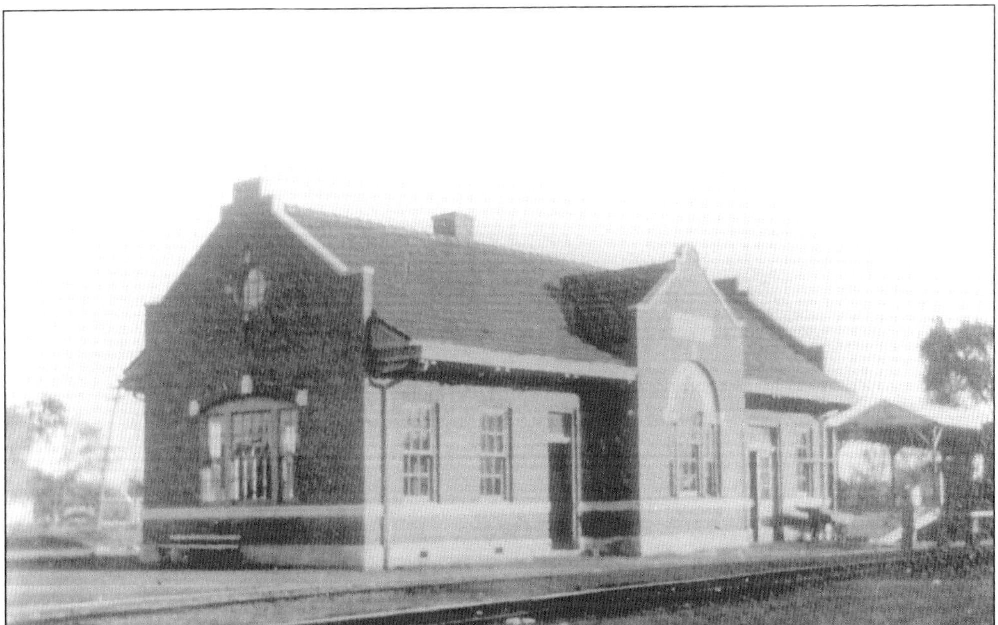

The Fort Dodge, Des Moines, and Southern Railroad Interurban Depot, new in 1915, was located where the ISU Credit Union stands today.

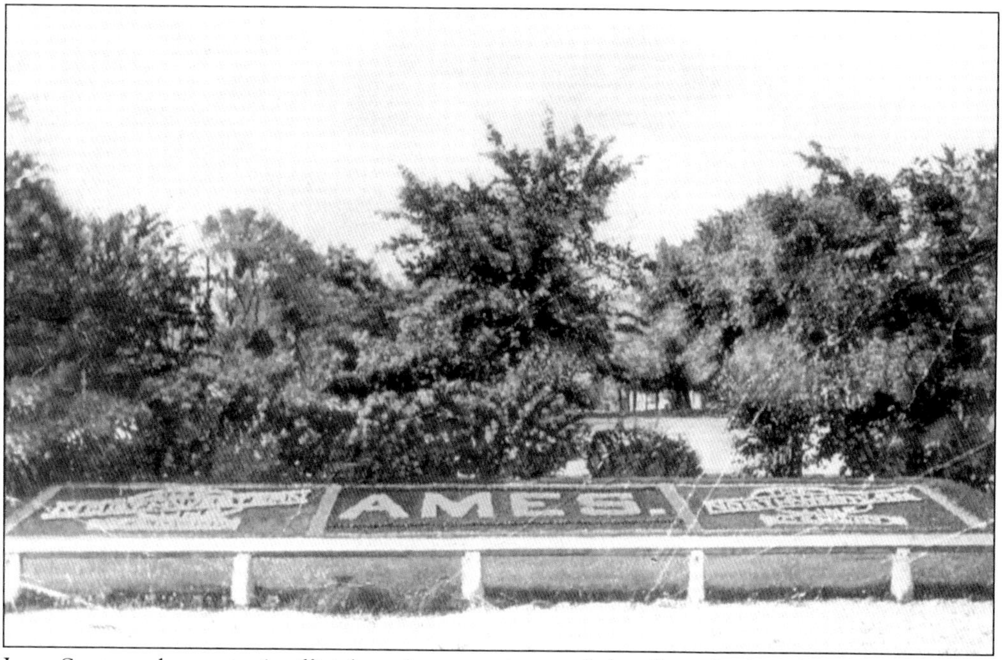

Jerry Sexton, the station's official gardener, maintained this flowerbed at the east end of the Chicago & North Western Railroad Depot to let train passengers know this was Ames.

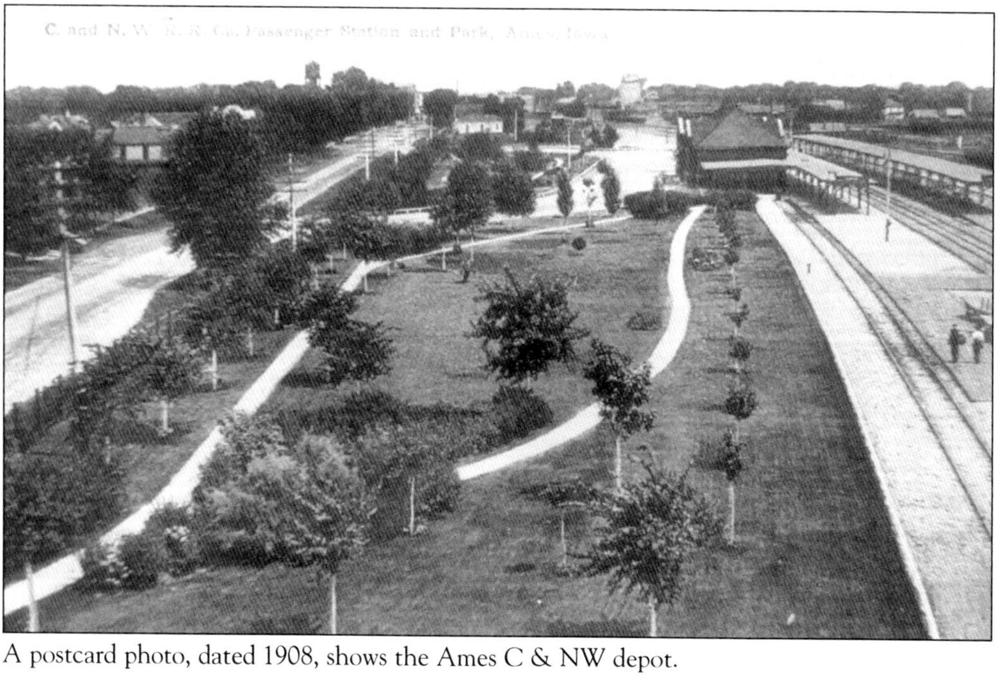

A postcard photo, dated 1908, shows the Ames C & NW depot.

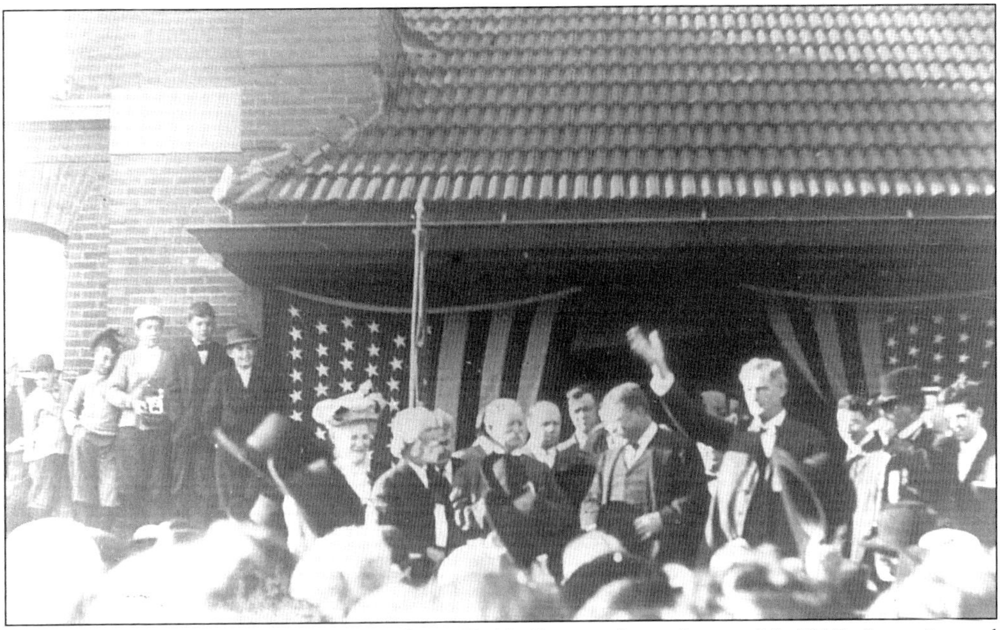

Parley Sheldon, mayor of Ames, introduces Teddy Roosevelt on August 26, 1910. An estimated crowd of five thousand people gathered at the steps of the C & NW Railroad Depot to hear the president speak.

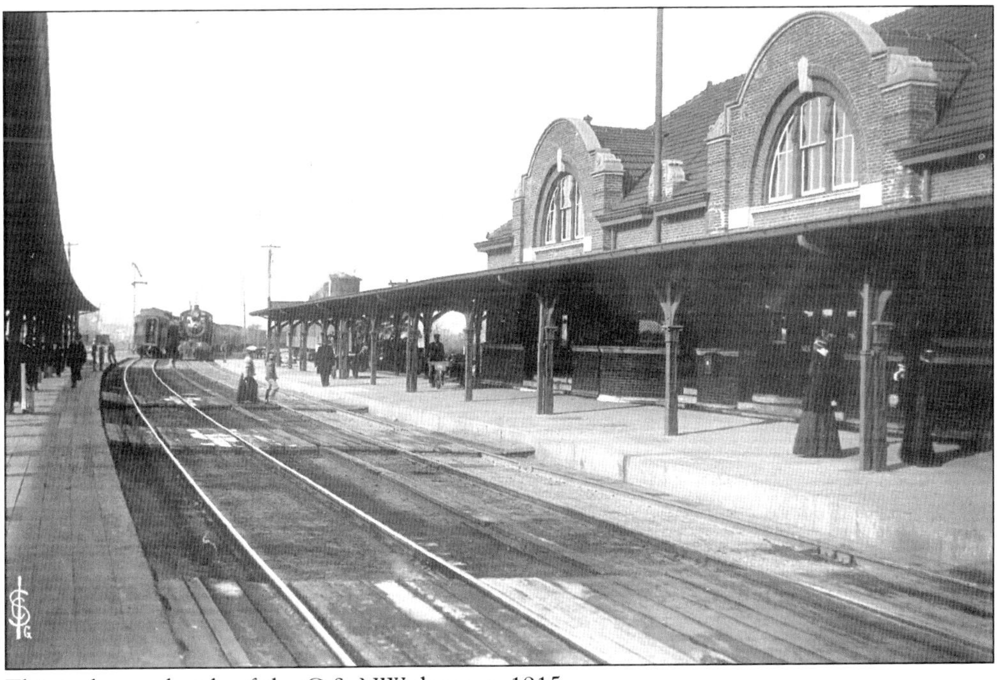

This is the south side of the C & NW depot, c. 1915.

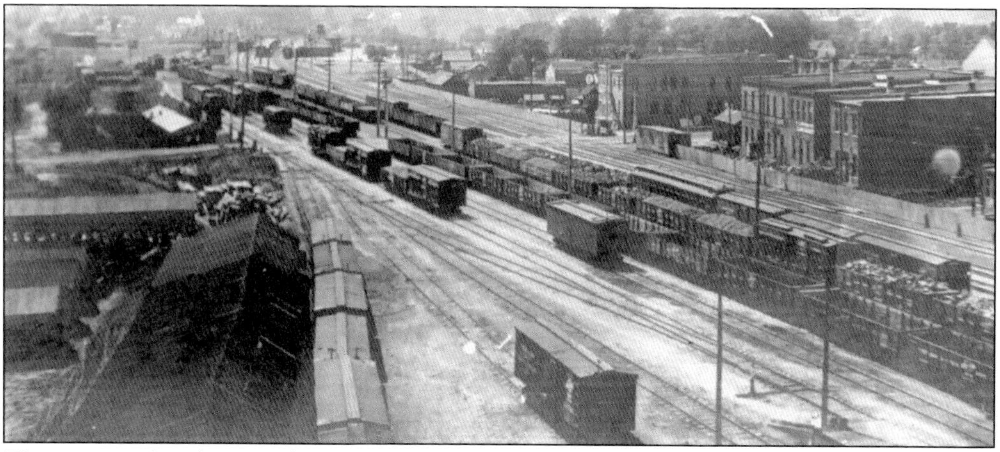

The cars are lined up at the Chicago & North Western Railroad yard, looking west from Duff, around 1915.

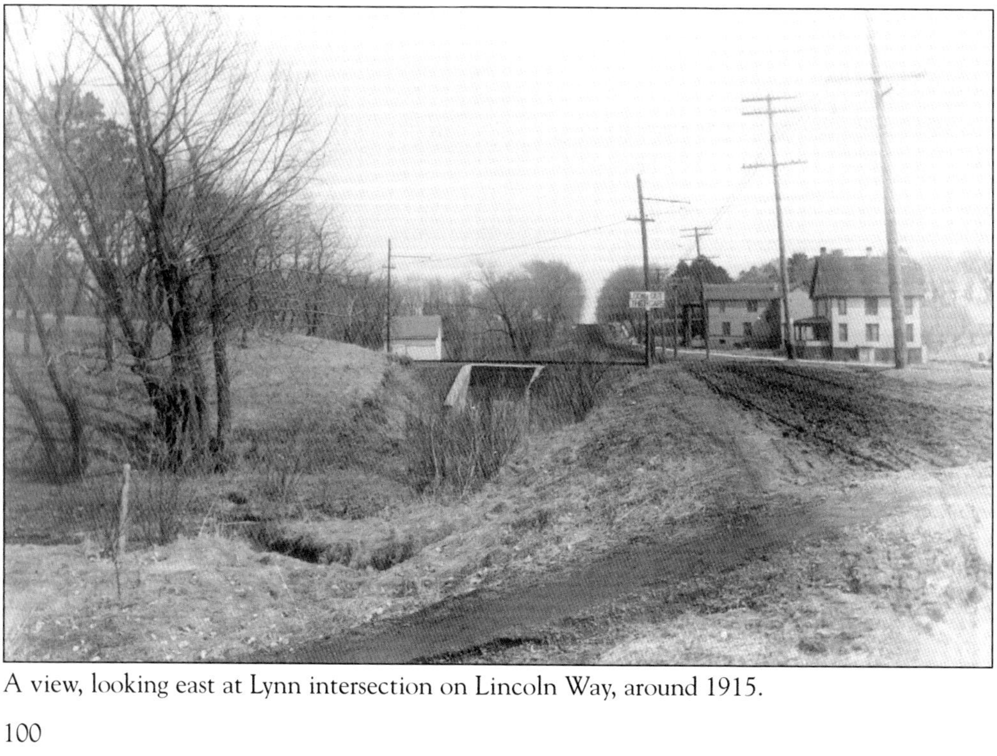

A view, looking east at Lynn intersection on Lincoln Way, around 1915.

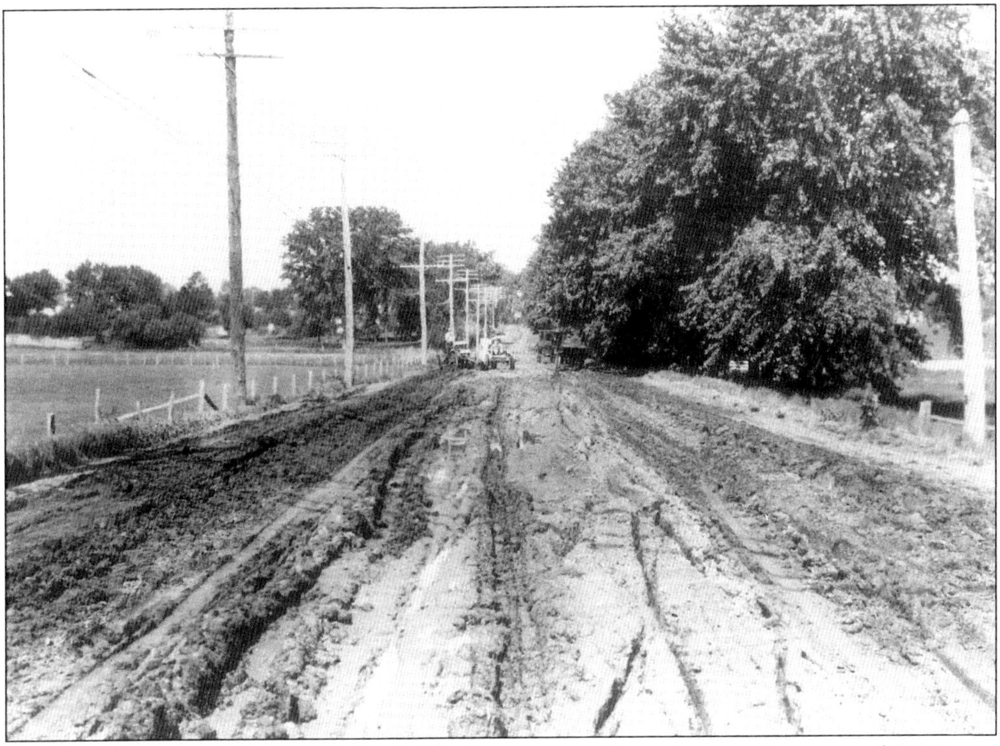

Looking west on Boone Road (Lincoln Way), just east of Lynn intersection, around 1914.

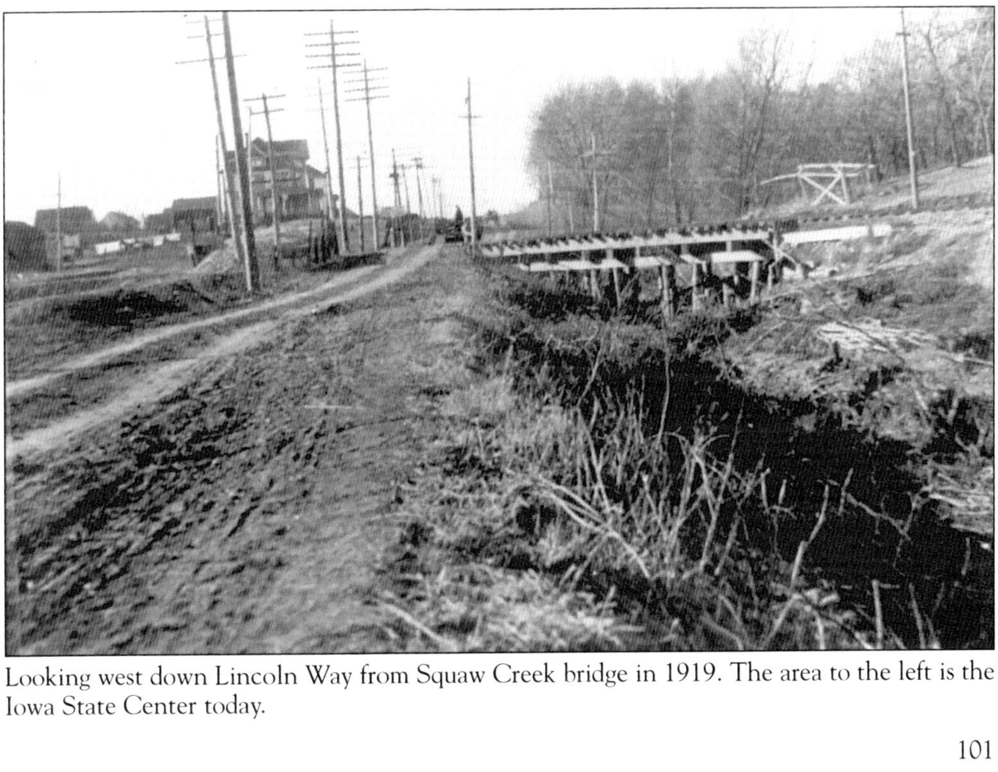

Looking west down Lincoln Way from Squaw Creek bridge in 1919. The area to the left is the Iowa State Center today.

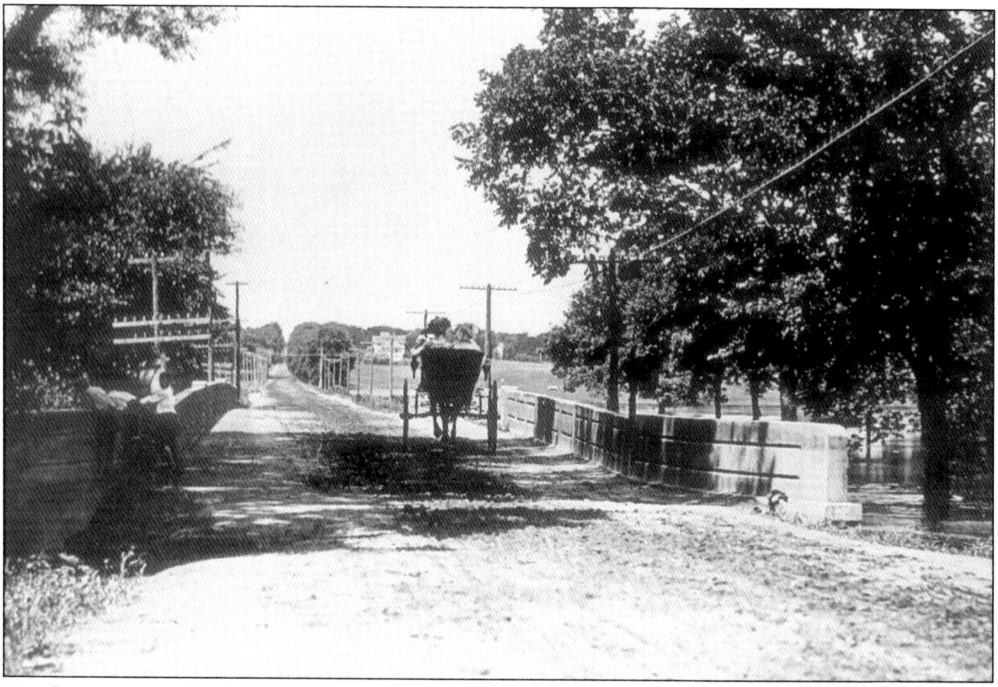

Heading west on Boone Road (Lincoln Way), toward ISC campus, the Herman Knapp family and their horse Milo are seen traveling on an unpaved road, muddy from excess rain. Squaw Creek was nearing flood stage, *c*. 1909.

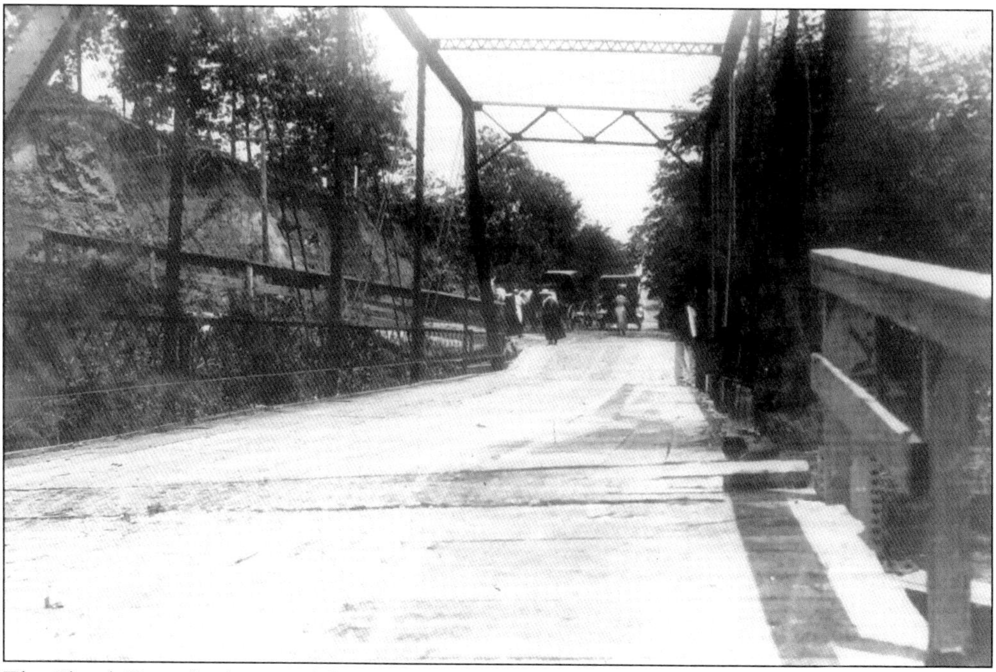

The Skunk River bridge on 13th Street was severely damaged following the flood of 1918.

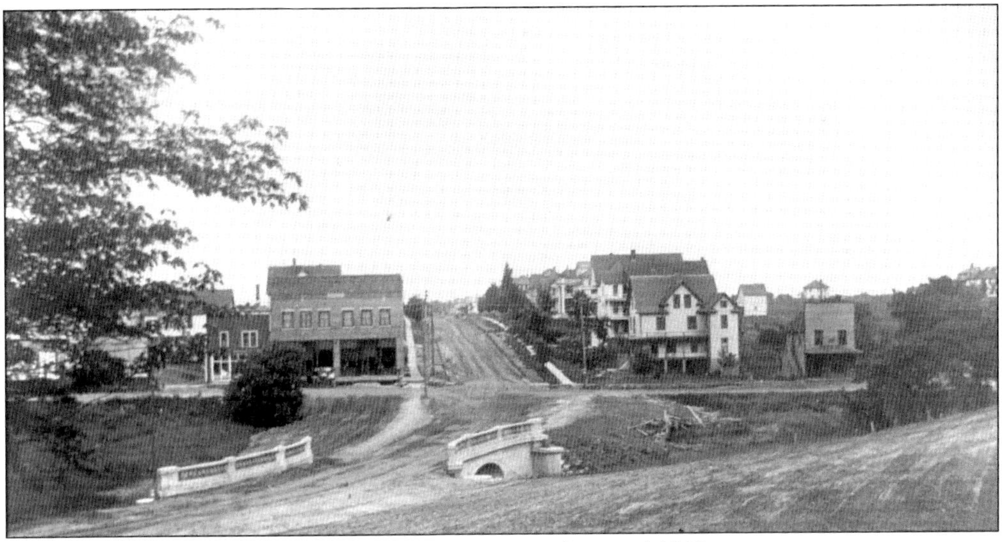

This is how Welch Avenue in Campustown appeared around 1912.

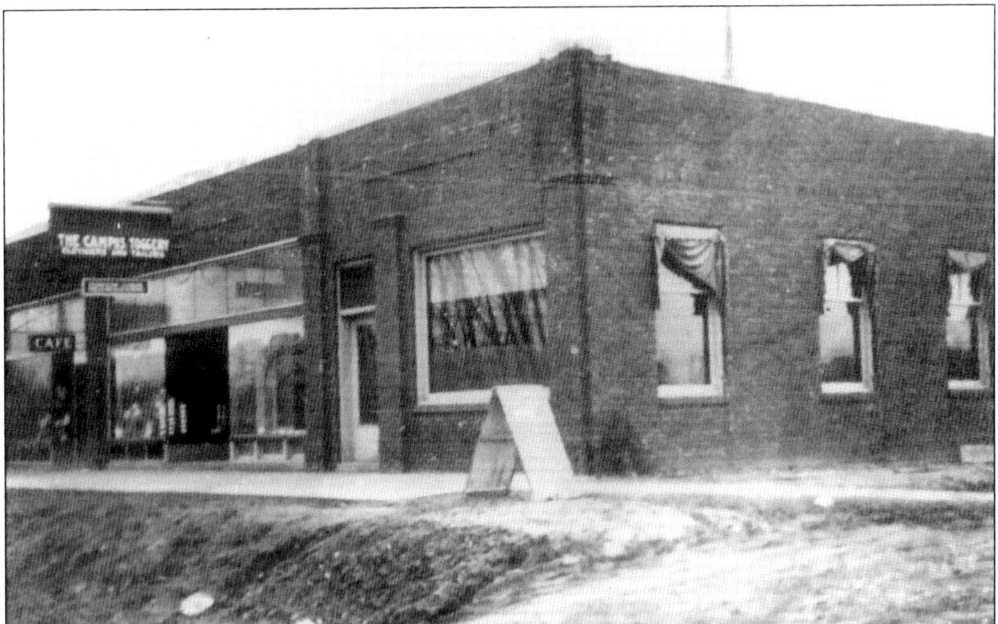

College Savings Bank, organized by C.J. Lynch in 1915, was built on the corner of Lincoln Way and Hayward in 1916. Enlarged in 1962, the building is now part of Firstar Bank in Campustown.

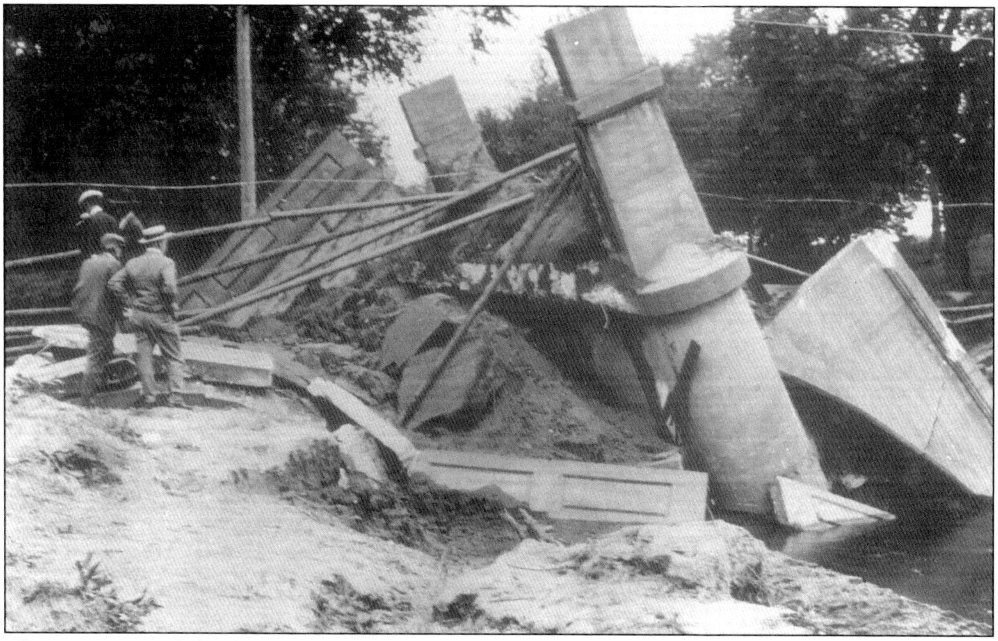

The Squaw Creek bridge on Lincoln Way collapsed shortly after the flood of June 3, 1918. The bridge was only ten years old, and had been flooded at least once before. The Goddard family was on the bridge at the time of collapse, but was rescued with only damage to the car. A new bridge was not built until 1921.

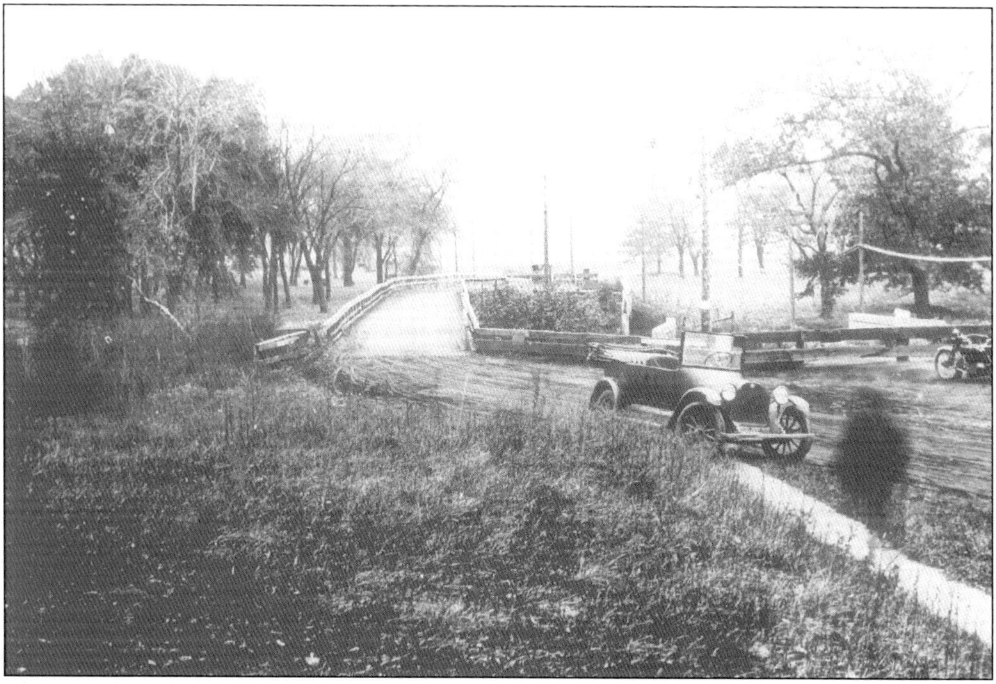

This is what the temporary bridge over Squaw Creek looked like after the collapse of Lincoln Way bridge during the 1918 flood. This bridge was used until 1921, when the new bridge was completed.

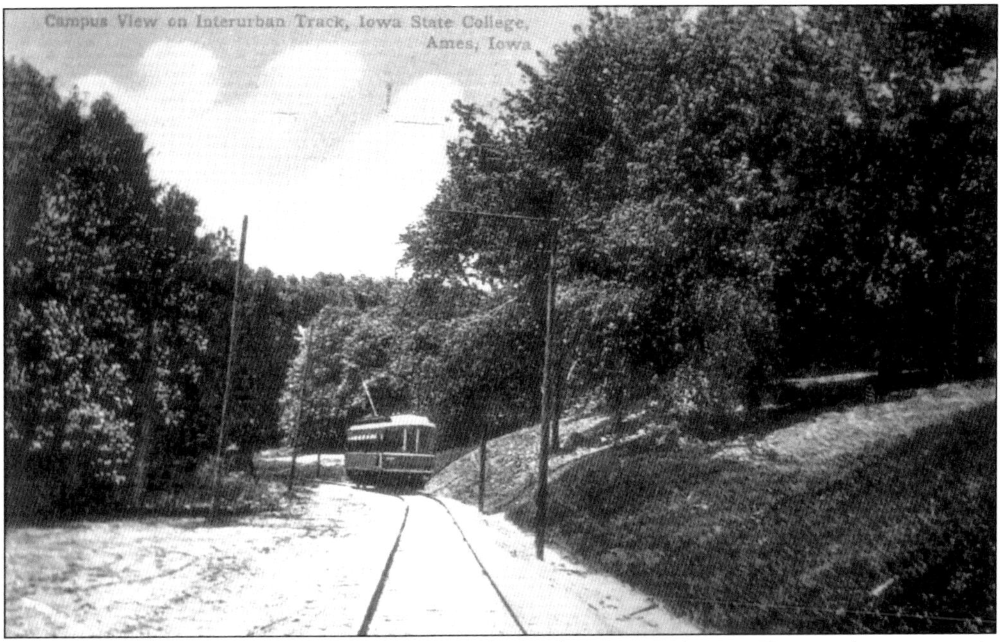

The interurban car crosses campus and heads for downtown Ames. This track was exactly where the exit ramp from the Memorial Union parking ramp now stands.

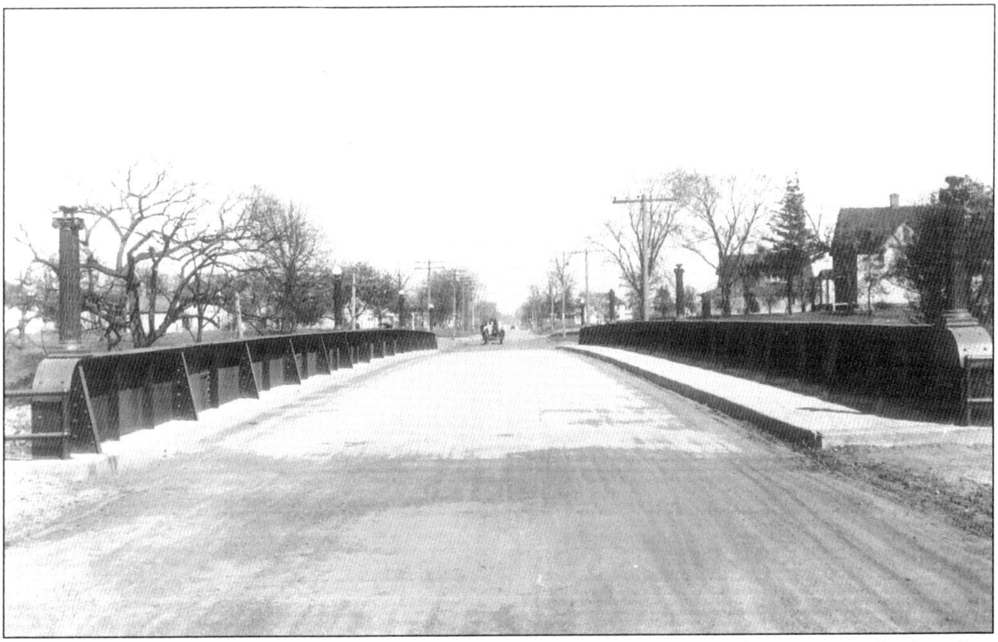

The new Lincoln Way bridge, which opened in May 1921, replaced a concrete bridge that collapsed in the 1918 flood on Squaw Creek. The bridge was a joint project of the city of Ames and Story County.

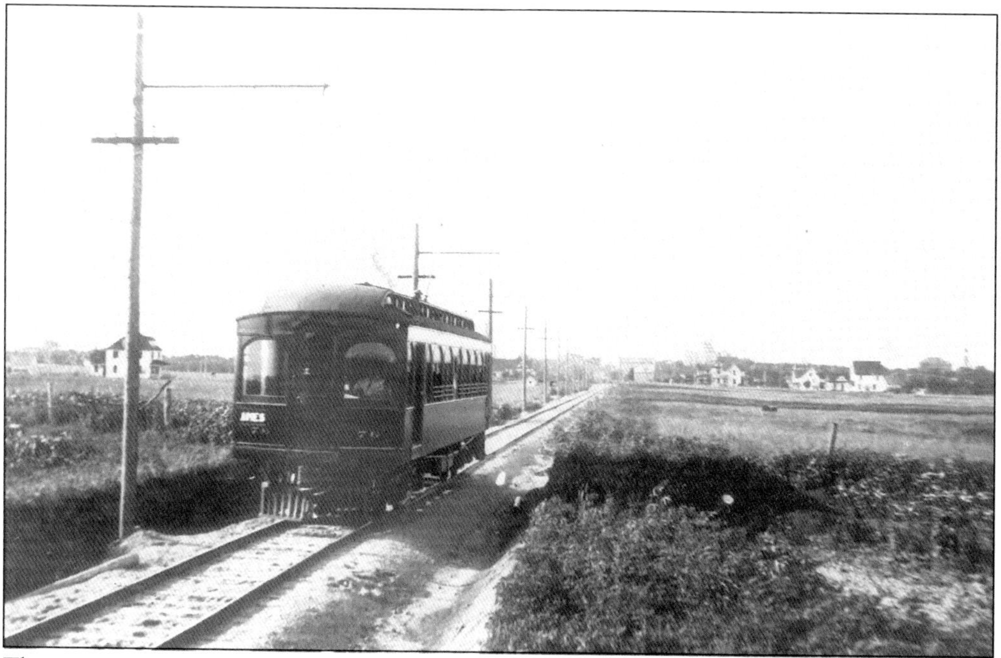

This is an interurban train south of the ISC campus.

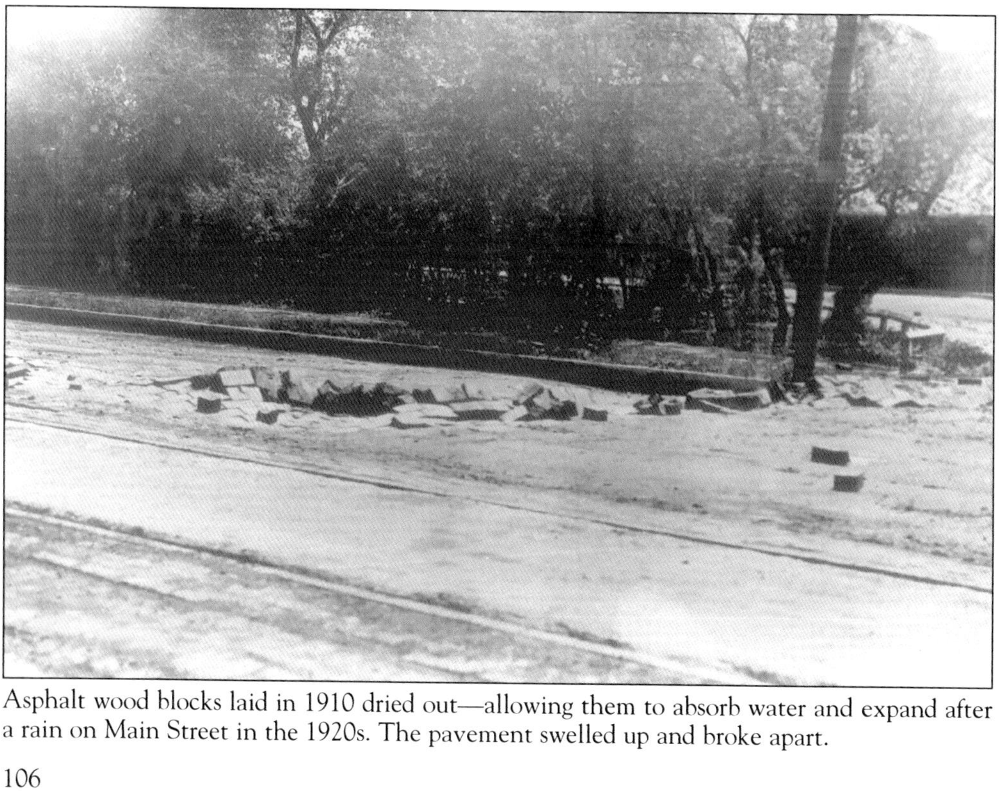

Asphalt wood blocks laid in 1910 dried out—allowing them to absorb water and expand after a rain on Main Street in the 1920s. The pavement swelled up and broke apart.

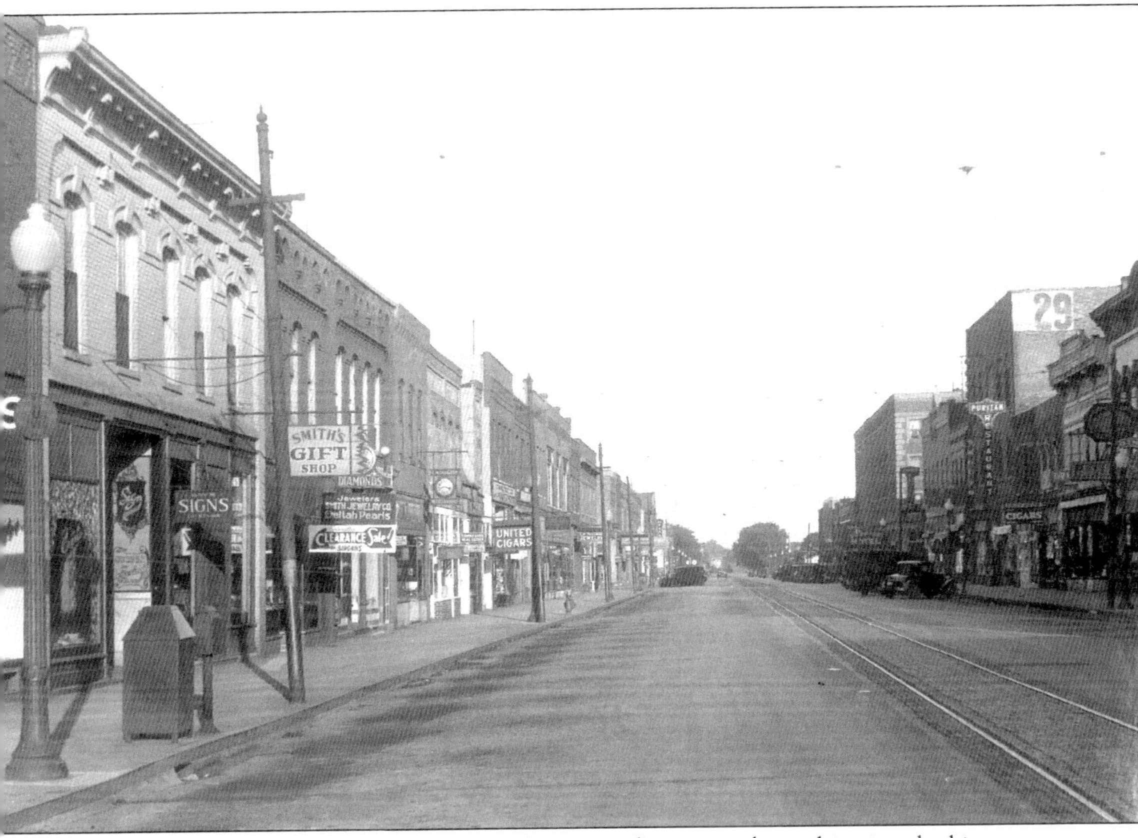

Smith Jewelry Company appears to be conducting a clearance sale in this view, looking west down Main Street, c. 1930.

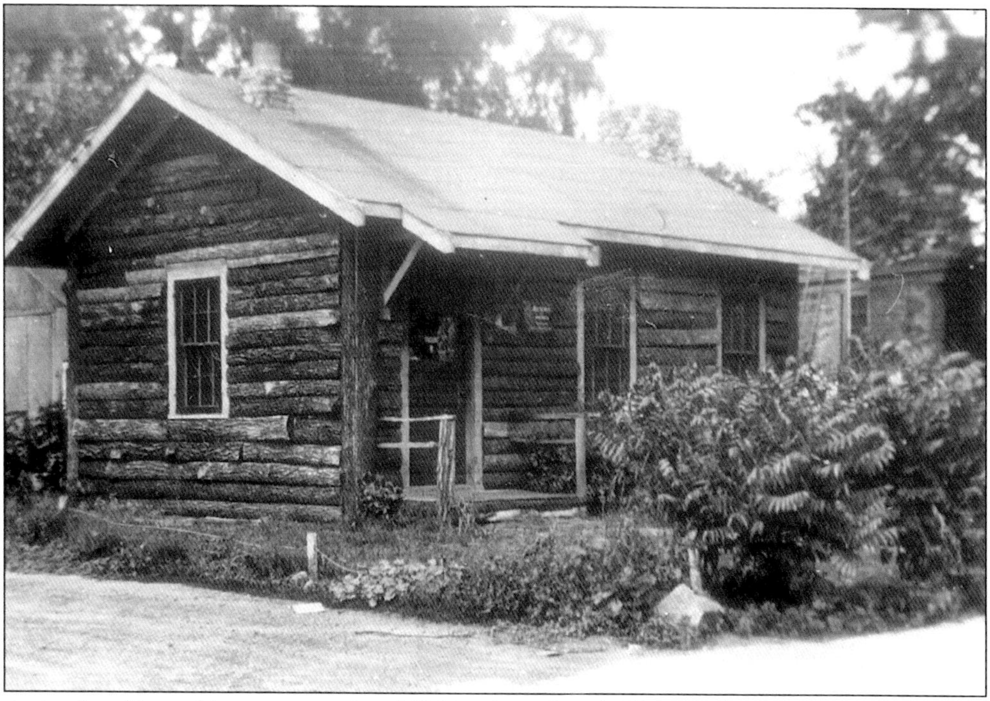

A simulated log cabin constructed in 1926 by Ames Lion's Club was headquarters of the Ames Boy Scouts on Fifth Street (present day backside of the Ames Public Library). The cabin was moved in the late 1930s to South Riverside Drive and converted into a private residence.

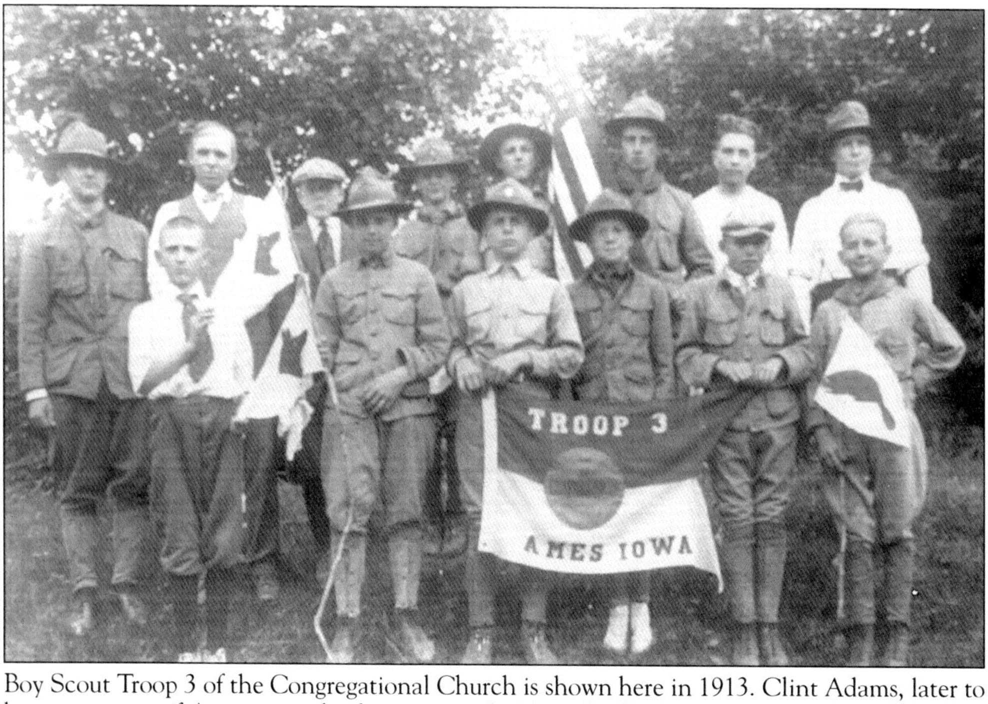

Boy Scout Troop 3 of the Congregational Church is shown here in 1913. Clint Adams, later to become mayor of Ames, is in the front center, holding the flag.

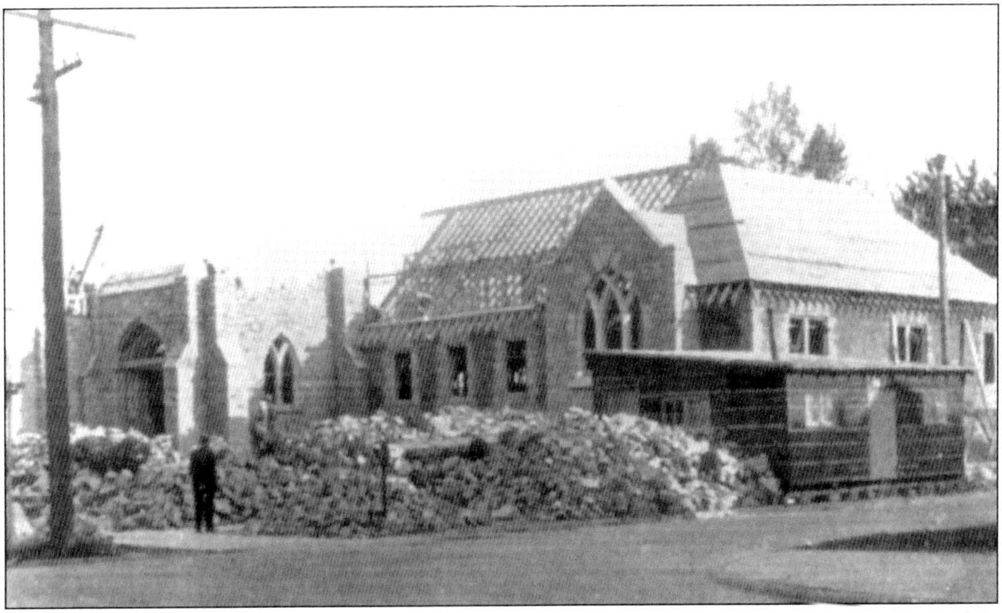

St. John's Episcopal Church on the corner of Lincoln Way and Stanton was completed in 1929.

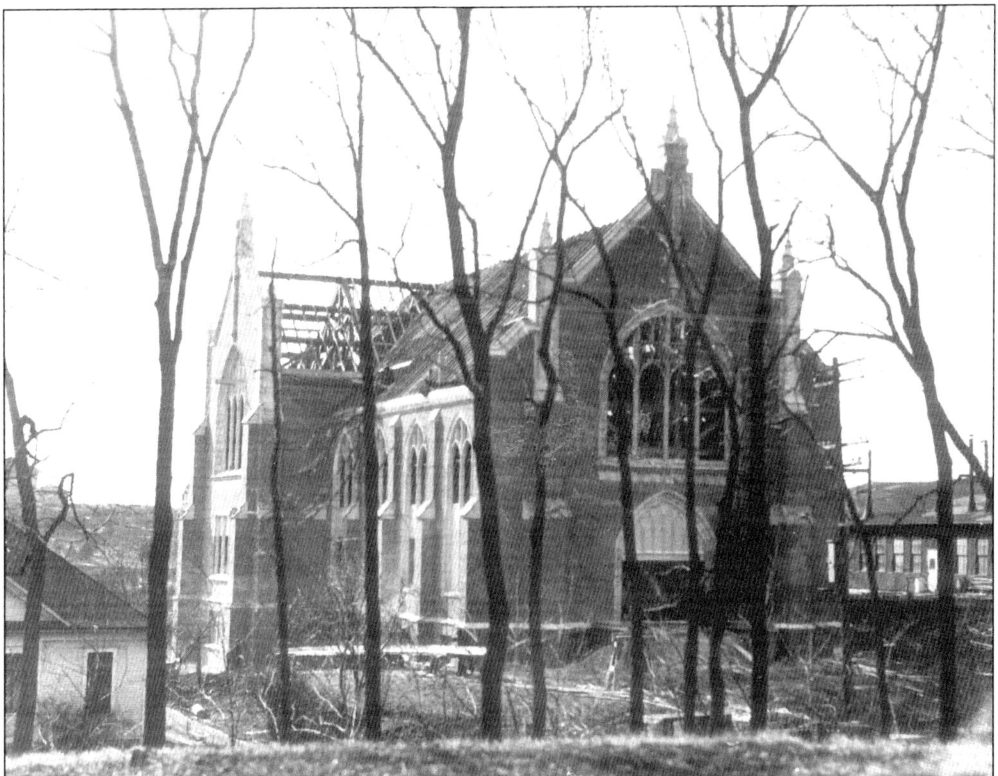

Collegiate Methodist Church, here under construction on Lincoln Way across from the ISU campus, was dedicated on June 6, 1926.

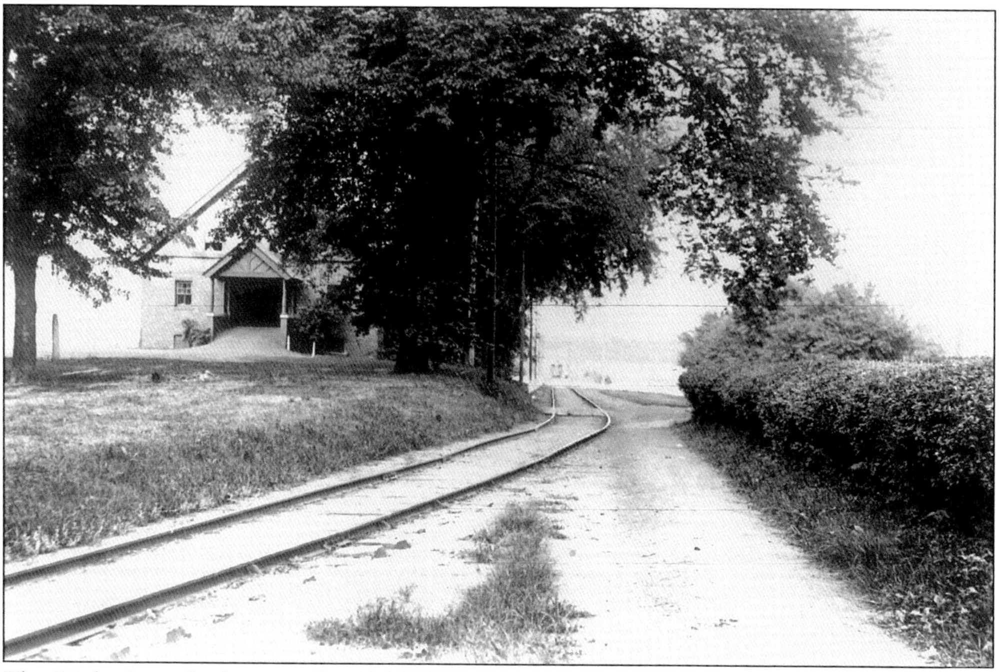

The Dinkey's tracks (seen in this 1907 photo) ran next to the old horse barn, which was later remodeled as the Landscape Architecture Building.

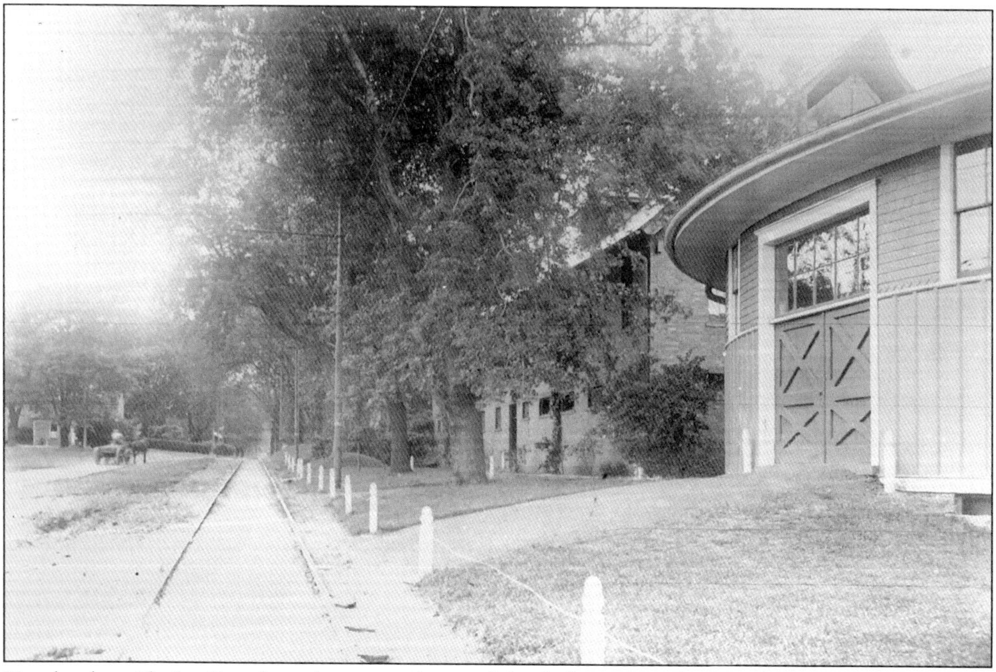

Newly electrified railroad tracks ran in front of the Judging Pavilion in this 1910 image.

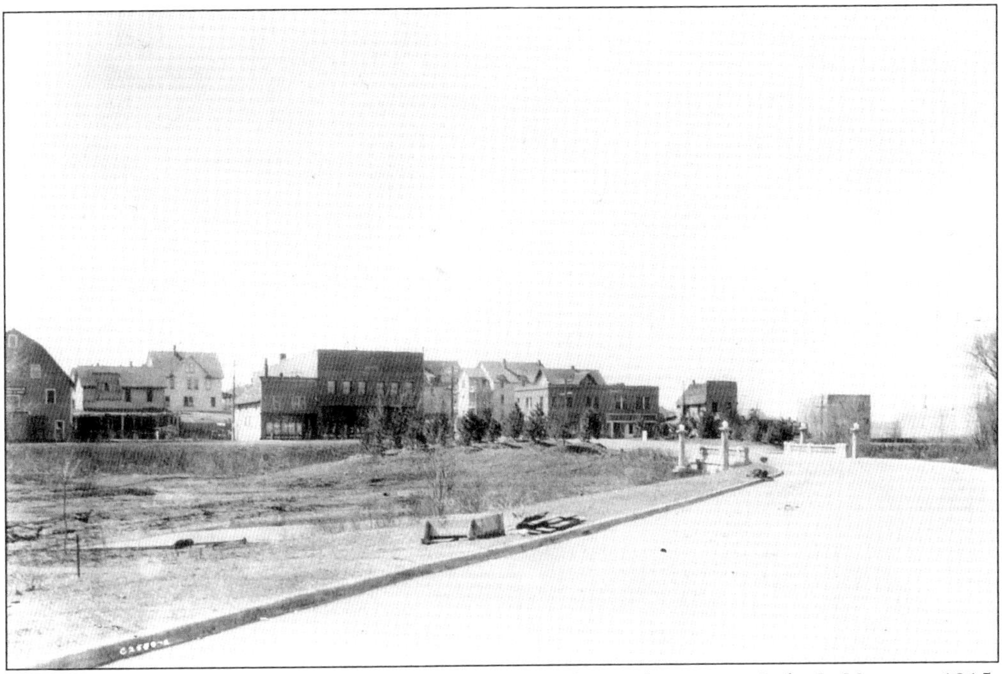

Looking at ISC Campustown on Lincoln Way across from what is now Lake LaVerne in 1915.

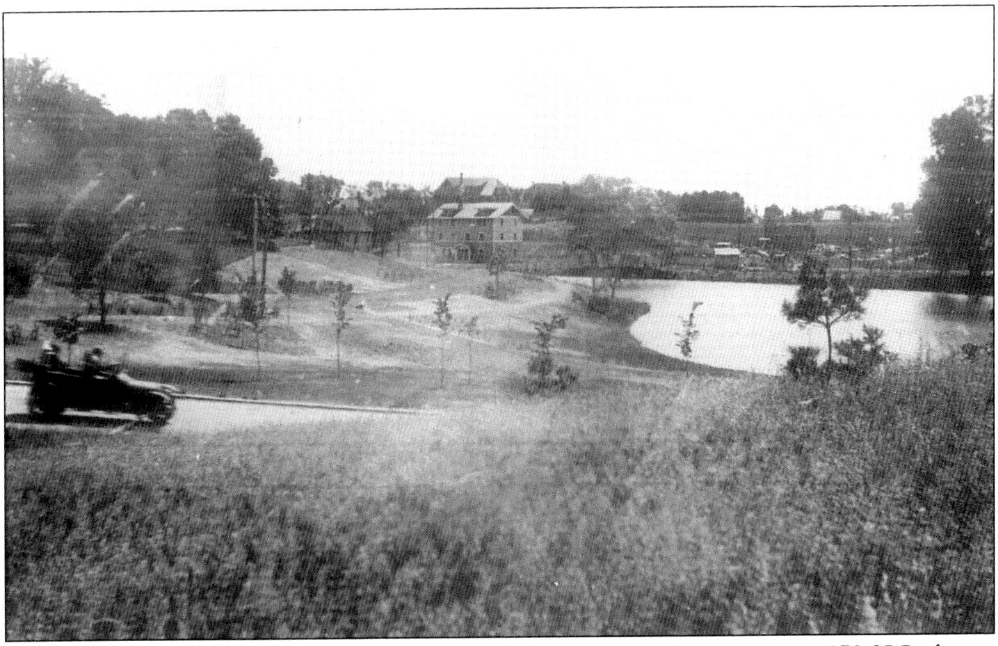

Lake LaVerne, constructed in 1916, was named for LaVerne W. Noyes, an 1872 ISC alumni who paid for its design and construction. This view of the lake was taken c. 1916.

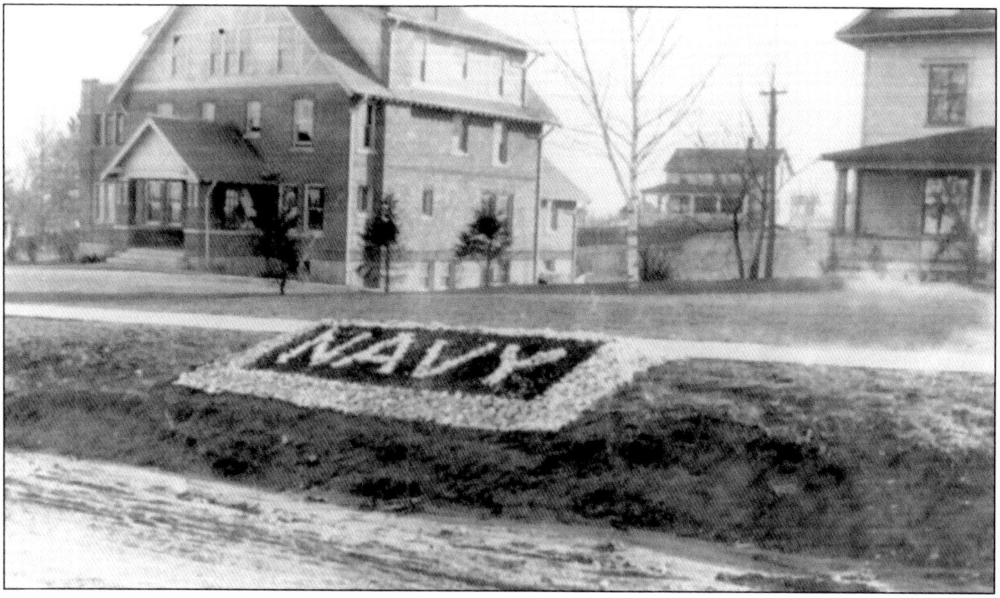

The fraternity houses on Lincoln Way near Beach Avenue served as barracks for a Navy unit brought to the ISC campus during World War I.

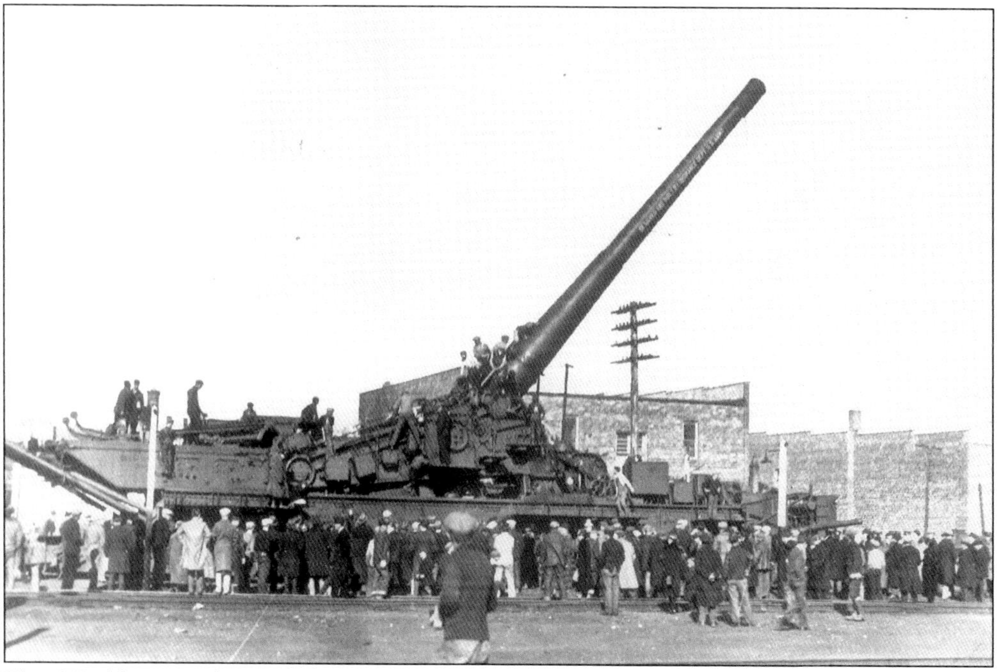

This World War I "big gun," on tour from the U.S. Army, was placed on the siding near the Clark Avenue railroad crossing on July 8, 1929. The weapon was one of the 14-inch guns that were first manufactured in 1908 at the Watervliet Arsenal in Watervliet, New York. Several models were produced, including the M907M1 and the M1908. Production of these guns ended sometime in the early 1920s when most large-weapon manufacture ended prior to World War II production.

Dwight D. Eisenhower first visited Ames in 1919. The occasion was the Army's coast-to-coast motorcade.

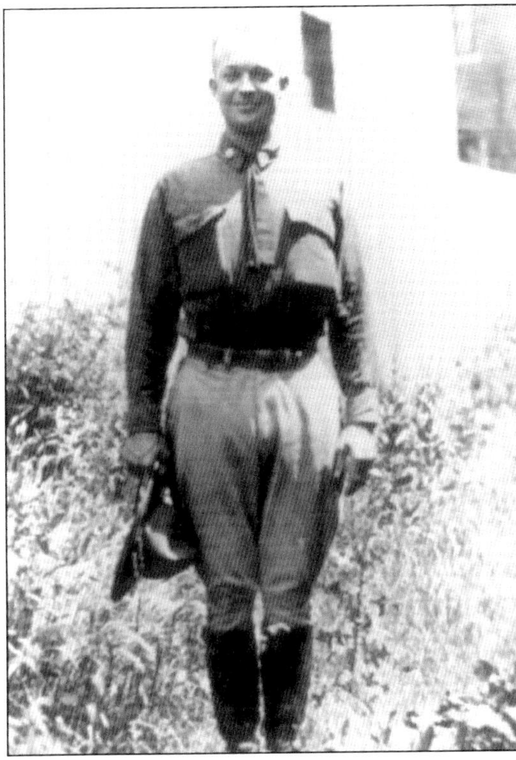

Dwight D. Eisenhower also visited Ames as a presidential candidate in 1952. The wife of Governor Leo Hoegh is at left, and Mamie Eisenhower is at right.

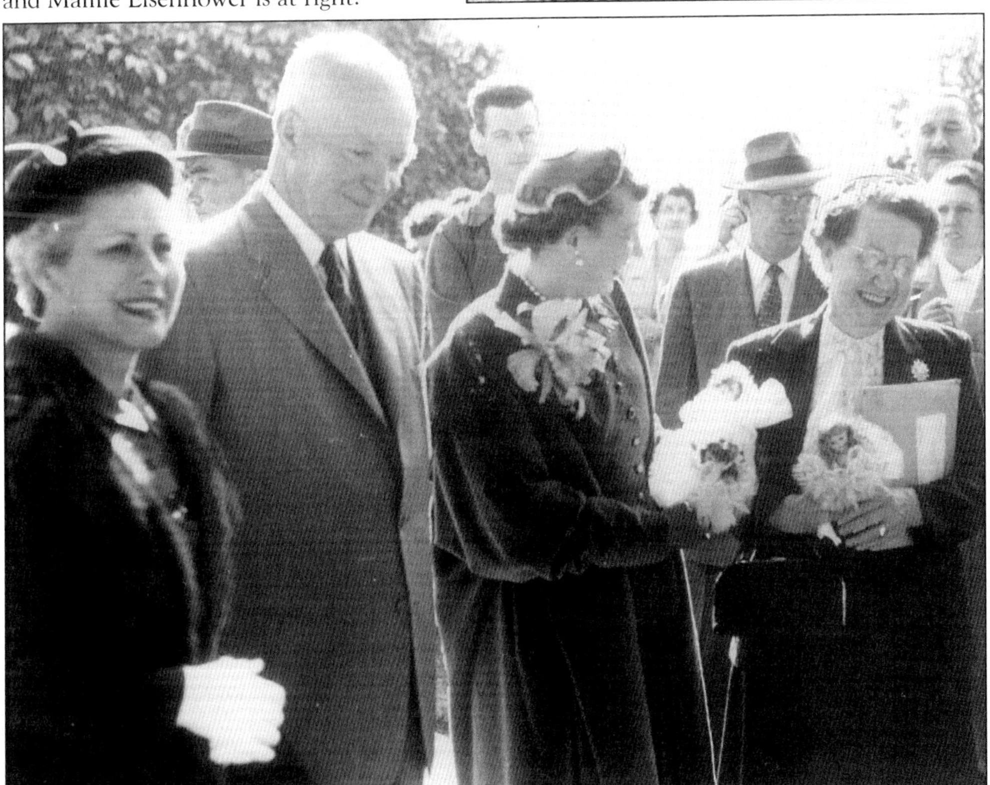

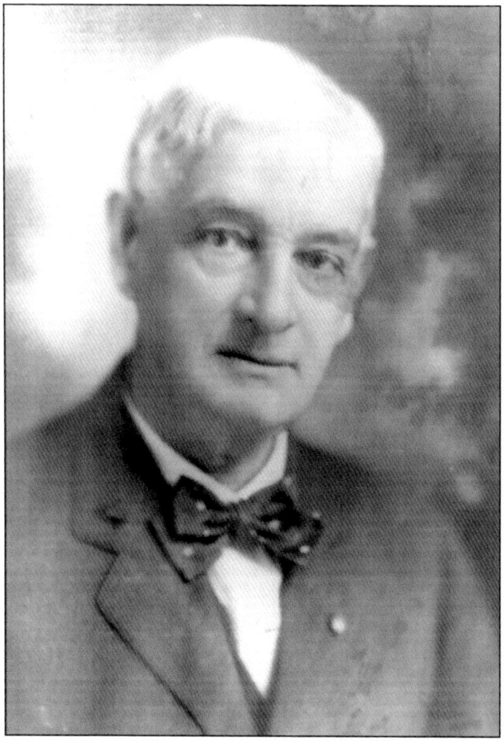

Parley Sheldon was mayor of Ames for 18 years in non-concurrent terms over a 32-year period—from 1884 to 1916.

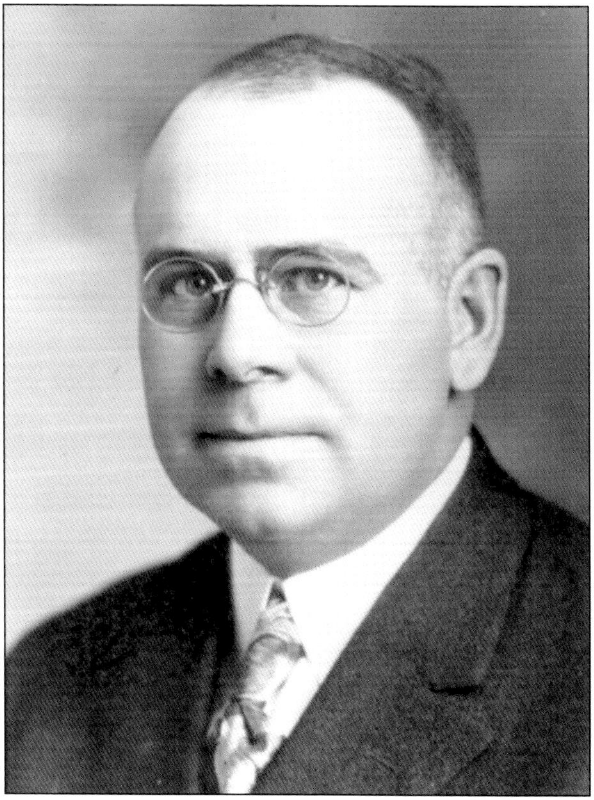

Thomas H. MacDonald, ISC class of 1904, was appointed that same year as the first chief engineer of the Iowa Highway Commission. He left Ames in 1919 to become the first Chief of the U.S. Bureau of Roads in Washington D.C.

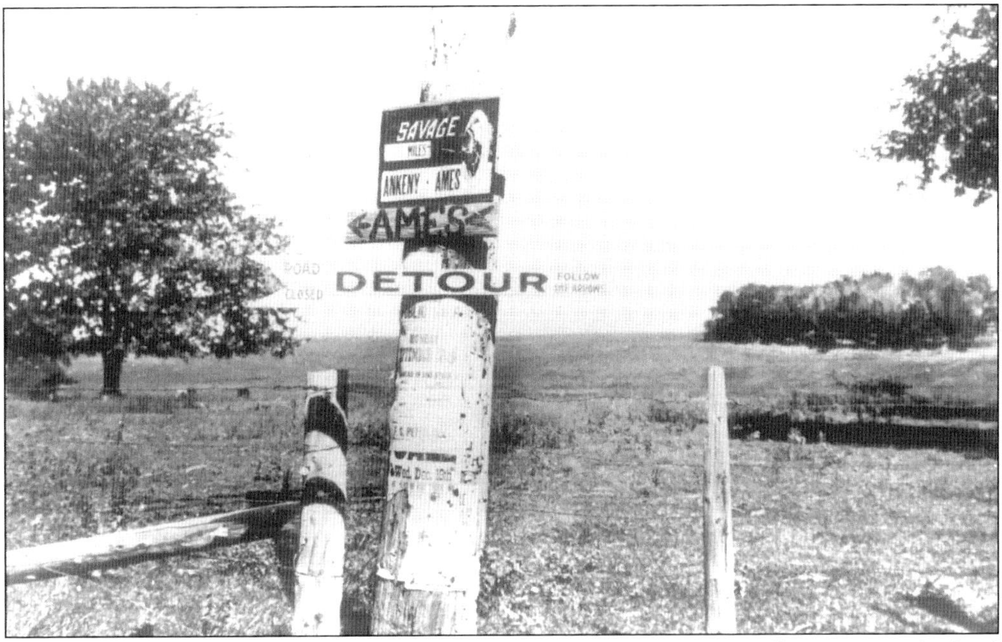

This Ames "road sign" appears to be clear enough, but such signs were still not yet standardized by the 1920s.

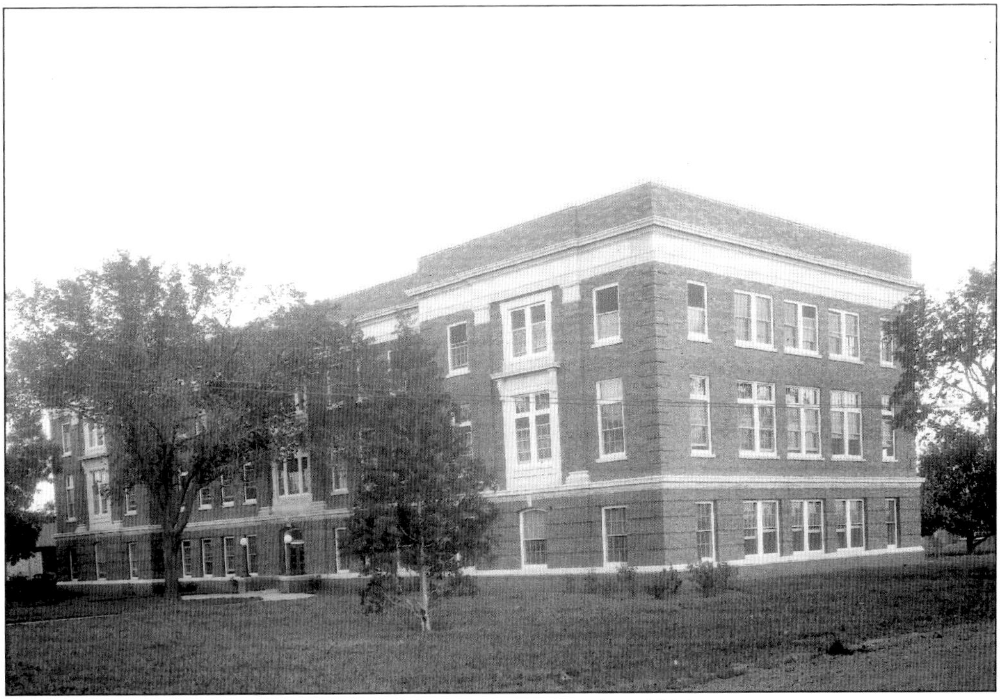

This is the Highway Commission Building as it appeared in 1924.

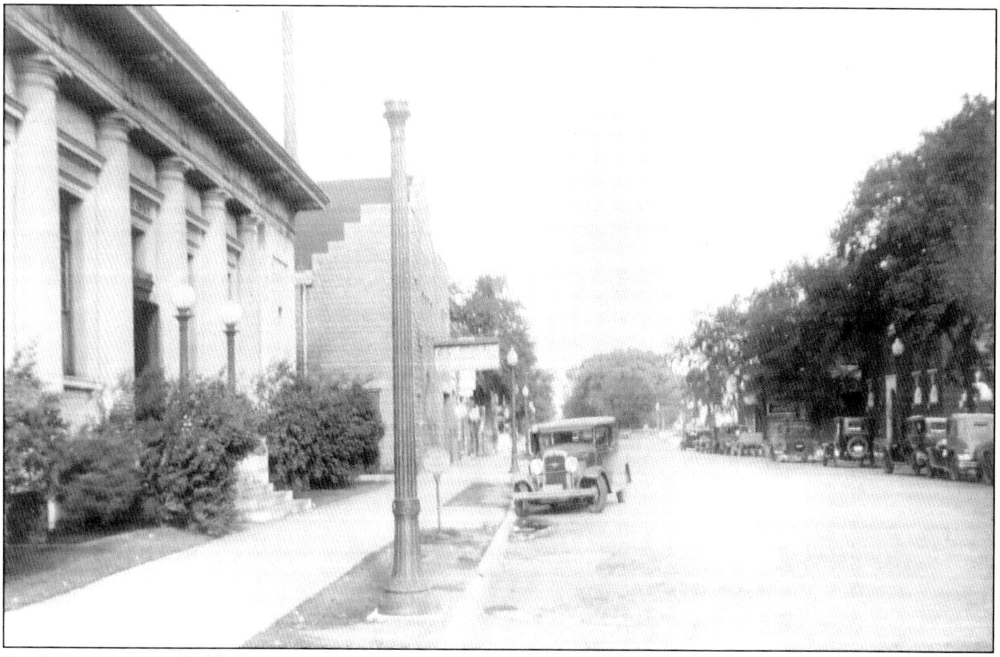

Looking west on Fifth Street around 1927, the post office and O'Neil Dairy are on the left and the Tribune Building (built around 1926) is on the right.

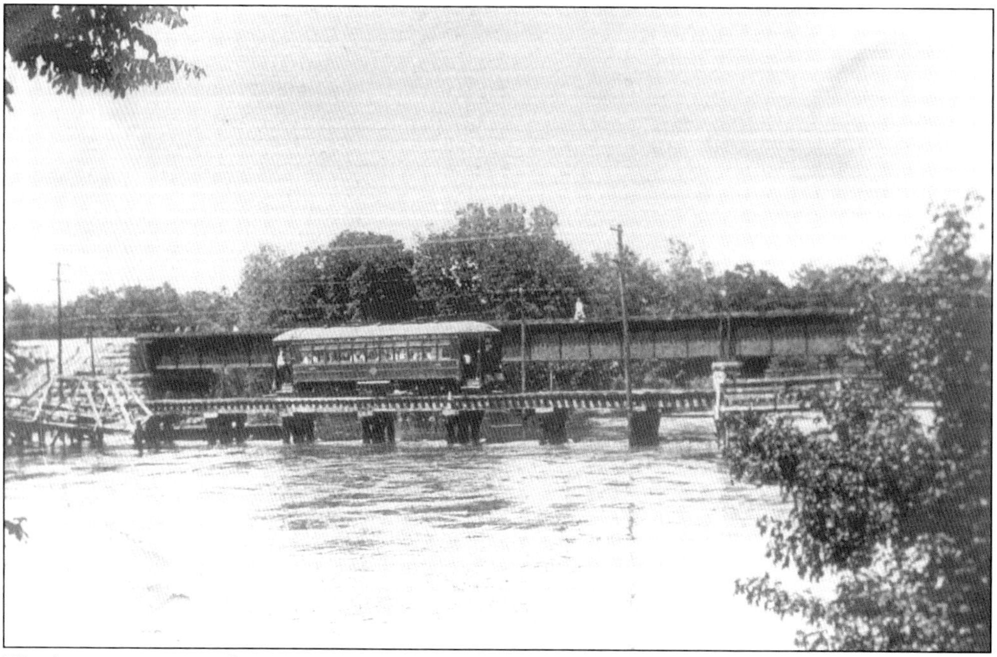

The best way to see the Squaw Creek flood of 1918 was to take the streetcar to the campus. Here, the high water has taken out the footbridge located on this side of the streetcar bridge.

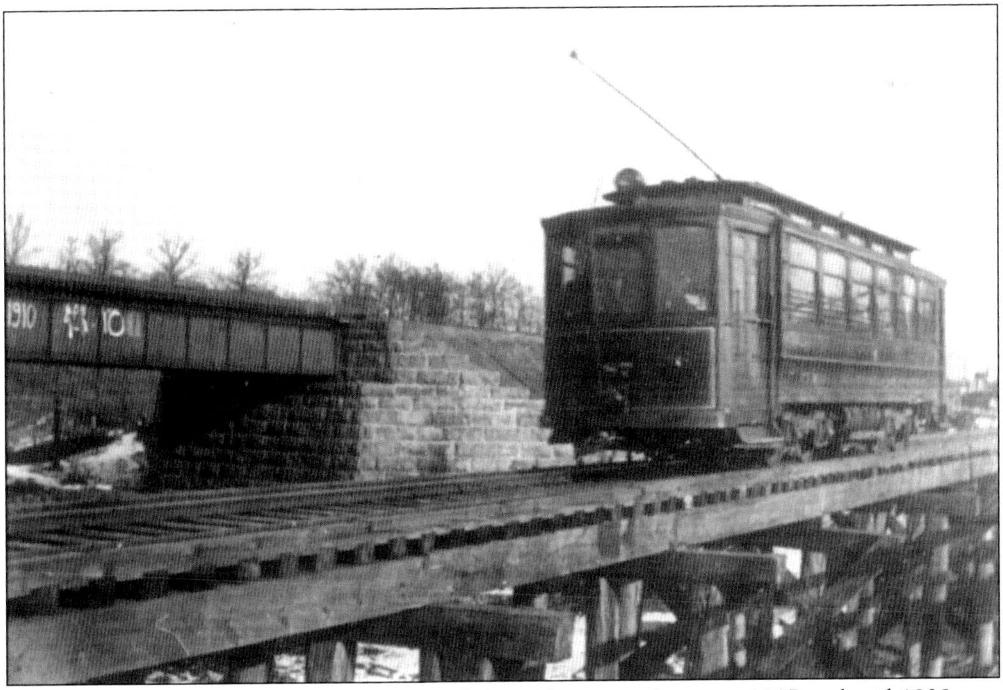

Streetcars operated between downtown and the ISC campus between 1907 and mid-1929.

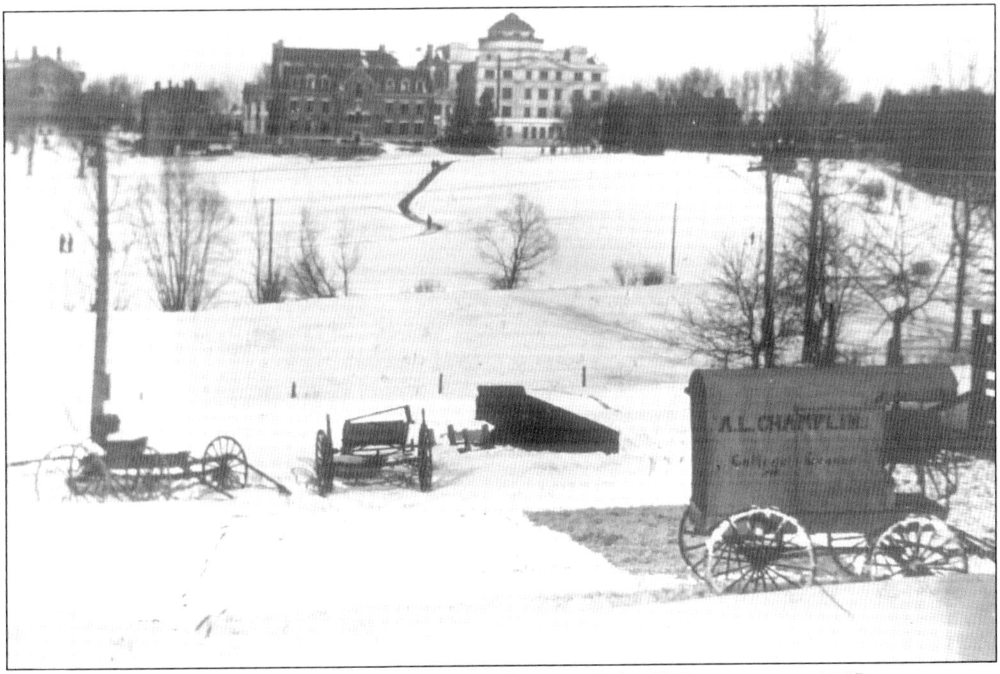

This is the farm of A.L. Champlin looking north toward the ISC campus, c. 1907.

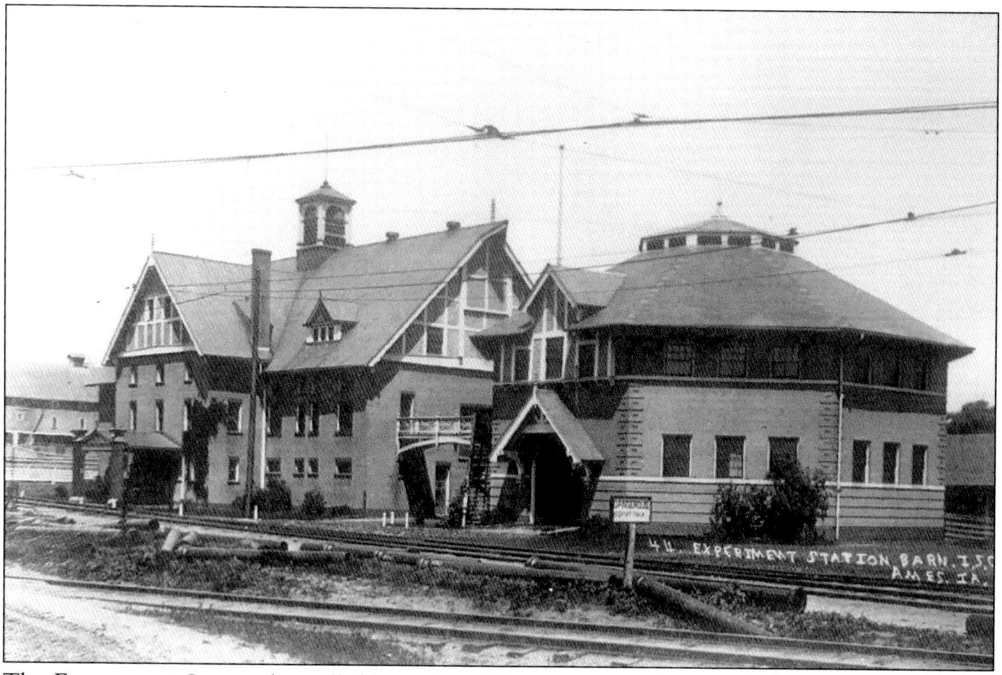

The Experiment Station barn (left) on the ISC campus was built in 1902 to replace a barn, which had burned in 1901. This barn was struck by lightning in 1922 and also burned.

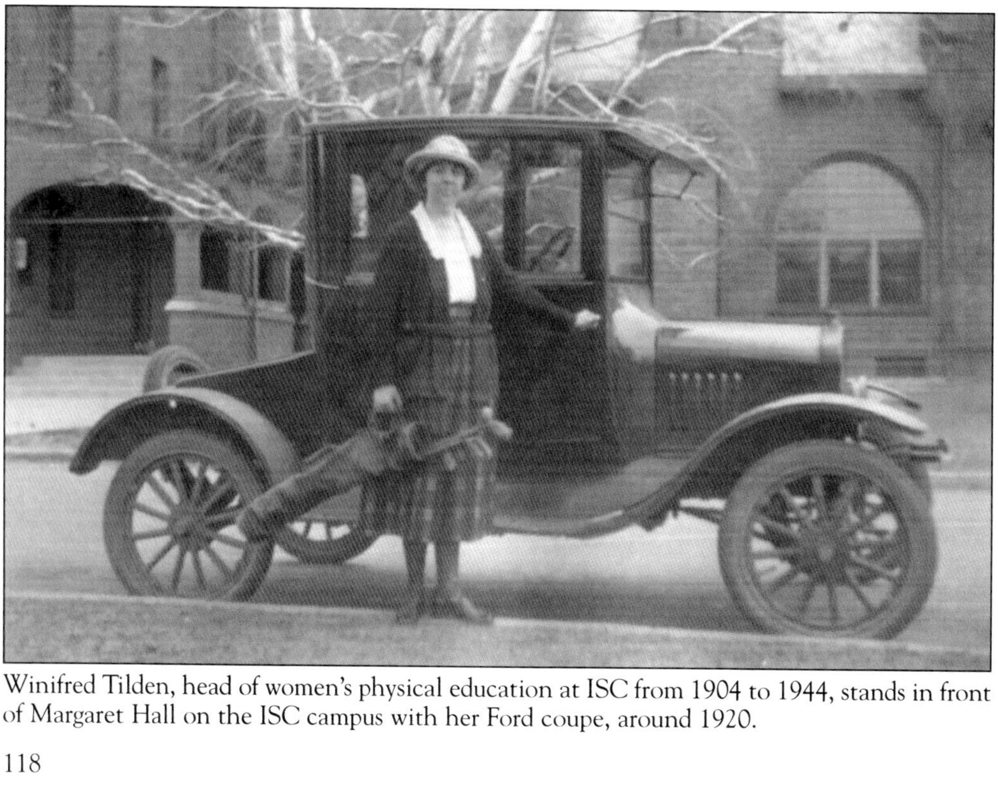

Winifred Tilden, head of women's physical education at ISC from 1904 to 1944, stands in front of Margaret Hall on the ISC campus with her Ford coupe, around 1920.

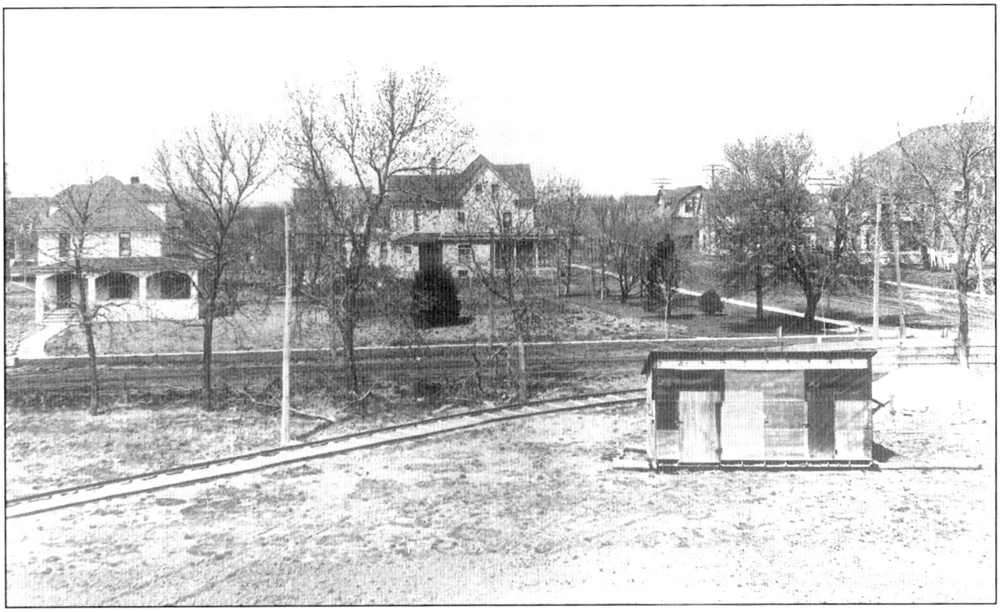

This is a view looking west toward the corner of West Street and Sheldon in 1913, with the rail tracks having been extended to the State Gym construction site.

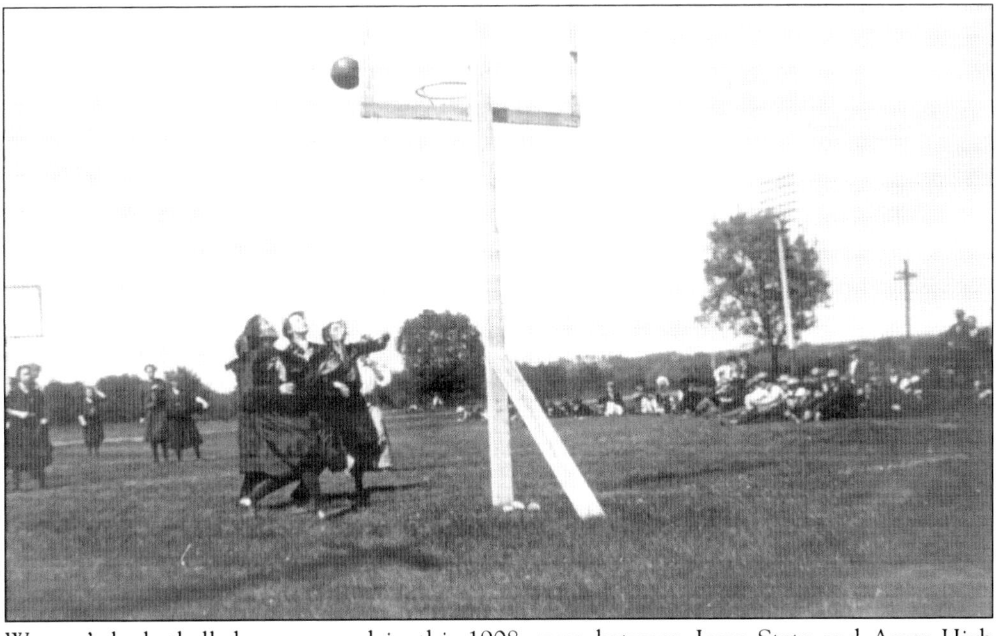

Women's basketball drew a crowd in this 1908 game between Iowa State and Ames High School. Women also played basketball on the Margaret Hall dining-room floor after the tables were removed.

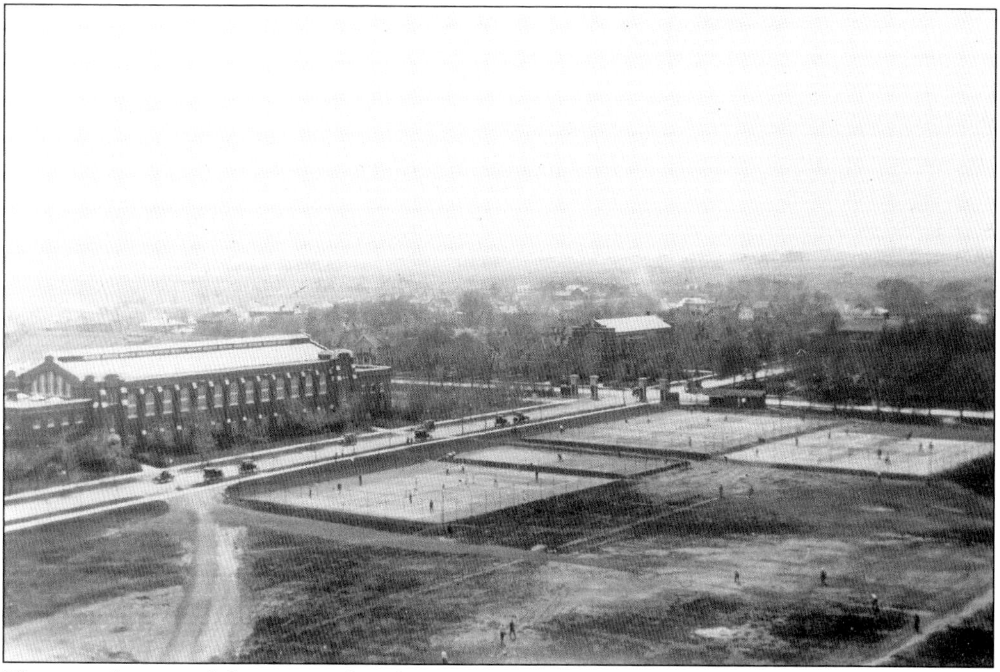

This aerial view of the west side of campus was taken in the mid-1920s. The Collegiate Presbyterian Church, dedicated in 1917, can be seen at the West Gate.

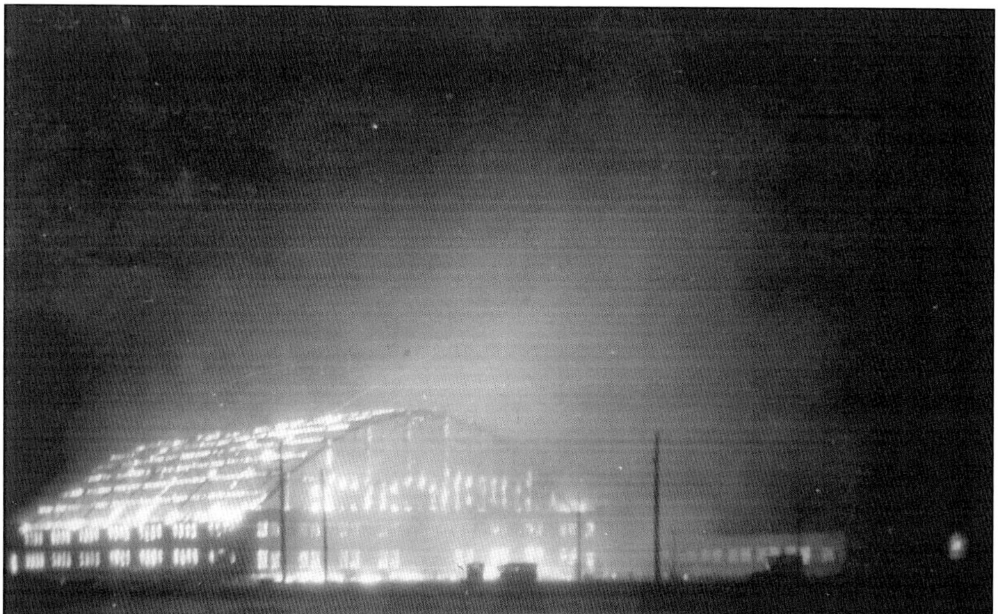

The Iowa State College armory fire occurred on December 16, 1922. The armory was rebuilt in 1923.

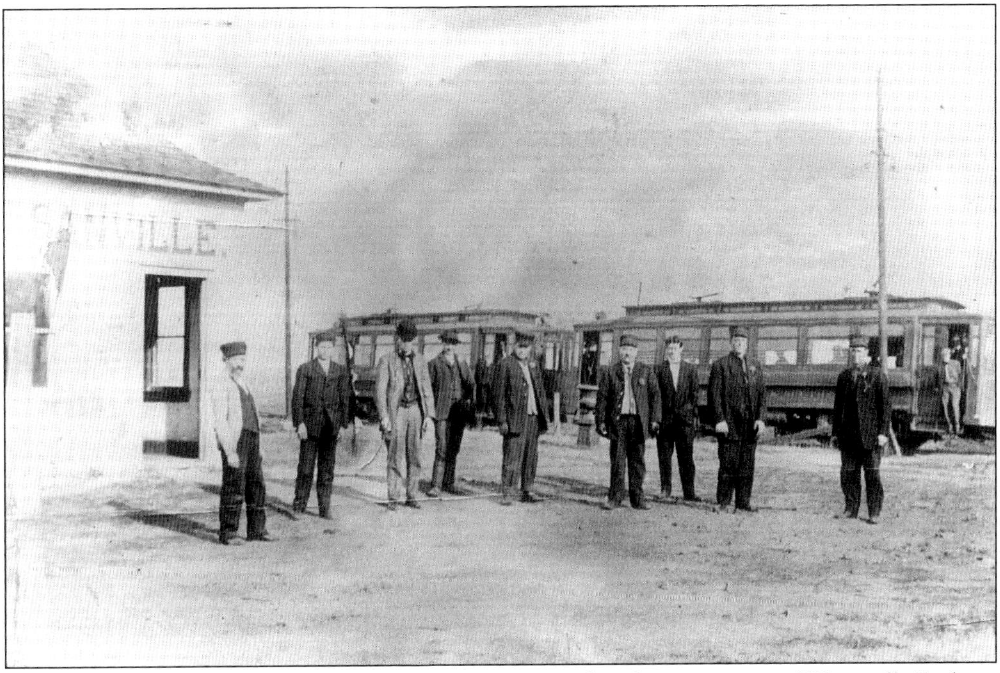

The conductors operating the electric line gather together for a picture at "Olsanville," where the loop line passed near Olsan's Greenhouses, *c.* 1916. Today, this is a parking lot west of the College of Design.

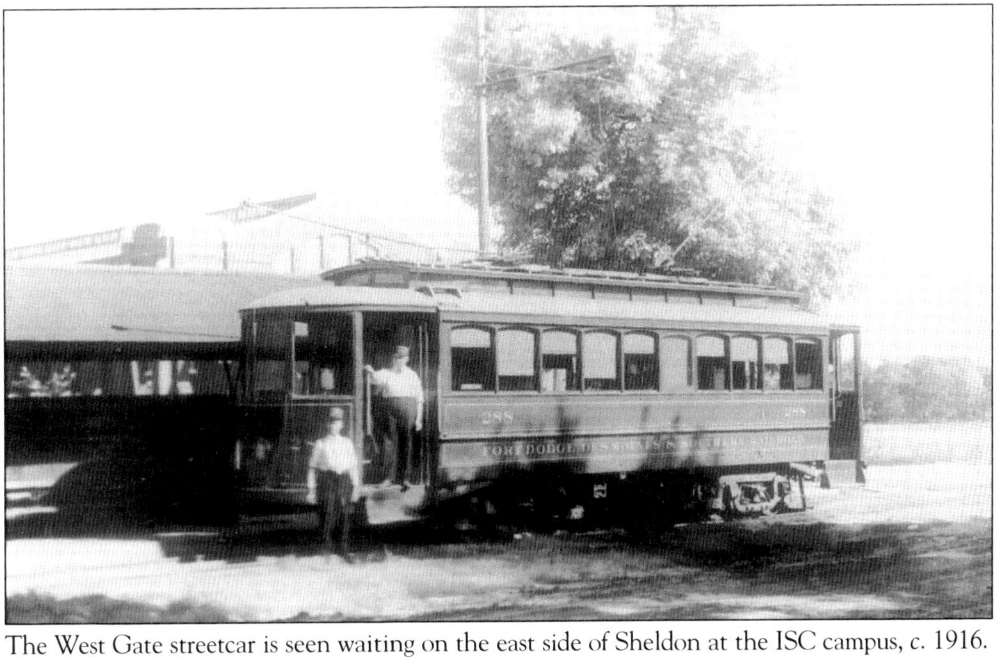

The West Gate streetcar is seen waiting on the east side of Sheldon at the ISC campus, *c.* 1916.

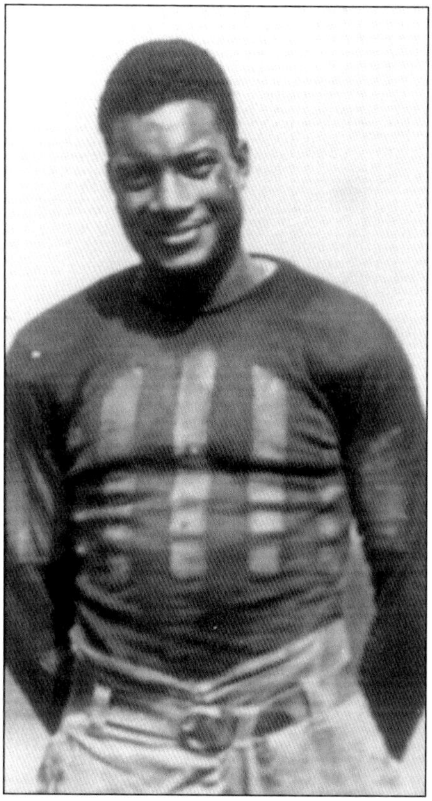

Jack Trice, a member of the Iowa State football team, suffered a fatal injury during a game with Minnesota in 1923. The ISU football stadium is today known as Jack Trice Stadium.

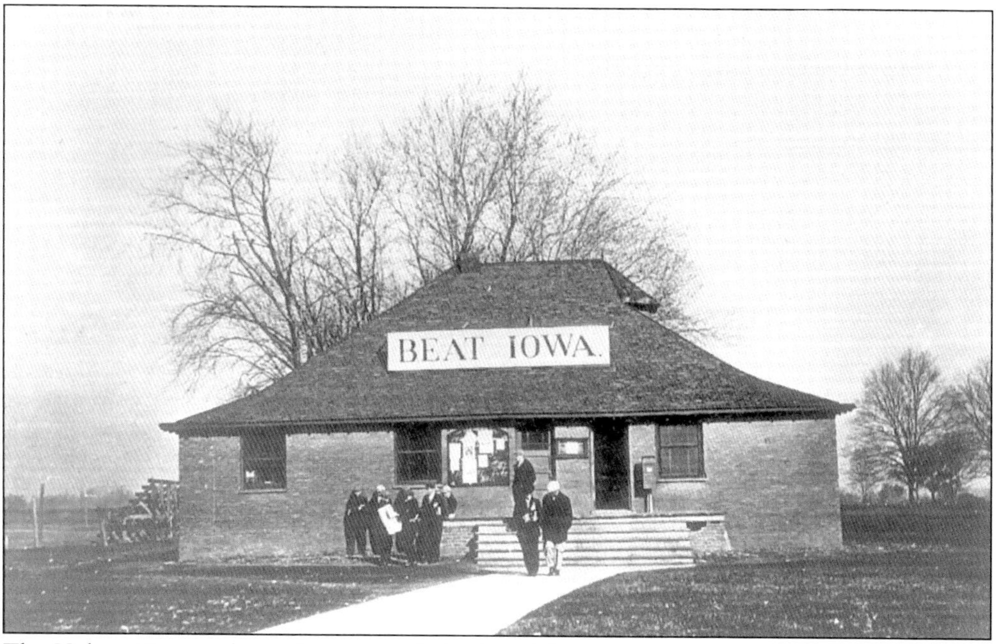

The Hub at ISC, in about 1916, was a U.S. Post Office and a bookstore. It was originally the Dinkey's campus depot, dating from 1892. In 1983, the Hub was torn down and reconstructed according to the original depot structure plans.

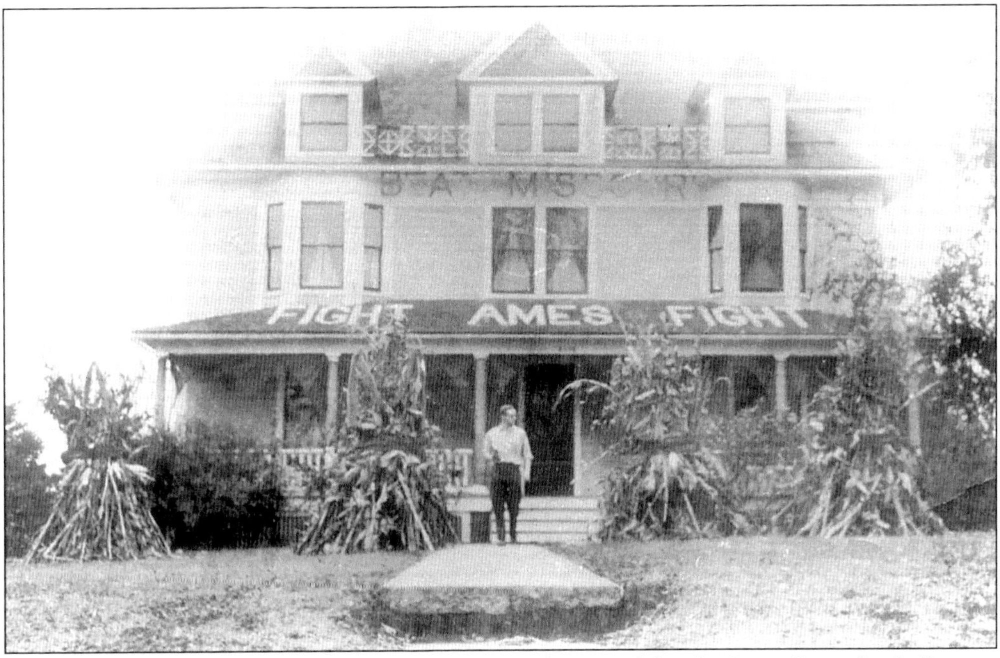

The Chi Phi fraternity house on Lincoln Way is decorated for the Iowa State football game with the University of Minnesota in 1926.

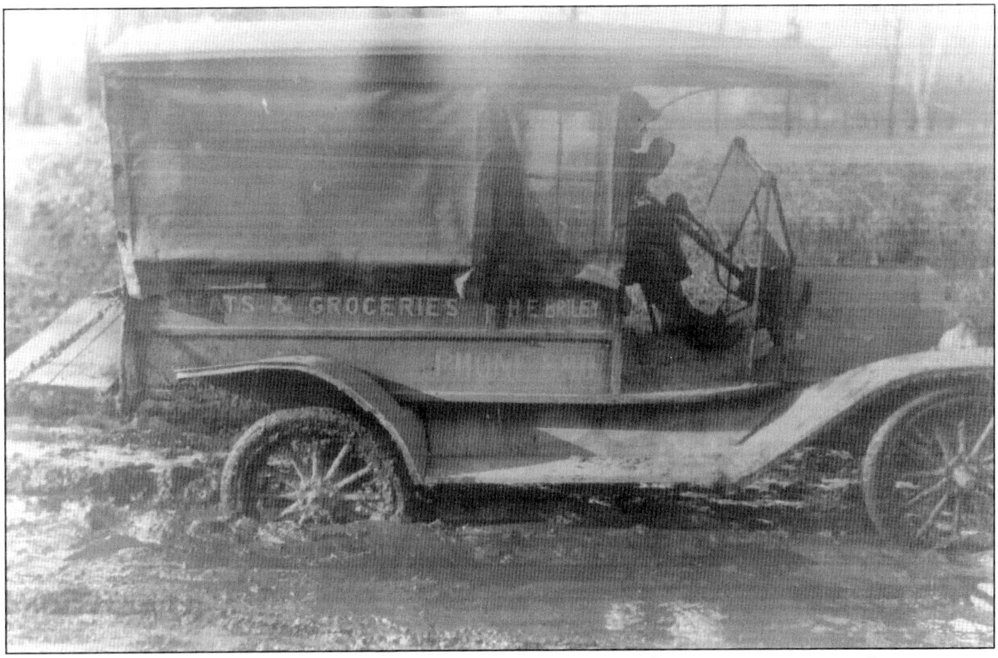

This is the very muddy H.E. Briley Groceries delivery truck in Campustown after a spring rain, c. 1916.

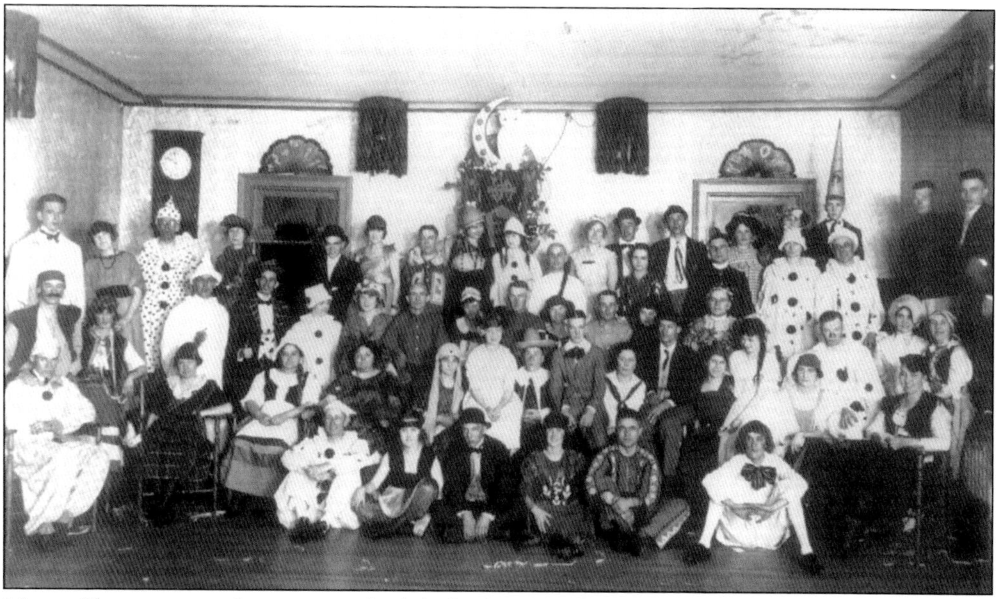

Mono Clan, a young businessmen's club, had a "Hard Time" party in Smiths Hall in 1920. After 1920, the Mono Clan's room was on the second floor of the new Tribune Building on Fifth Street.

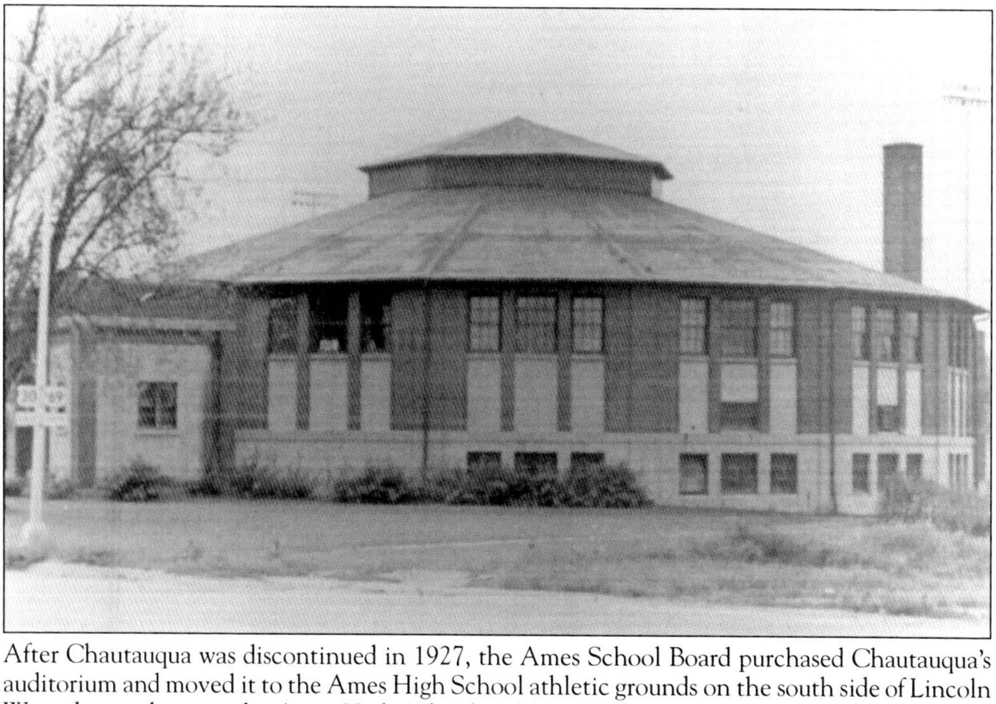

After Chautauqua was discontinued in 1927, the Ames School Board purchased Chautauqua's auditorium and moved it to the Ames High School athletic grounds on the south side of Lincoln Way where it became the Ames High School Field House, until it was removed in 1965.

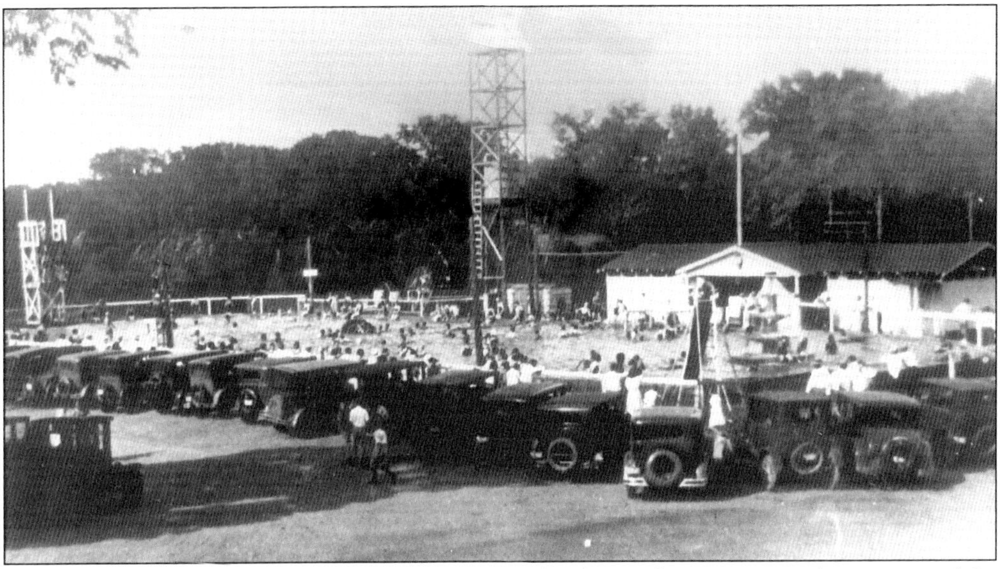

R.E. Carr built Carr's Pool in 1926. For a short while, the 50-foot tower seen here was used for exhibitions, until "Dad" Carr decided that it was too dangerous. This image is from c. 1930.

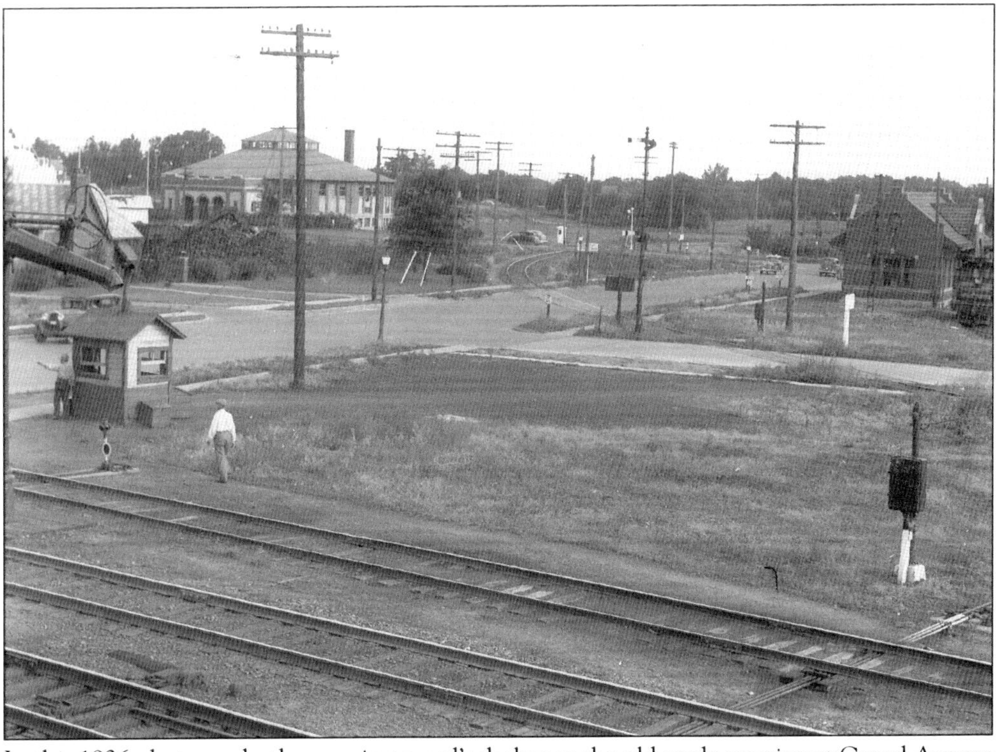

In this 1936 photograph, the crossing guard's shelter at the old grade crossing at Grand Avenue can be seen.

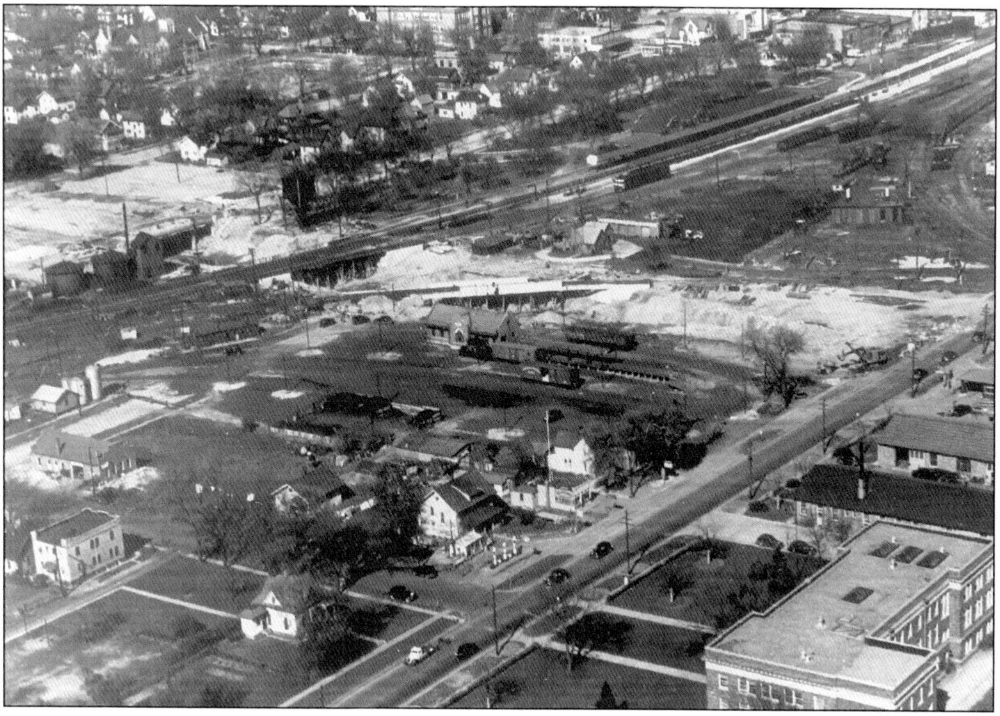

This aerial photo is looking northeasterly over the Highway Commission building in 1936. It shows the Grand Avenue underpass under construction. The Interurban Depot is at left-center, and the C & NW station is at the top-right, toward the center.

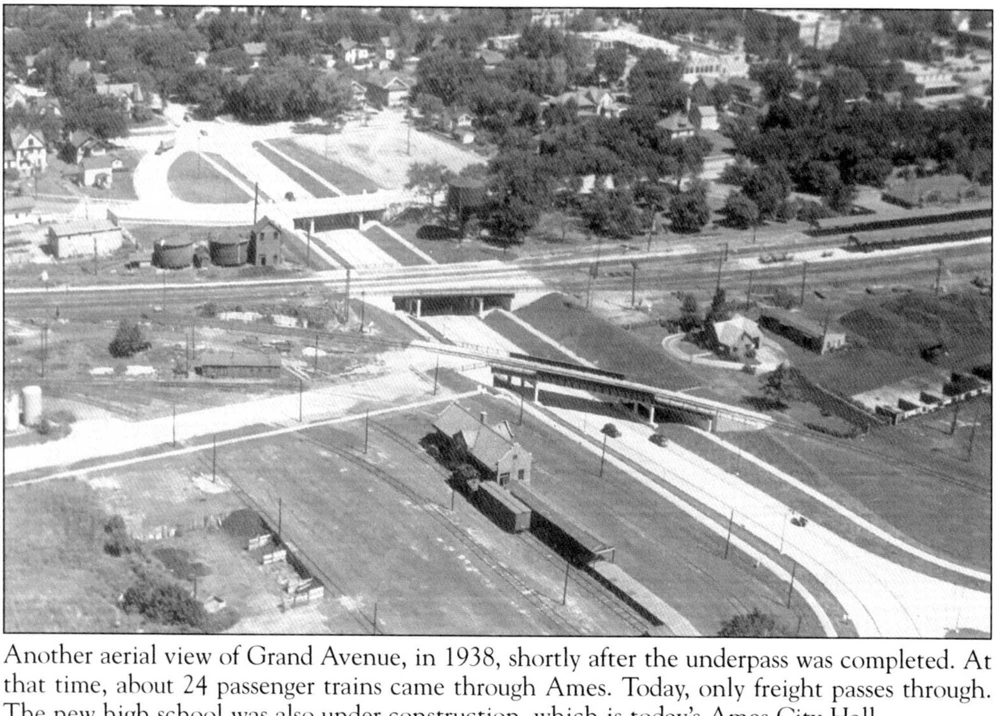

Another aerial view of Grand Avenue, in 1938, shortly after the underpass was completed. At that time, about 24 passenger trains came through Ames. Today, only freight passes through. The new high school was also under construction, which is today's Ames City Hall.

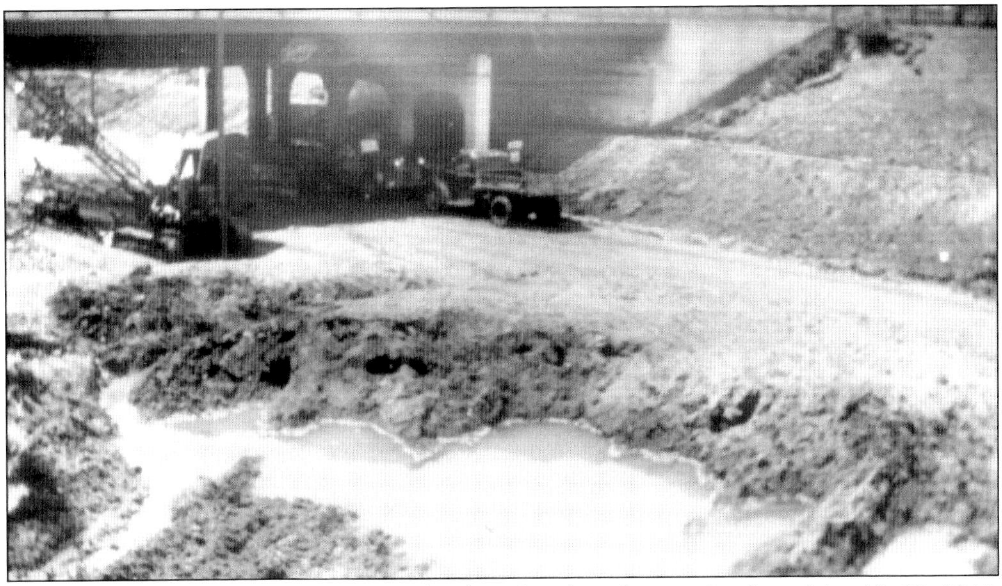

This is the Grand Avenue underpass, the day after Ames' worst flood, on May 18–19, 1944, when 8.21 inches of rain fell within 24 hours. Two cars were abandoned beneath the underpass and the drivers had to swim to safety.

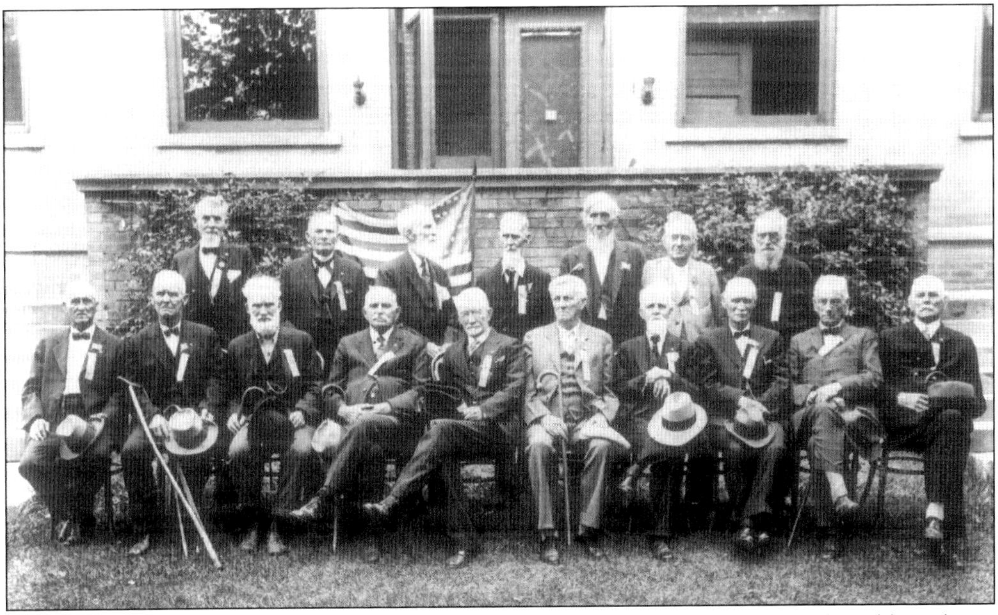

Story County's Civil War veterans stationed themselves in front of the Nevada Public Library during Story County's Jubilee Celebration in 1928. They are, from left to right, as follows: (front row) Mr. Weneklies, J.C. Moore, John Ridgeway, George Barnard, Oley Nelson, F.C Tilden, T.J. Miller, Elias Shearer, Parley Sheldon, and Charles Hamilton; (back row) Eli R. Cramblit, Cyrus Hiland, H.A. Hendrickson, Jack Gasaway, unidentified, and H. Toms. Charles Hamilton was the last surviving Civil War veteran in the county when he died in 1941.

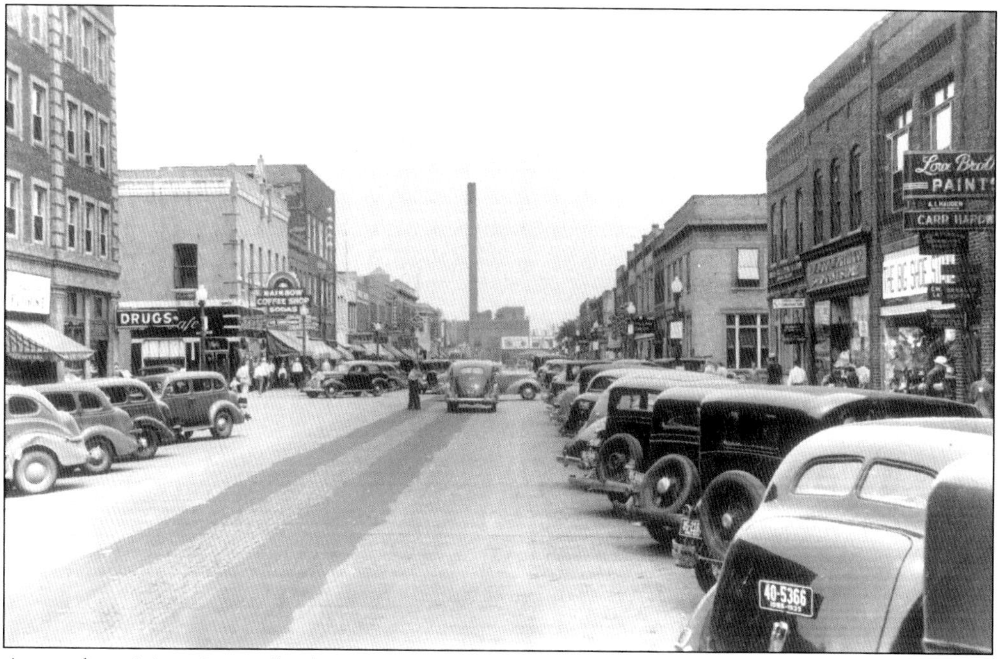

A very busy Main Street (looking east) is filled with cars, in this 1939 photo.

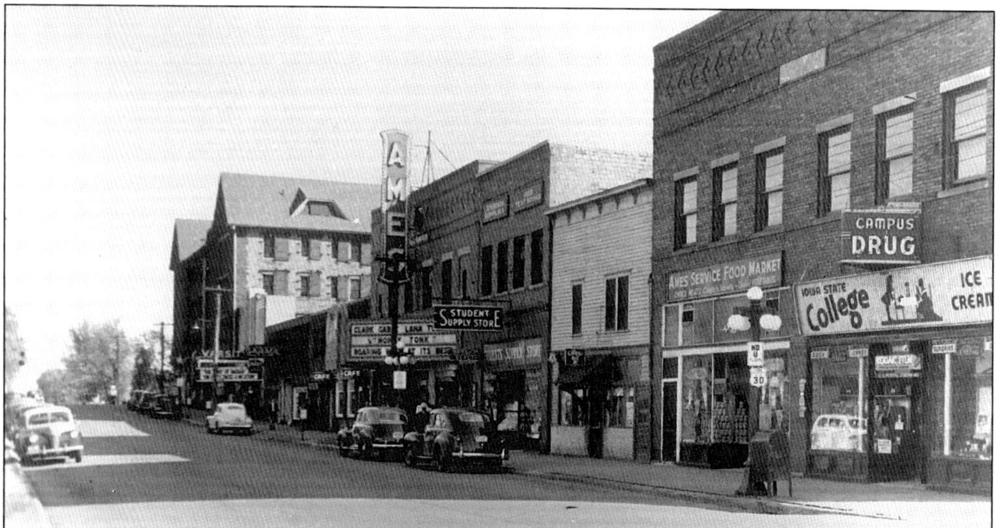

Honky Tonk, starring Lana Turner and Clark Gable, is playing at the Ames Theater on Lincoln Way in Campustown in this 1941 scene. The Ames Theater opened in 1919.